# Sibling Aggression

*Assessment and Treatment*

**Jonathan Caspi, PhD, LCSW**, is Associate Professor and Graduate Program Coordinator in the Department of Family and Child Studies, Montclair State University, Montclair, New Jersey. His areas of scholarship include sibling process, sibling aggression, intervention development, and clinical supervision. Dr. Caspi teaches sibling relationships, child development, interpersonal relationships, and family counseling courses to graduate and undergraduate students. He maintains a small private practice that includes family counseling, clinical social work supervision, and parent consultation services.

# Sibling Aggression

## *Assessment and Treatment*

Jonathan Caspi, PhD, LCSW

Springer Publishing Company, LLC
11 West 42nd Street
New York, NY 10036
www.springerpub.com

*Acquisitions Editor:* Jennifer Perillo
*Composition:* Techset

ISBN: 978-0-8261-2415-9
E-book ISBN: 978-0-8261-2416-6

11 12 13/ 5 4 3 2 1



**CIP data is available from the Library of Congress**



Printed in the United States of America by Gasch Printing

*For Barbara and Daniel, truly superb and loving parents*
*. . . but even better grandparents!*

---

*Dedicated to the memory of William J. Reid*

# Contents

# Preface

The first time I came across a research article that claimed sibling violence to be the most prevalent form of interpersonal aggression and child maltreatment, I did not believe it. How could that be possible? I had been reading about families for years before I was presented with this information. How is it that I could have gone through college, graduate school, doctoral study, professional workshops, and agency trainings and not encountered any discussion of sibling aggression along the way?

Sibling aggression is an invisible social phenomenon. It has received little attention in the practice, development, and research literatures, despite solid evidence that it is widespread and harmful. Strangely, it has not been invisible in other domains. Sibling aggression themes are prevalent in personal, historical, pop culture, and religious narratives. Children often complain about the treatment they receive from siblings, and parents frequently voice frustrations about their children being "at each other all the time." However, these narratives have not been viewed as overly problematic. The only exception is the abundance of self-help books on sibling rivalry available to parents, but even these tend to focus more on the annoyance of parents and not on the protection of children.

Indeed, sibling aggression is typically considered to be developmentally expected and normal. As a consequence, such behavior is viewed as mundane, typical, and not damaging or problematic. Yet, a growing body of research has demonstrated that sibling aggression *is* destructive, with considerable negative consequences. Moreover, it often rises to the level of abuse—a dangerous, widespread, and underdiagnosed form of maltreatment. The dominant view of sibling aggression as harmless promotes practice that avoids engaging in systematic sibling evaluation, and risks missed victimization and client safety. Even bickering, considered to be a fairly mild form of conflict, is disruptive to family life and negatively affects sibling relationships. Sibling aggression is not just a problem of childhood. It occurs throughout the life course and has been linked to an array of other social problems. In short, sibling aggression constitutes a serious social concern.

At the same time, siblings represent a valuable personal resource. This relationship is simultaneously if not paradoxically characterized by intense closeness and support (e.g., "We are more than best friends, we are like sisters"), and hostility. It is important that sibling aggression be stopped. It is equally important to preserve and develop positive sibling relationships, which are associated with many substantial benefits, including serving as a protective factor against unfavorable environmental conditions. Sibling relationships are a valuable source of strength and resilience, and need to be bolstered.

Practitioners receive little, if any, training about sibling aggression—as my own experience demonstrates. It is rarely included in university classes, practice curricula, or textbooks. Few interventions have been developed for this area of practice. Surprisingly, no current volumes offer clear practice guidelines for the full range of aggression. The time is ripe for such a book.

This book attempts to address current voids in the academic and professional literatures by offering a comprehensive volume that (a) provides an in-depth overview of current understandings of sibling aggression, (b) offers a new emerging "sibling theory" for development and practice, and (c) puts forth a coherent, empirically derived model that provides well-explicated series of steps and task strategies for the systematic treatment of sibling aggression, the Task-Centered Sibling Aggression (TCSA) treatment approach. TCSA integrates task-centered, structural family therapy and behavioral methods. It is a two-pronged approach that aims to stop aggression *and* facilitate positive sibling relationships.

This book should be of interest to a wide audience from a range of different backgrounds. First and foremost, it should be of great interest to clinical practitioners from the human service professions, including family therapy, social work, psychology, counseling, nursing, and family and child studies. Second, it should appeal to both graduate and undergraduate students and educators in these disciplines. Third, the book should be of interest to researchers who study siblings, family process, and treatment.

It is hoped that this book will be a valuable resource for practitioners, educators, and researchers. Focusing on siblings in practice offers a unique and revealing lens for teaching individual development and behavior, family process, and intervention work. I hope that this book advances the sibling aggression conversation, prompts future research, theory, and intervention development, and contributes to fostering a new cultural narrative in which sibling aggression is seen as abnormal, hurtful, and needing immediate attention. Finally, I hope that practitioners, researchers, educators and their students, and society at large engage in "thinking siblings."

# Acknowledgments

First and foremost, I would like to specially thank my amazing wife, Jennifer, and our wonderful children for generously giving up their time, and time with me, so that I could complete this book. I certainly could not have completed it without their support. I would also like to give special credit to Jennifer Perillo, senior acquisitions editor at Springer Publishing Company, for her expert feedback, creative insights, and very patient support. Also, a big thank you to Dr. Ada Beth Cutler, dean of the College of Education and Human Services, and Dr. Katia Goldfarb, chair of the Family and Child Studies Department, for their encouragement to pursue a sabbatical in order to give this work my central attention. Gratitude also goes out to Jane Eigenrauch and the fine staff at the Red Bank Public Library for providing a welcoming and ideal setting to work on this endeavor. I would also like to show appreciation toward my students who have shared their personal stories and challenged me with thoughtful questions that forced me to think about sibling relationships in new ways. Finally, I want to thank and recognize two incredibly important pioneers in family treatment, Dr. William J. Reid and Dr. Salvador Minuchin. Their contributions have had great influence on me professionally and personally, and provided the foundation for the model presented in this volume.

# Sibling Aggression

*Assessment and Treatment*

# 1

# An Overview of Sibling Aggression

Few will be surprised to read that siblings engage in a good deal of aggression. Sibling conflict is prevalent (Dunn & Munn, 1986), particularly troublesome to parents (Pakula, 1992), and is frequently dangerous (Caffaro, 2011). Sibling conflict themes are currently popular, religious, media, and cultural narratives. Despite the common view that aggression between siblings is normal, parents are troubled by sibling bickering as evidenced by the abundance of self-help books for the general public. What may be a surprise to many is that there is strikingly little available to psychotherapists and family practitioners (e.g., social workers, psychologists, family therapists) for understanding and treating sibling aggression. While some attention has been given to the most severe form of sibling aggression—that is, sibling abuse (Caffaro & Conn-Caffaro, 1998; Wiehe, 1997)—there has been little with regard to working with lesser forms of sibling aggression such as constant bickering and insults. This book hopes to address this void and offer practitioners treatment considerations and a clearly defined and empirically based approach for the full range of sibling aggression severity. The exception is sibling sexual abuse treatment that involves unique dynamics and treatment considerations from nonsexual forms of aggression. Although sexual abuse is included and discussed, treatment strategies offered in this book are not intended for this type of hostility.

This chapter will provide an overview of sibling aggression. It will begin by answering the question, "What is sibling aggression?" and offering definitions of its various types. This will be followed by a review of its prevalence, and its multiple problematic short- and long-term consequences. Processes that normalize sibling aggression will be considered next because not only is it both exceptionally widespread and deleterious, but seems to go relatively unnoticed. The chapter will continue with a discussion of risk factors, or factors that support sibling aggression, including family and parenting processes. Sibling aggression will then be considered in a sociocultural context as sibling relationships have different meanings, influence, and structure across environments. Finally, the chapter will briefly present research and prior offerings related to sibling violence treatment.

*Please note that "practitioners" is used throughout this book to refer to degreed and licensed professionals who provide therapy, counseling, or other direct human services to families and individuals, such as family therapists, social workers, psychologists, counselors, psychiatrists, mental health nurses, and nonclinical licensed professionals such as parent educators and social service administrators.*

## WHAT IS SIBLING AGGRESSION?

*Sibling aggression* is used here as an all-encompassing term to refer to all types of aggressive behavior ranging from competition to abuse. The term has not been used consistently in the literature, and no universal definition exists. Researchers have employed a variety of terms to capture aggressive sibling interactions, including violence (Reid & Donovan, 1990), conflict (Graham-Bermann, Cutler, Litzenberger, & Schwartz, 1994), maltreatment (Whipple & Finton, 1995), abuse (Caffaro & Conn-Caffaro, 1998), hostility (Stocker, Ahmed, & Stall, 1997), rivalry (Prochaska & Prochaska, 1985), and victimization (Finlkelhor & Jones, 2006). Many of these terms have been used interchangeably in the literature. The term "rivalry" is particularly present in the self-help literature but is not a helpful construct as it does not distinguish between mild and extreme aggression, and may confuse conflict over shared living space with competition for parental investment. Childhood aggression in general is complex with diverse conditions, etiologies, and consequences, which in part may explain the numerous constructs used to describe it (Connor, 2002).

As indicated earlier, *sibling aggression* is conceptualized here as an umbrella construct that refers to behaviors that range from nonviolent to abusive behaviors. It is viewed here on a severity continuum reflecting four categories ranging from mild-to-extreme aggression: competition, conflict, violence, and abuse (see Figure 1.1). A discussion of each follows.

### Competition

Sibling competition generally involves nonviolent behaviors aimed at winning in a particular area or activity, without the intent to physically or psychologically harm the other. Competition is often beneficial as it can motivate and challenge children to develop increased skill and achievement (Sulloway, 1996). The famous sister tennis players, Venus and Serena Williams, are an example of how competing with a sibling has such benefits. It could be argued that neither would be as proficient without the benefit of sibling competition. However, competition can also be hurtful when the end game is to systematically outdo a sibling, particularly with the aim of highlighting the other's inadequacies. Generally, siblings can be bested without injury to sense of self. In most cases, a child's self-esteem is not damaged by having a sibling who is more skilled in an activity like basketball, dance, or mathematics. Indeed, such discoveries may be educational in that they promote honest self-appraisals and help individuals make well-informed decisions about pursuits. Some evidence,

**FIGURE 1.1** Severity continuum of sibling aggression.

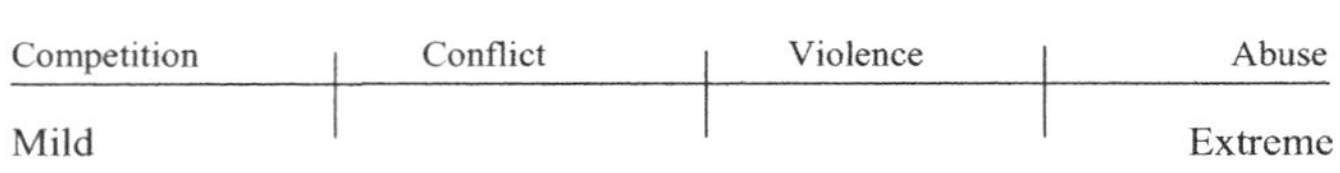

| Competition | Conflict | Violence | Abuse |
|---|---|---|---|
| Mild | | | Extreme |

however, suggests that competition to be the "good" versus "bad" child in families may be problematic for both the sibling relationship and individual development (Schachter & Stone, 1985). Finally, overly competitive siblings are often an ongoing aggravation with a resultant negative and unpleasant family environment, which frequently leads to resentment and lack of support between members.

## Conflict

Sibling conflict is a frequent aspect of family life (Dunn & Munn, 1986) and a major source of parent aggravation (Pakula, 1992; Ralph et al., 2003). Conflict is an expected part of all relationships and, like competition, can be both destructive and constructive (Howe, Rinaldi, Jennings, & Petrakos, 2002). Ross, Ross, Stein, and Trabasso (2006) make the distinction by defining destructive conflict as antagonistic, unresolved behavior that damages relationships, whereas "constructive conflict includes reasoning, resolutions of differing goals, and enhanced interpersonal understanding" (Ross et al., 2006, p. 1730).

Constructive sibling conflict is important for development as it increases social and emotional competence (Bedford, Volling, & Avioli, 2000), and the act of resolution may bring relationships closer. Accordingly, practitioners should avoid objectives aimed at simply halting sibling conflict that may result in apathetic and disengaged relationships (Kramer, 2004). Instead, practitioners should focus on the development and enhancement of prosocial skills such as emotional regulation and problem solving to promote supportive relationships (Kramer, 2011). Additionally, constructive conflict management skills learned with siblings have potential positive long-term benefits for future peer, romantic, and other relationships. By comparison, destructive conflict is problematic. For example, it has been related to sibling negativity (Rinaldi & Howe, 1998) and conduct problems (Garcia, Shaw, Winslow, & Yaggi, 2000).

Whether conflict is productive or debilitating may depend upon the siblings' relational context. Stormshak, Bellanti, and Bierman (1996) found that conflict in warm and supportive sibling relationships was associated with increased social competence and behavioral control, while conflict in relationships that lacked warmth and support was associated with behavioral problems. Similarly, Ross et al. (2006) and Recchia and Howe (2009a) reported that relationship quality was linked to the nature of conflict. Children in positive sibling relationships were more likely to utilize constructive conflict strategies, whereas those in poor-quality relationships employed negative behaviors. The causal direction is unclear as to whether positive relationships generate prosocial conflict strategies (e.g., compromise) or whether it is the use of prosocial strategies that results in enhanced relational quality. The process is likely reciprocal. Nevertheless, the two seem to be linked and practitioners may be able to help families change negative sibling relationships into positive ones by teaching constructive strategies for managing disagreements. Positive sibling relationships are linked to an array of beneficial results (e.g., Stormshak et al., 1996; Updegraff, McHale, & Crouter, 2002), whereas poor ones are associated with problematic outcomes (e.g., Bank & Burraston, 2001).

It seems that while sibling disagreements are more often about shared living (e.g., possessions) and invasion of personal space than about favor and fairness (Campione-Barr & Smetana, 2010; McGuire, Manke, Eftekhari, & Dunn, 2000), parents do play a role in their children's conflicts (Perlman & Ross, 1997; Piotrowski, 1999; Smith & Ross, 2007). Parental favoritism and differential treatment have been found to be influential in sibling conflict (e.g., Brody, Copeland, Sutton, Richardson, & Guyer, 1998; Updegraff, Thayer, Whiteman, Denning, & McHale, 2005b; Volling & Elins, 1998). It presumably raises parental stress (Patterson, 1986), and how parents manage both their own stress and their children's disagreements influences the sibling relationship. For example, Updegraff et al. (2005b) reported that lower levels of parental acceptance, the less time fathers spent with their children, and the use of authoritarian parental interventions increased sibling relational aggression. In another example, Felson and Russo (1988) found that parents typically intervene in sibling conflicts by protecting the younger child, a pattern that may increase sibling conflict.

While conflict may be more often about shared living (e.g., borrowing sibling's items without permission, mimicking, having alone time with friends, chores, bathroom time), my professional experiences suggest that more serious forms of sibling conflict such as violence and abuse are often tied to perceptions of parental favoritism. That said, conflict should not be taken less seriously than violence, as it can be frequent and intense, and is often a precursor to violence.

The nature of sibling conflicts change's with age. At younger ages, children are more self-focused and lack perspective (Recchia & Howe, 2009b), whereas older children may rely more on verbal self-justification tactics (e.g., retaliation for perceived personal violations). The frequency of sibling conflict seems to peak during early adolescence (Buhrmester & Furman, 1990; Campione-Barr & Smetana, 2010; McGuire et al., 2000). Conflicts at this age are commonly related to shared living but often include violent behaviors such as teasing, maliciousness, and property damage (Campione-Barr & Smetana, 2010).

Conflict in adulthood has received less attention but remains a feature of sibling relationships. Disagreements regarding parental care have been particularly noted in the literature (e.g., Lashewicz & Keating, 2009; Strawbridge & Wallhagen, 1991). Shifting culturally based family rules regarding responsibility for parents may contribute to sibling conflict in adulthood. For example, in a South Korean study, Sung, Lee, and Park (2008) reported that confusion over parent caretaking roles created tensions in the sibling relationship. Traditionally, the oldest brother had primary care responsibilities for aging parents, but recent legal and cultural value shifts have changed this expectation. In the study, older brothers tended to rely on modern equality social rules regarding parental care, whereas younger brothers emphasized traditional hierarchical norms, expecting their oldest brothers to do the caretaking work.

To make conflict distinct from other levels of aggression, it can be understood as typically occurring out of frustration rather than systematic domination and is usually contained to verbal assault, with occasional fleeting physical acts (e.g., grabbing the television remote, slapping). Conflict is particularly expected when children are very young and lack skills of cognitive reasoning, conflict resolution, or restraint (Newman, 1994). With only primitive strategies for managing frustration and obtaining objectives with siblings, young children may turn to violence (e.g., shoving, hitting) as a means of handling disagreement. If not addressed early, children will likely continue relying on aggressive tactics as they grow, often with increasing severity.

## Violence and Abuse

Both sibling violence and abuse entail a range of physical and verbal acts perpetrated with the intent to do harm, and involve the same behaviors. The terms sibling *violence* and *abuse* are often used interchangeably in the literature, but are distinguished here according to the balance of power in relationships. Violence reflects mutual or bidirectional aggression, in which both siblings' aim is to harm the other, in the context of a perceived egalitarian relationship. Abuse is unidirectional hostility where one sibling seeks to overpower the other via a reign of terror and intimidation and reflects an asymmetrical power arrangement. The intent of abusive behavior is control, intimidation, and the overpowering of another. Research indicates that siblings overwhelmingly perceive their violent interactions to be mutual (Kettrey & Emery, 2006). However, it is important to note that what may appear to be a mutually violent encounter may, upon closer inspection, reveal a clear perpetrator with a victim defending himself or herself.

Sibling violence and abuse are typically organized into three classifications that include physical (e.g., hitting, stabbing, tickling), sexual (e.g., leering, rape), and psychological (e.g., belittling, threatening) (Caffaro & Conn-Caffaro, 1998). A fourth recognized form of violence known as relational aggression has just begun receiving attention with regard to siblings (Ostrov, Crick, & Stauffacher, 2006; Updegraff et al., 2005b). Relational aggression (a.k.a. *indirect* and *social* aggression) are behaviors that intentionally hurt others through relationships (e.g., gossip, peer exclusion, distributing embarrassing pictures) (Goldstein & Tisak, 2004), and some evidence suggests that it occurs between siblings more than physical or verbal violence (Crick et al., 2001).

Brief discussions of the four types of sibling violence and abuse follow. These include physical, sexual, psychological, and relational. The nature of and considerations for each are described.

### *Physical*

Physical violence has been defined as the use of willful force to cause physical injury or pain (e.g., Caffaro & Conn-Caffaro, 1998; Wiehe, 1997). It is likely the most common form of child victimization. Estimates suggest that it occurs more frequently than parental abuse of children and domestic violence combined (Button & Gealt, 2010; Gelles, 1997; Gelles & Straus, 1988; Kolko, Kazdin, & Day, 1996). Its incidence also far outnumbers peer bullying (Felson, 1983, Finkelhor, Turner, & Ormrod, 2006). Although prevalence rates vary, research consistently demonstrates that it is pervasive throughout childhood and into adulthood, moderately declining with age. In their landmark study on family violence, Straus et al. (1980) found that violent sibling acts occurred in approximately 80% of families in the past year. Subsequent research has reported that between 85% and 96% of children (Kolko et al., 1996; Roscoe, Goodwin, & Kennedy, 1987) and 62–66% of older adolescents (Goodwin & Roscoe, 1990) have perpetrated and/or experienced sibling violence. In college samples, Hardy (2001) found that 48% recalled having been victimized by and 41% had perpetrated childhood sibling physical aggression, whereas Kettrey and Emery (2006) reported that 70.5% had either perpetrated or experienced "severe" sibling violence. While some studies have reported lower prevalence rates, ranging from 28% to 42% (Button & Gealt, 2010; Duncan, 1999; Finkelhor et al., 2006; Graham-Bermann et al., 1994), as Duncan suggests, "Whether 30% or 98% of children are victimized by siblings, it is evident that this is a prevalent source of violence in a child's life" (Duncan, 1999, pp. 881–882). Similarly, because of its prevalence, Button and Gealt (2010) call for sibling hostility to be systematically included in family violence prevention initiatives.

Like other types of family violence, capturing prevalence rates for sibling physical hostility poses real challenges. Rates may be overestimated in research due to the difficulty in distinguishing between "rough and tumble play" (Tannock, 2008) and problematic aggression. Conversely, prevalence may be underestimated due to coerced secrecy, threats of further violence, or fear of family disruption. In cases when sibling violence is known, it is often not reported (Wiehe, 1997). Moreover, systematic mechanisms for tracking this type of data are essentially nonexistent and child protection workers' definitions of sibling abuse vary widely (Kominkiewicz, 2004). Prevalence estimates have also been impeded by parents' beliefs that sibling aggression is normal. Parents often disregard abusive sibling interactions and obstruct efforts at determining its incidence (Rosenthal & Doherty, 1984) by minimizing it, blaming the victim, reacting with disbelief when told (Wiehe, 1997), and even ardently defending the perpetrator (Randall, 1992).

*Rough play and violence.* A frequent challenge for practitioners, parents, and researchers has been distinguishing the line between violence and rough play, which often also includes the intent to do harm. While rough play between a parent and a child or in intimate partner relationships is seen as problematic (Sanders, 2004), such sibling behavior fails to raise concern. It may be that such behavior is viewed as acceptable via rationalizations such as "it is just play" and "that's how siblings play." This complicates the ability to distinguish play from violence, as rough play often quickly changes from fun to anger and violent domination. The view presented here is that sibling physical violence should almost always be taken seriously as it is in all other interpersonal relationships, except perhaps when siblings are engaged in sports that require willful perpetration of pain (e.g., boxing). However, many believe that rough play between siblings holds important developmental functions such as learning one's own strength and how to limit aggression, and that it may represent a socially acceptable way for boys to be affectionate via physical contact (e.g., Gnaulati, 2002). Accordingly, I do not recommend putting a stop to playful aggression (e.g., wrestling) but that it should be done in the context of rules for behavior. Sports offer such structures for rough play and competition. Families can take this approach and create rules for rough play. For example, wrestling must end immediately when one becomes angry, makes claims of pain, or lashes out physically. Another rule could be that when one member says the playing should stop, the other abides. Parents must work together with their children to establish parameters for rough play. I take the view that all intent to harm is problematic and should not be permitted so that children feel safe in their homes. As such, teaching children skills to employ when they want to perpetrate harm is important from as early as before a child's first birthday (e.g., restraint). Wiehe (1997) offers criteria to distinguish abusive and nonabusive behaviors by evaluating the age-appropriateness, frequency, duration, degree of victimization, and purpose of the aggressive acts.

Compared with rough play, sibling physical violence and abuse are destructive and have no known developmental benefits for either the perpetrator or the victim. Parents sometimes believe sibling violence to be beneficial, thinking it makes children "tough" and readies them for peer aggression (Gelles, 1997), but there is no empirical evidence to support this. Even if sibling violence does result in peer toughness, it would likely come at the risk of poor sibling relationships (Updegraff et al., 2005b). Conversely, positive sibling relationships benefit individual development (Stormshak et al., 1996) and seem to serve as a protective buffer for children experiencing the negative effects of parental conflict (Caya & Liem, 1998; Jenkins, 1992), domestic violence (Lucas, 2002), stressful life events (Gass, Jenkins, & Dunn, 2007), and peer isolation (East & Rook, 1992). Positive sibling relationships seem more valuable than potential but improbable toughness.

### *Sexual*

Sibling sexual abuse represents a particularly harmful and fairly widespread form of aggression. It has unique features and considerations from nonsexual abuse and suggests different treatment concerns.

Similar to physical assault, no clear and consistent criteria have been utilized to define sibling sexual abuse (Carlson, Maciol, & Schneider, 2006) or for distinguishing it from "natural curiosity" (Caffaro, 2011). Moreover, sibling sexual abuse has received scant attention in the research and as such, little is understood about the complexities of sexual interaction between siblings. Individuals sexually abused by a sibling may not recognize the experience as abusive and may even see themselves as willing participants, complicating the ability to distinguish abuse from experimentation using a "coercion or consent" criteria. Similar to the earlier discussion of physical abuse, behaviors that appear to be mutual may truly be unidirectional and abusive. Because an act is physically stimulating (e.g., "feels good") does not constitute consent. Young children likely do not understand the implications of sexual interactions and may participate for a variety of reasons that look like consent. For example, a child who looks up to her older brother may go along with his actions to win or keep his approval, or because it is physically pleasurable. It may be only later that she recognizes the behavior as problematic and is confused by her role in the encounters, believing she consented. In order for consent to be authentic, one has to understand what they are agreeing to.

Abuse can be distinguished from experimentation (e.g., "playing doctor") by features that include coerced secrecy and power differential (Canavan, Meyer, & Higgs, 1992). As with all interpersonal abuse, sibling sexual abuse is an abuse of power and an act of domination. The interest of the perpetrator, although it appears to be sexual gratification, is primarily about overpowering and controlling another through coercive measures, although some have suggested that it may be tied to seeking emotional nurturance in violent and emotionally barren families (Brennan, 2006; Haskins, 2003). Perpetrators often threaten victims with physical harm (even death), or injury to others, pets, or prized belongings as a way to keep the behavior private. Because of the unidirectional nature of this type of aggression, I prefer the term *sibling sexual abuse*, which implies exploitation and makes clear what the behavior is (i.e., abusive), over the term *sibling incest*, which suggests mutuality in an egalitarian relationship and serves to confound and hide the experience of maltreatment.

A challenge for practice and research is that child victims of sibling sexual abuse are less likely to disclose than victims of other types of sexual abuse (Carlson et al., 2006). This may be due to victims' confusion over sibling encounters. For example, Carlson et al. (2006) reported that only about one in five victims disclosed at the time of the abuse. Similarly, Hardy (2001) noted that the number of respondents in her study who perceived their sibling sexual encounters to be abusive changed from 6.6% at the time they originally occurred to 33.3% at the time they completed the study as undergraduate college students. As children grow, their understandings of sexual behavior become more sophisticated, and again, encounters thought to be normal during childhood may later be understood as abusive.

Fear of disclosure, changing perceptions of the meanings of sexual encounters, and inconsistent and unclear notions of what constitutes sibling sexual abuse all complicate understandings of prevalence. Evidence suggests, however, that it is the most widespread of the intrafamilial sexual abuses (Flanagan, 2003; Welfare,

2008), with an estimated one fourth perpetrated by a sibling (Rudd & Herzberger, 1999). Between 5% and 17% of women and approximately 10% of men report having been sexual abused by a sibling (Finkelhor, 1980; Hardy, 2001). Brother–sister dyads seem to be the most common form with older brothers initiating the abuse (Caffaro & Conn-Caffaro, 1998).

Sibling sexual abuse also seems to be the most severe with higher rates of sexual penetration than other intrafamilial sexual abuses (O'Brien, 1991). But it is not limited to intercourse and includes nonpenetration touching (e.g., groping) as well as nontouching behaviors such as leering, forcing a sibling to view pornographic material, and sexual proposals. All have potentially harmful psychological effects on the victim. Although father–daughter sexual abuse has received more attention, there is some evidence that sibling sexual abuse is as harmful with regard to psychological distress (Cyr, Wright, McDuff, & Perron, 2002).

A fairly wide range of effects for sexual abuse victimization in general exists that include guilt, shame, lower self-concept, promiscuity, age-inappropriate knowledge of sexual behavior, substance abuse, eating disorders, revictimization, and posttraumatic stress reactions. Few empirical explorations of *sibling* sexual victimization consequences exist. Recently, a study by Carlson (2011) compared the psychological adjustment of adult women sexually abused by siblings in childhood with a matched comparison group. Those who experienced sibling sexual abuse reported lower self-esteem and higher anxiety, depression, hostility, and adult victimization. Anxiety seemed to be a unique feature of those victimized by sibling sexual abuse compared to other forms of abuse. Other long-term consequences of sibling sexual abuse in this study included a distrust of men, fear of getting close to others, and the perception that a normal life is not possible. Others have suggested that posttraumatic stress disorder, eating disorders, and problems with intimate relationships in adulthood represent additional consequences (Wiehe, 1997). Male victims of sexual abuse are usually less willing to disclose it, often because of concerns they have for what it means about their own sexual orientation and masculinity (Lisak, 1994). Such concerns are also likely consequences of sibling sexual victimization of males.

### *Psychological*

Psychological (a.k.a. verbal, emotional) abuse is nonphysical behaviors that intend to psychologically or emotionally harm (e.g., lower self-esteem, raise anxiety), such as name calling, belittling, teasing, and threatening injury to person, pets, or property. Sibling psychological maltreatment has been found to be the most prevalent behavior in sibling conflict (Stormshak et al., 1996), although few researchers have investigated this area of sibling life (Martin, Anderson, Burant, & Weber, 1997). It is likely that almost all siblings engage in verbal hostility, but it is unclear as to how often and when verbal assaults are intended to be about domination and emotional injury, or about simple expressions of frustration. Repetitive hurtful themes (e.g., "you're ugly," "you're stupid") reflect dominance intentions, and sibling teasing seems to be particularly problematic. It has been associated with less trust and relationship satisfaction (Martin et al., 1997), and girls teased by siblings were found to have higher body dissatisfaction, bulimic behaviors, depression, and lower levels of self-esteem (Keery, Boutelle, van den Berg, & Thompson, 2005). In another study (Mackey, Fromuth, & Kelly, 2010), the experience of later anxiety correlated with individuals who identify themselves as emotionally abused.

Psychological maltreatment also involves threats to and destruction of personal property, behaviors that have negative consequences (Norris & Kaniasty, 1994). In their national study of child victimization, Finkelhor et al. reported that siblings engaged in a "considerable quantity" of property vandalism and robberies (Finkelhor et al., 2005, p. 14). Because name calling, insults, and threats are hurtful, I recommend that practitioners and parents institute "no name calling, insults, or threats" rule to create safety for children, and to create and model a nonviolent environment.

### *Relational*

Relational hostility, sometimes called social or indirect aggression, entails nonphysical behaviors intended to psychologically and emotionally hurt its victims by socially injuring and isolating them. These behaviors are typically not exhibited face-to-face and the actions are sometimes even unknown to the victim. It is a more ambiguous type of violence than physical, which is overt and involves direct confrontation. As such, relational aggression perpetrators can more easily deny involvement. Examples of this behavior include persuading a circle of friends to exclude a member from a social event, ignoring a peer, starting rumors, and posting embarrassing material on an Internet website.

As investigation into sibling relational hostility has only just begun, evidence suggests that it is common, although prevalence is unknown. Studies have found that preschoolers used more relational aggression with siblings than peers (Stauffacher & DeHart, 2005), that school-aged children utilized it more frequently with their siblings than physical or verbal tactics (O'Brien & Crick, 2003), and that siblings may teach relational aggressive behavior by modeling it (Stauffacher & DeHart, 2006). Such tactics have been associated with poor sibling relationships (McHale, 2005; Updegraff et al., 2005b), and more generally, are distressing and psychologically hurtful to their victims.

Once thought to be employed more by girls than boys, research indicates that there does not seem to be significant gender differences in its use with siblings (Card, Stucky, Sawalani, & Little, 2008), although the role of sibling gender positions may be linked to its use with peers. As examples, Ostrov et al. (2006) reported that older sisters used more relational aggression with peers than do older brothers, who rely more on physical behaviors, and Goldstein and Tisak (2004) found that girls thought more about using it and found it more hurtful than boys did.

Interest in family dynamics that support sibling relational aggression has begun to emerge. Yu and Gamble (2008) reported that family environment is linked to sibling relational aggression, with positive families having less. They also reported that perceived maternal psychological control (i.e., using behaviors such as shaming and conditional approval to manage children's behavior) has been linked to sibling relational aggression.

General findings, primarily derived from research focused on peer aggression, provide considerations for possible sibling behavior. For example, peer relational aggression has been associated with *higher* prosocial behavior (Card et al., 2008), particularly for those who experience more jealousy (Culotta & Goldstein, 2008). Jealousy is a major theme in sibling life, usually cast as sibling "rivalry." It is possible that children who make greater use of prosocial skills in their sibling relationships rely on more relational aggression. That is, positive relationships may have more relational aggression, whereas poor ones use more confrontational (e.g., physical, verbal) behaviors. Alternatively, it may be that children view physical assault as prohibited or view it unfavorably, and become creative by using indirect tactics when being aggressive.

## NORMALIZATION OF SIBLING AGGRESSION

A likely explanation for the comparatively limited attention given to sibling aggression is that it is largely considered to be normal behavior (Finkelhor, Ormrod, Turner, & Hamby, 2005), and therefore not a pressing concern. Sibling aggression is often dismissed as playful and "what siblings do." In research, respondents have reported that hitting a sibling is considered to be acceptable and not violent or abusive behavior (Hardy, 2001), even when it may be (Kettrey & Emery, 2006). Although a growing body of research demonstrates its deleterious effects, the mistaken belief that sibling violence is not harmful further normalizes it. Statements such as "My brother beat on me and I am fine" and "Boys will be boys" minimize honest appraisals of possible effects and validate its continued use. The very acts deemed abusive in parent–child, partner, and stranger interactions (e.g., punching, kicking, throwing objects) are often considered ordinary sibling behavior.

Practitioners were raised and reside within a social context that considers sibling aggression as normal and frequently underestimate its prevalence (Begun, 1995). This internalized social construction obstructs consideration of sibling violence in practice, education, and research. For example, mental health and human service practitioners rarely receive training on managing, assessing, or treating sibling aggression. An obvious danger is the practitioner inadvertently supporting ongoing victimization because he on she does not see sibling aggression as potentially dangerous. It has been noted that professionals and persons in authority positions fall prey to minimizing serious injury and known acts of violence as normal sibling rivalry (Phillips, Phillips, Grupp, & Trigg, 2009). Families also may not recognize hostile sibling interactions as problematic and are unlikely to raise them as an issue of concern, even when violent and abusive.

It is possible that many of the problems practitioners encounter are directly related to hostile sibling relationships (e.g., school-related problems, peer problems, bullying, marital conflict, date rape, anxiety disorders), but not identified as such. Practitioners who do not view sibling aggression as problematic will overlook these connections. For example, a child may be struggling academically because of anxieties related to maltreatment by an older sibling (e.g., threats of after-school harm made in the morning). Practitioners who fail to assess for sibling aggression may be tempted to attribute the academic difficulties to individual characteristics (e.g., learning disability) or marital problems, both of which may exist but neither of which fully explains the child's struggle.

As in the case of other forms of interpersonal violence (e.g., wife battering, peer bullying, child abuse), which were once overlooked and thought to be rarely occurring, private matters, or normative development, a cognitive shift with a new understanding of the dangers and prevalence of sibling aggression is necessary. Both Kettrey and Emery (2006) and Phillips et al. (2009) have highlighted the role of dominant cultural discourses in "silencing" attention for sibling violence. Challenging social norms is a necessary part of practice and can be done via formal practitioner training, parent education, public awareness campaigns, and social reflection efforts.

## CONSEQUENCES

The consequences of sibling aggression have not been adequately studied (Hoffman & Edwards, 2004), but research has linked it to a variety of psychosocial problems across age groups. Although there has been a presumption that exposure to violence is less harmful to younger children than to older ones, recent evidence suggests that early and later childhood victimizations are equally problematic (Finkelhor et al., 2006). Practitioners should address aggression at young ages with the same seriousness as when working with older children or adults.

A brief overview of consequences linked to problematic sibling aggression (i.e., destructive conflict, violence, abuse) is provided here. It is important to note the use of the research literature here. The following overview was culled from the extant research on sibling relationships in order to develop empirically derived ways to inform treatment practices. There is a great variation in both the rigor and the terminology used in the research discussed, and few used clinical samples. Again, my intent is to provide practitioners with a general look at what researchers are discovering to inform the direction of enquiry during practice. It should also be noted that much of the research does not offer a causal direction for links to sibling aggression. The mechanisms and processes that underlie the following associations are not always well understood. That said, I have attempted to organize the research by likely consequences, representing outcomes or reciprocal processes, and factors that support sibling aggression, or causes. Both the causal direction and division of research is theoretical and in large part artificial. For example, arrests in adolescence are linked to sibling aggression. I handled this as a consequence, believing that it is unlikely that arrests cause sibling aggression, but rather that sibling aggression may lead to problematic behaviors that result in arrest.

It is clear that sibling aggression is linked to a variety of adverse conditions. Considered as consequences, practitioners can use them as indicators to guide assessment. For example, if working with an adolescent who has been arrested, and struggles with depression and substance abuse—all linked to problematic sibling aggression—enquiry into sibling victimization is indicated.

In childhood, sibling violence has been associated with school misconduct (Garcia et al., 2000), academic difficulties (Kingston & Prior, 1995), peer bullying (Duncan, 1999; Ensor, Marks, Jacobs, & Hughes, 2010), physical aggression with peers (Berndt & Bulleit, 1985; MacKinnon-Lewis, Starnes, Volling, & Johnson, 1997), behavior and emotional problems (Deater-Deckard, Dunn, & Lussier, 2002), poor peer relations (Dunn & McGuire, 1992; Ensor et al., 2010; Stormshak et al., 1996), unhappiness, helplessness, more medical illness, and destructive thoughts about family members (Rosenthal & Doherty, 1984), and anxiety and depression (Duncan, 1999). Cuevas et al. (2009) found that having a psychiatric diagnosis was associated with sibling victimization. Similarly, Kessler and Magee (1994) reported that children victimized by a sibling or multiple other family members were six times more likely to experience a major depressive disorder in adulthood than nonvictims. They add that exposure to sibling violence in childhood likely affects individuals throughout the life course in additional ways such as being more violent, emotionally reactive, and stressed, as well as more likely to be revictimized and to develop maladaptive conflict resolution skills.

In adolescence and early adulthood, experiencing sibling aggression has been linked to arrests (Bank, Patterson, & Reid, 1996), interpersonal aggression (Williams, Conger, & Blozis, 2007), depression, insecurity, and feelings of incompetence (Hoffman & Edwards, 2004), date violence (Noland, Liller, McDermott, Coulter, & Seraphine, 2004), greater consideration for using violent behaviors with others (Gully, Dengerine, Pepping, & Bergstrom, 1981), and anxiety and possible enduring anger, resentment, and challenges with expressing emotion (Graham-Bermann & Cutler, 1994). Recently, Button and Gealt (2010) reported a link between sibling violence and substance use, delinquency, and aggression in a sample of 8,122 eighth and 11th grade students, but noted that the causal direction is not known. Sibling negativity and lack of intimacy have also been associated with sibling aggression (Updegraff et al., 2005b) although it not clear as to whether these are causes or consequences and probably reflect reciprocal interactional processes. Long-term consequences include lowered self-concept (Garey, 1999), depression, insecurity, feelings of incompetence (Hoffman & Edwards, 2004), relationship problems, and possible posttraumatic stress disorder (Wiehe, 1997) in adulthood. Recently, Morrill-Richards (2010) found that college students emotionally and physically abused by a sibling during childhood reported lower self-esteem and social competence as young adults.

It is likely that sibling violence shares many if not most outcomes associated with other types of childhood victimization, but this needs further study. Of note is that sibling violence may be *more* detrimental than parental abuse because victims simultaneously experience two types of abuse, the sibling hostility and parental neglect (i.e., neglecting to protect the child from harm) (Green, 1984).

As noted, sibling aggression is linked to aggression in other relationships. It is important to note that it may be a *precursor* to other forms of violence (Caffaro & Conn-Caffaro, 1998; Ensor et al., 2010; Garcia et al., 2000). The sibling relationship is the first and most likely fertile training ground for learning social skills with individuals close in terms of age, and for how to manage frustrations and achieve objectives. Violent sibling behavior may "set the stage for violent interactions with peers, and later with spouses and children" (Caffaro & Conn-Caffaro, 1998, p. 82). Serious violence typically starts with more mild forms and becomes increasingly severe. Abusive behavior rarely spontaneously emerges and most often starts with verbal aggression such as name calling and belittling, and escalates to physical violence such as shoving, hitting, and beatings. As such, acceptance of seemingly mild aggression between siblings may give tacit permission to become increasingly more aggressive until it reaches the level of severe violence and abuse. From a practice perspective, it is much easier to halt mild than severe aggression, and as such it is recommended that practitioners help families institute "no violence" rules that include prohibitions of verbal as well as physical aggression.

## FACTORS THAT SUPPORT SIBLING VIOLENCE

A review of the literature offers an array of factors that seem to support sibling antagonism. These factors differ from consequences in that they likely reflect causes or reciprocal associations that exacerbate problematic aggression. For example, spousal abuse is understood as a consequence, not a cause. By comparison, academic problems (discussed earlier under "Consequences") are seen as a result or reciprocal process and not a direct cause of sibling aggression. Similar to the discussion on consequences, the following overview of associations represents a wide array of research rigor and terminology, and few used clinical samples. The aim is to provide an introductory overview of what has emerged in the literature for the purpose of informing practice.

Building upon organizing frameworks offered by Caspi (2008) and Hoffman and Edwards (2004), the following review attempts to arrange linked factors into conceptual categories that include family system, parenting, individual, and additional considerations. Additionally, conditions that theoretically support sibling aggression but are yet to be investigated are offered. The list of factors that follows was compiled from sibling and family literatures, primarily relying on empirical findings. The factors that support sibling aggression can be considered to be risk factors that can inform assessment and prevention, and have been organized as such in Appendix A.

## Family System

Most of the factors that support sibling aggression are linked to family dynamics such as negative and conflictual parent–child relationships (Hoffman, Kiecolt, & Edwards, 2005), parent hostility toward a child (Williams et al., 2007), spousal abuse (Haj-Yahia & Dawud-Noursi, 1998; Hotaling, Straus, & Lincoln, 1990), partner conflict (Hoffman et al., 2005), marital conflict (Stocker & Youngblade, 1999), mother's marital dissatisfaction and negative emotional expressiveness (Stocker et al., 1997), maternal self-criticism (Garcia et al., 2000; MacKinnon-Lewis et al., 1997; Volling & Belsky, 1992), financial stress (Hardy, 2001; Williams et al., 2007), low family cohesion (Brody, Stoneman, & McCoy, 1994), family disorganization and husband's loss of temper (Eriksen & Jensen, 2006), low maternal education (Ensor et al., 2010), and household chaos (Kretschmer & Pike, 2009). Sibling aggression is likely linked to family triangulation (Haskins, 2003; Kerig, 1995; Kiselica & Morrill-Richards, 2007) and its related parent–child coalitions (Vuchinich, Wood, & Vuchinich, 1994). Such coalitions are typically tied to split-parent identification (Schachter, 1985), in which parents disagree on disciplinary practices and do not operate as a unified team.

With regard to family structure, outcomes seemed to be inconsistent. For example, Finkelhor, Ormrod, and Turner (2007) found that polyvictimization which may include harm perpetrated by siblings, occurs more in step- and single-parent families than traditional two-parent and single-parent families. Others, however, have reported that full siblings were more aggressive than half- or step-siblings (Deater-Deckard et al., 2002), perhaps because step-siblings are more likely to be disengaged (Hetherington & Stanley-Hagan, 1999). Deater-Deckard et al. (2002) also found support for higher sibling hostility in single-mother families.

## Parenting

The ways in which parents behave with their children influence sibling aggression. Behaviors related to sibling hostility include parental differential treatment of children (Dunn, 1991), by fathers (Brody & Stoneman, 1994), and particularly by fathers favoring later-born sisters (Updegraff et al., 2005b). Differential treatment is a form of family triangulation, and is likely exacerbated by stress (Crouter, McHale, & Tucker, 1999). Also linked to sibling aggression are active and direct judgmental comparison (Feinberg & Hetherington, 2001), particularly in the form of polarized or complementary labeling of children into categories of bad/good and easy/difficult (Schachter, 1985; Schachter & Stone, 1985), low parental involvement, particularly by fathers (Updegraff et al., 2005b), ineffective parenting (Bank, Burraston, & Snyder, 2004), inconsistent discipline (Bank et al., 1996), coercive parenting (Means-Burleson, 2002), maternal coercive, rejecting, and overcontrolling behaviors (Eriksen & Jensen, 2006; Yu, 2008), parental abuse of children (Button & Gealt, 2010; Wiehe, 1997), parents' use of violence to resolve parent–child conflict (Graham-Bermann et al., 1994), parental neglect and approval of aggression (Rosenthal & Doherty, 1984), and possibly corporal punishment (Eriksen & Jensen, 2006).

A number of behaviors that parents *do not undertake* have also been tied to sibling violence, including providing supervision (Whipple & Finton, 1995), intervening in sibling conflict (Bennett, 1990), acknowledging child-voiced claims of maltreatment (Wiehe, 1997), and reinforcement of prosocial behaviors (Bryant & Crockenberg, 1980).

Finally, Sulloway (1996) explained sibling conflict using Darwin's principle of divergence, which posits that the more siblings diversify their interests, the more they can access parental favor and resources (e.g., time, attention), while minimizing direct competition. Accordingly, children who employ similar strategies for garnering parental investment will engage in more conflict. Although yet to be empirically tested, it puts forth a compelling reason for sibling aggression. For example, parents who encourage sameness (e.g., enmeshed families) and disapprove of difference may be more likely to experience sibling violence than those who promote uniqueness.

## Individual

Investigations of individual factors linked to sibling aggression have focused more on the perpetrator than victim characteristics. Perpetrators often lack empathy for their victims (Silverman, 1999), possess aggressive temperament (Munn & Dunn, 1988), and have either lower (Hanson et al., 1992) or higher (Graham-Bermann et al., 1994) self-esteem than peers. While yet to be researched, sibling violence has also been viewed as a way to satisfy unmet personal needs for physical contact in emotion-deprived environments (Bank & Kahn, 1997; Haskins, 2003). Additionally, it is not uncommon for offenders to also be victims of abuse, including by siblings (Caffaro & Conn-Caffaro, 2005).

The consequences for victims were reviewed earlier in this chapter. However, whether or not there are individual characteristics that promote initial victimization by siblings is yet to be investigated. It does seem that characteristics related to the consequence of violence victimization raise the risk of subsequent victimization. For example, Cuevas, Finkelhor, Clifford, Ormrod, and Turner (2010) recently reported that the psychological distress (e.g., anger, depression, anxiety) from violence victimization by siblings and others sources may serve as a precipitant for revictimization. Indeed, sibling victims are more likely to experience victimization from multiple sources (i.e., "poly-victimization") than siblings who do not experience violence (Turner, Finkelhor, & Ormrod, 2010).

## Additional Factors

Birth order and age spacing, gender, sociocultural background, and other issues have also been associated with sibling violence. They are briefly discussed here.

### *Birth order and age spacing*

Firstborn children are more likely to be aggressors (Martin & Ross, 1995), and caretaking, a task often given to firstborns, has been linked to sibling hostility (Baum, 1998). Younger children are influenced by their older sibling's aggressive behavior, and often imitate it (Patterson, 1986). Wiehe (1997) reported a cascading dynamic for sibling abuse in which the firstborn attacks the second, which goes after the third and so on. By comparison, first- and thirdborns (i.e., "jump pairs") have been found to be more alike than middleborns (Schachter, Gilutz, Shore, & Adler, 1978), and may join against their middleborn siblings. That is, when a secondborn picks on the thirdborn, the firstborn may aggressively protect the third, giving the third permission to initiate conflict with the old secondborn. Finally, close age spacing seems to increase frequency of conflict (Aguilar, O'Brien, August, Aoun, & Hektner, 2001) and violence (Noland et al., 2004); however, wider age spacing may be more common with abuse.

### *Gender*

Gender is likely a factor in sibling aggression although findings have been generally inconsistent. Some have suggested the presence of a male increases the likelihood of violence (Ensor et al., 2010; Hoffman et al., 2005; Lockwood, 2002; Randall, 1992), particularly with preschool-age children, perhaps because parents seem to be more tolerant of male than female aggression (Martin & Ross, 2005). While some have reported that older brother–younger sister pairs represent the most common combination for sibling violence (Aguilar et al., 2001; Button & Gealt, 2010; Buhrmester, 1992; Caffaro & Conn-Caffaro, 2005; Graham-Bermann et al., 1994), earlier studies have found no relationship between sex pairings (Dunn & Kendrik, 1981). Nevertheless, females may experience greater harm related to mechanisms of gender bias (Atwood, 2001), and seem to perceive physical aggression as more violent than men (Rapoza, Cook, Zaveri, & Malley-Morrison, 2010). Finally, Edwards and Weller (2011) suggest that sibling aggression can be understood as a gendered process in which conflict may represent negotiations and contestations about gender identity and development.

### *Sociocultural background*

Social context considerations such as culture practices (e.g., primogeniture, patriarchy) (Hoffman & Edwards, 2004; Sulloway, 1996), issues related to disability (Hanson et al., 1992; Linares, 2006), and family economic pressure are potential factors for sibling hostility (Williams et al., 2007). Cross-cultural research on siblings, although fairly scarce, has demonstrated important group distinctions (Caspi, 2011a; Cicirelli, 1995; Goetting, 1986; Steinmetz, 1981; Updegraff, McHale, Killoren & Rodriguez, 2011; Zukow, 1989), but how these distinctions support or minimize sibling aggression has received scant attention. Sibling violence is likely perceived, enacted, and addressed uniquely across cultures (Caffaro & Conn-Caffaro, 1998; Steinmetz, 1981), as it is with other forms of family violence (Malley-Morrison & Hines, 2004). For example, Rapoza et al. (2010) asked their respondents from a variety of different ethnic groups for examples of different levels of sibling violence, ranging from mild to severe. All the groups in their study perceived physical violence to be more severe than psychological violence, with the exception of Asian Pacific Americans who held an opposite view. The authors also reported that South Asian Americans focused more on beating and hitting than the other groups, and that European American participants gave the most instances of sexual abuse.

It is necessary for family practitioners to understand both the core similarities and unique dynamics of different groups. For example, poorer families rely on their older children to act as primary caregivers for their siblings more often than do middle- and upper-class families. Excessive sibling caregiving has been linked to sibling aggression (Green, 1984). Another example, discussed earlier in this chapter, is that parents from violent neighborhoods may be more likely to view sibling aggression as beneficial because it teaches their children to be "tough," and that it prepares them for what they are likely to encounter on the "streets." Children with homosexual siblings may experience unique dynamics that include aggression related to homophobia. Cultural groups that emphasize masculine power (e.g., machismo) may engage in overt favoritism that promotes sibling aggression. For example, in at least one study Hispanics along with Whites reported higher rates of assaults by siblings than other groups (Finkelhor et al., 2005).

Immigrant families often experience hierarchical disruptions due to learning a new language. Young children, who often learn the new language more quickly, frequently become the family's spokesperson when engaged with individuals who do not speak their native language, giving them a unique position of power. In the United States, for example, younger siblings who grow up with English may have more power in public endeavors than older siblings who are learning it as a second language. In another example, in families with a child with a disability, typically developing children may resent both their siblings and parents for the increased attention given to the child with the disability (Goeke & Ritchey, 2011).

It is critical that clinicians recognize and attend to sociocultural differences in their sibling work, but there has been little to help them in this regard. A recent volume on sibling development, however, offers important implications for practice across groups and issues (Caspi, 2011a). Practitioners are encouraged to incorporate "difference" in their work with aggressive siblings, and to recognize how socializing and social power structures influence such relationships.

### *Additional factors*

Additional factors derived from both the literature and the author's practice experiences are added here. Many of these factors have already been linked to other forms of child victimization. These factors include parental alcoholism, parental support of child aggression (e.g., wanting their children to be tough), and social glorification of violence in the media (e.g., television, video games). Boredom is also a likely predictor (Prochaska & Prochaska, 1985)—for example, consider two siblings sharing the back seat on a long car trip.

## SIBLING AGGRESSION AND PRACTICE

Considering the widespread nature of sibling aggression and its known problematic consequences, relatively few practice interventions exist. Indeed, practice information for working with siblings in general is scant (Sanders, 2011). As noted earlier, the primary focus of sibling aggression treatment has been on its most severe forms: physical and sexual abuse (e.g., Caffaro & Conn-Caffaro, 1998; Haskins, 2003). While no comprehensive models for less severe forms of sibling aggression treatment have been offered, a handful of discrete interventions have been put forth, such as using "time outs" (e.g., Adams & Kelley, 1992; Jones, Sloane, & Roberts, 1992; Olson & Roberts, 1987). Additionally, a wide array of advice has been offered for parents, but little is empirically supported (Kramer, 2004).

Only a few empirically supported sibling aggression offerings have been put forth. The aim of most is to stop hostilities, usually by training parents (usually mothers) in behavioral management strategies. These have shown promising results but have been limited by small sample sizes, lack of controls or comparison groups, and no follow-up (for a review, see Kramer, 2004). Similarly, teaching conflict resolution skills has received scant attention but has had promising results, when targeting both parents (Siddiqui & Ross, 2004; Smith & Ross, 2007) and children (Gentry & Benenson, 1993).

Only three empirically tested intervention offerings have targeted a change in family dynamics, such as cross-generational coalitions (Caspi, 2008; Kelly & Main, 1979; Reid & Donovan, 1990). All three showed fairly dramatic reductions in sibling antagonism but used small samples using single-case designs.

Fewer empirically considered approaches have been put forth, which focused on promoting sibling positivity. A growing awareness of the importance of supporting prosocial skill development as a way to address sibling negativity in practice has been emerging (Brotman et al., 2005; Kennedy & Kramer, 2008; Kramer, 2011; Kramer & Radey, 1997; Olson & Roberts, 1987; Tiedemann & Johnston, 1992). As noted, although aggression-halting strategies seem to be effective, they may inadvertently generate disengaged sibling relationships—a problematic practice outcome. Prosocial skills interventions have been quite effective in improving sibling positivity but its utility as a treatment approach for sibling violence is yet to be clearly established. An approach that integrates both violence-stopping and positivity-building strategies is needed. The sibling aggression treatment model put forth in this book offers such an approach: a new two-tier intervention model that integrates empirically tested aggression-halting *and* prosocial-development strategies.

## Untested Interventions

Examples of additional important offerings, which have yet to receive empirical examination, include three family systems approaches for sibling abuse and maltreatment (Caffaro & Conn-Caffaro, 1998; Kiselica & Morrill-Richards, 2007; Wiehe, 1997) and two that focus on sibling sexual abuse (DiGiorgio-Miller, 1998; Haskins, 2003). Theory-driven frameworks rely on conceptual frameworks to broadly inform practice, but do not provide step-by-step strategies for intervention work. Other theory-guided frameworks include a psychodynamic model for sexual abuse (Mitchell, 2004) and an approach that integrates feminist, conflict, and social learning theories (Hoffman et al., 2005). Theoretical frameworks are particularly useful for guiding practice in areas for which few technologies exist.

Other examples of yet to be tested sibling intervention work include a release play therapy framework for sibling rivalry (Kaduson, 1997), and a systemic approach that makes use of a "prescribing ambivalence" strategy (Wagner, Hunter, & Boelter, 1988). Finally, Gnaulati (2002) puts forth "sibling therapy" as an underutilized but viable treatment modality and offers clinical considerations for treating sibling hostility.

## Implications for Practice

Despite the limited sibling aggression treatment offerings for practitioners, developmental and intervention research findings can be used to inform practice. Strategies that have been tested and shown to be effective are preferable but, as noted, few such approaches exist. The next best approach is to look to empirically derived practice, where practitioners utilize developmental and intervention research findings to inform their practice (Caspi, 2011a). Empirically derived practice is preferable to idiosyncratic approaches. As presented earlier, the research literature offers an array of information about empirical links to sibling aggression with regard to promising treatment strategies. Assessment and intervention implications based on the literature are presented here.

### *Assessment*

The consequences and links to social problems presented earlier in this chapter can be utilized as a list of risk factors to guide assessment of sibling aggression. For example, knowing that marital dissatisfaction is linked to sibling aggression suggests practitioner exploration of sibling relationship quality when marital conflict is observed. Attending to risk factors can help identify sibling hostility and screen for physical safety—the primary assessment concern with all forms of interpersonal violence. Additionally, when sibling aggression is the identified treatment problem, an understanding of risk factors assists enquiry into related issues (e.g., academic struggles, peer relationship problems, parents' marital conflict).

The literature provides additional offerings in the form of tools that can be useful for sibling aggression assessment. These include Caffaro and Conn-Caffaro's (1998, 2005) questions for sibling abuse assessment (i.e., *Sibling Abuse Interview*), and research inventories that measure sibling conflict (e.g., *Scale of Negative Family Interactions*; Simonelli, Mullis, & Rohde, 2005). Standardized inventories can assist both practice and research endeavors (see Chapter 4 for using research inventories in practice).

Specific assessment strategies are offered in subsequent chapters and include exploration of family dynamics, empirical understanding of problems, and a simple strategy I put forth to assist the identification of abuse (see Chapter 5). It is likely that many of the risk factors commonly associated with child maltreatment by parents (see, e.g., Miller-Perrin & Perrin, 2007) overlap with those in cases of sibling victimization and should be explored. Assessments that suggest immediate danger require safety plans (Kellogg & Menard, 2003). An in-depth discussion of safety plans is taken up in Chapter 6.

It is common for sibling hostility to be present, problematic, and even directly related to a family's primary complaint, but not identified as such. For example, families may seek treatment for divorce or academic problems, but assessment reveals that sibling aggression is also a central concern. Practitioner identification of issues linked with sibling aggression indicates exploration into sibling discord, initially for the purpose of assessing child safety, and then as a potential treatment objective (often to address the primary complaint). More mild forms of sibling aggression (e.g., constant bickering) may not be considered problematic, but is often a serious source of family stress and can escalate to more serious hostility. Name calling, threats, and other forms of psychological maltreatment should not be dismissed as normal sibling behavior but rather as damaging (Keery et al., 2005) and as potential gateway behaviors to more severe and physical forms of aggression. Addressing mild aggression may serve as an important violence prevention strategy. In addition, family issues are often linked and sibling bickering may be serving a family function (e.g., stabilizing a conflictual marriage).

### *Intervention*

The assessment considerations gleaned from the literature inform the intervention process. For example, an assessment of parental favoritism suggests an intervention that disrupts this dynamic. A father who intervenes in sibling conflict by regularly protecting the younger from the older may be directed to temporarily side with the older, or to help the children problem solve in a more neutral way. Such restructuring of family interactional patterns is a common family intervention (Minuchin, 1974). In another example, an assessment of high sibling negativity suggests interventions that promote prosocial relationships (e.g., Kramer, 2011).

Helping siblings negotiate and create clear rules for managing sibling conflict has been found to be empirically promising (Reid & Donovan, 1990), particularly when it involves future-oriented planning, and avoids review of past grievances (Ross et al., 2006). Parent training aimed at assisting their children with sibling conflict problem solving has also been shown to be effective (Siddiqui & Ross, 2004). Positive sibling conflict resolution skill likely mediates conflict in other relationships (Reese-Weber & Kahn, 2005), as teaching such skills may reduce aggression in relationships outside the family.

Unless a child's safety is at risk, intervention should focus on developing and reinforcing prosocial and problem-solving behaviors with the goal of promoting supportive sibling relationships. Positive reinforcement of sibling prosocial behavior (e.g., sharing, complimenting, listening) can reduce conflict and increase support (Kramer & Radey, 1997). Intervention can help parents' change their focus on noting and inadvertently reinforcing sibling problems to supporting and praising positive encounters. Kramer (2011) offers prosocial competencies that can be implemented as intervention tasks.

Reid and Donovan (1990) suggest that practitioners should systematically quantify the severity and frequency of sibling conflict as an intervention strategy. Measuring aids the determination of intervention success and provides practitioners and families with insight into whether or not treatment strategies should be maintained, refined, or abandoned. Decreases in the severity or frequency of sibling assault suggest that interventions are working. No change or increases in conflict indicate that a different course of action should be pursued.

Sibling aggression is best understood as embedded within the multiple systems that support it. While family systems occupy most of the focus of this book, sibling hostility is supported across environmental systems, including schools, hospitals, communities, and by the culture at large. Interventions must frequently attend to multiple systems and systems levels. For example, a hospital emergency department practitioner may need to work with the intake staff to highlight the seriousness of injury caused intentionally by siblings. Raising awareness about problematic sibling aggression and voicing opposition to its use as comedy in the media should also be part of standard practice.

Finally, prevention of sibling violence has received scant attention but is a pressing social concern because it is both a widespread and deleterious form of child and adult maltreatment. Evidence is fairly strong that youth violence prevention interventions aimed solely at individuals, or framed as the problem being located within individuals, are ineffective (Mattaini & McGuire, 2006). Effective violence prevention efforts utilize strategies that attend to both individual risks and environmental factors, including individual prosocial skill development, parent training, and changing the social climate (U.S. Surgeon General, 2001). In a review of effective youth violence prevention programs, Mattaini and McGuire found that "basic behavioral strategies (e.g., skills training, substantial increases in positive reinforcement for prosocial behavior, moderation of aversives, and on-going, systematic evaluation) appear to be at the core of the effective interventions that have been identified, often explicitly" (Mattaini & McGuire, 2006, p. 213). Although their review did not speak specifically of sibling violence, it can be argued that these core elements bolster the effectiveness of sibling aggression treatment and prevention. These components run through the center of the model put forth in this book.

## CONCLUSION

This chapter provided an overview of sibling aggression, its definitions, prevalence, consequences, and the factors that support it. Empirical links to sibling aggression were put forth as potential risk factors to guide assessment in practice. Available treatment approaches were reviewed, and I provided implications for practice. A review of the sibling aggression literature provides support for presentation and implementation of the treatment model put forth in subsequent chapters. It suggests a two-tier approach that involves stopping problematic hostility while also working to enhance the quality of sibling relationships. It also indicates that sibling relationships cannot be understood or addressed without considering the contexts in which it exists. The family is the most immediate and powerful environment and as such, a family treatment approach makes sense. Although research provides some general directions, a related guiding theoretical framework is needed to provide a cohesive approach to working with siblings. In the following chapters, I offer a developing theoretical framework for working with siblings.

# 2

# A Theoretical Framework for Siblings: Part 1

A cohesive and comprehensive theory for sibling relationships and their influence on human development does not exist. However, principles from a handful of theoretical approaches have been used to account for sibling behavior, including family systems, evolutionary psychology, and social learning theories. These principles have been chiefly applied to discrete aspects of sibling development (e.g., explaining similarity and difference, sibling violence), or to give meaning to specific sibling research findings, but have yet to be integrated into a cohesive framework (Caspi, 2011). Indeed, the primary focus of sibling research has been to investigate outcomes and not theory development (with perhaps the exception of Sulloway, 1996). The complexities of sibling relationships make the formulation of a truly functional comprehensive theory challenging. Such a model, however, has much utility for practitioners. Mostly drawing from family systems, but integrating principles from other frameworks as well, I introduce an emerging "sibling theory" here.

This chapter provides an overview of family systems theory and how it provides a helpful lens for viewing sibling interaction. The next chapter continues presentation of the framework, focusing on how interactional processes shape individual identities and influence sibling conflict. All the concepts presented in both chapters are linked by the principle of interdependence.

Possessing a theoretical framework informs practice for focused and structured work. Without guiding principles, practitioners are likely to rely on haphazard "trial-and-error" approaches that are difficult to reproduce when effective. Sibling behavior occurs in various contexts, but its most immediate and powerful environment is the family. Sibling behavior can only be understood by recognizing family dynamics. How parents interact and manage their individual children, and their relationships to them, has much to do with how siblings relate to each other. Accordingly, family systems principles make particular sense for application to sibling relationships. Although the central purpose of introducing this emergent integrative sibling theory is to inform treatment efforts for sibling aggression, the framework also offers direction for human development and behavior.

## FAMILY SYSTEMS THEORY

Family systems theory represents a collection of principles drawn from a variety of theorists. Its initial development began in the 1950s when it was brought to prominence by family communications researchers interested in discovering whether repetitive interactions between members (especially between mothers and children) were linked to schizophrenia (via the "double bind") (Bateson, Jackson, Haley, & Weakland, 1956). From these experiments, Gregory Bateson and his colleagues concluded that families operate by an unspoken and often unacknowledged set of rules that govern members' behaviors (Jackson, 1968). Family systems principles have emerged as the central framework for understanding family interaction and for informing the widespread practice of family therapy. A central belief of family systems is that the family is the most immediate and powerful environment for human development, and that individual behavior is inextricably tied to those of other members and to family process. This assumption of interdependence is central to family systems principles.

## INTERDEPENDENCE

The principle of interdependence suggests that no behavior is enacted independently, but happens in relation to one's environmental context, relationship history, and in reaction or in anticipation of others' behaviors. Interdependence is a process of mutual causality where a change in one part of the family system affects change in another part (Whitchurch & Constantine, 1993). Specifically, an individual's behavior is influenced by others in the family system, and that one member's behavior affects all others. All members' behaviors are linked. For example, if a child in the family becomes sick and must stay home from school, the parents must change their behaviors to make accommodations for the child. They usually behave differently with the child (e.g., spend more time, use more gentle voice) and with each other (e.g., deciding who should stay home to care for the child or take the child to the doctor). The sibling relationship also changes. Siblings may be instructed to keep distance from the sick child to minimize risk of contagion, and to keep quiet, restricting the ability to play freely. The healthy siblings may also experience less parental attention. It is not just the sick child who is changed by the illness; all family members and their relationships are altered.

The concept of interdependence contrasts with Western culture's emphasis on autonomy, independence, and individual responsibility. A cognitive shift is required to move from a "problem within the individual" focus to an understanding of actions as embedded in an interdependent network. Using a sibling lens enables such a shift and is helpful in identifying interdependence in action, which will become evident as additional family systems are discussed here.

## BOUNDARIES

Interpersonal boundaries refer to the rules that regulate the flow of information and emotional investment that occur between individuals or systems (Minuchin, 1974). It is understood in terms of *permeability*; how easy or difficult it is for information to travel across the boundary—that is, how fast or slow the flow is. To illustrate the concept of permeability, consider the metaphor of how milk interacts with two types of boundaries: cereal and a drinking glass. The cereal has high permeability and the milk enters it rather easily and makes it soggy. By comparison, the drinking glass has no permeability and the milk cannot cross its boundary. The higher the permeability the more impact the milk will have on the system. The cereal is dramatically influenced and changed by the infusion of milk. The drinking glass remains uninfluenced or unchanged. The cereal represents an *open system* with a *diffuse* external boundary, and the drinking glass is a *closed system* with a *rigid* boundary.

In family systems, two sets of boundaries are considered. *Systems boundaries* refer to the boundary that exists around the system, defining the system as separate from other entities, and describing the nature of the family's interactions with other systems. By comparison, *interpersonal boundaries* are located between individuals. It is important to emphasize that interpersonal boundaries emerge between pairs of individuals who both help to define them, which is quite different from the notion of "personal boundaries" described in many pop psychology books as located within or by individuals. In the family systems view, one does not have a single personal boundary, but many different and ever-changing boundaries depending upon with whom an individual is interacting. For example, one is likely to have a more permeable boundary with a best friend than with a stranger. It is also incorrect to refer to an individual as having "no boundaries" (e.g., "Jane shares everything with everyone, she has no boundaries!"). Rather, interpersonal boundaries are defined on a permeability continuum that ranges from high (i.e., *enmeshment*) to low (i.e., *disengagement*) (Minuchin, 1974). The permeability of sibling subsystem and interpersonal boundaries changes over time, and influences relationships with others.

### Interpersonal Boundaries

Interpersonal boundaries are considered on a permeability continuum that ranges from open or enmeshed to closed or disengaged (see Figure 2.1). Over the course of interpersonal relationships, the degree of permeability changes,

**FIGURE 2.1** The permeability continuum of interpersonal boundaries.

Most relationships

Enmeshed ______________________________ Disengaged

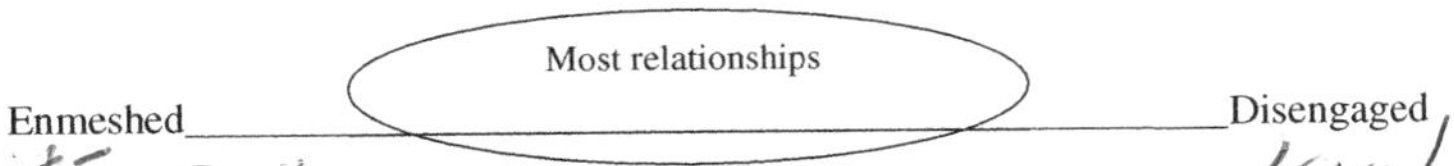

with most relational time spent somewhere in the middle portions of the continuum rather than the far ends. Enmeshment and disengagement are described here, providing a common language for discussing sibling and family relationships later in this book.

### *Enmeshment*

Enmeshment is used to describe an especially permeable boundary across which information flows easily and emotional investment is high. Enmeshed pairs know a great deal about one another and readily share intimate details about their lives with little filtering. They are exceptionally in tune with each other and are *highly reactive* to each other's emotions and behaviors. This elevated level of reactivity suggests that they are highly interdependent and have little ability to operate autonomously. Each one's behavior is linked to the other's. An example of this high degree of reactivity is illustrated by a child who describes the sky as "blue" and his sibling immediately responding that it is "black." The siblings operate in reaction to each other rather than independently. Their "selves" are lost in the enmeshed boundary. Because the pair is so invested in each other, they have little energy or ability to focus on other people or activities. The more enmeshed a pair becomes, the more *disengaged* they are with others.

An excellent example of enmeshment and its relationship to disengagement with others is of a mother and her newborn. She gazes into the infant's face for long periods of time, mimics the baby's faces and noises, and is able to fairly well distinguish the meanings of the baby's vocalizations (e.g., hunger, wet diapers, tired). The mother is fairly unaware of other events in her immediate surroundings and must redirect interest previously aimed at others in order to focus this amount of attention on her baby. That is, she must become more disengaged with her husband or partner, who in turn will become more disengaged with her. As the baby develops and learns how to be increasingly independent (e.g., feed self, potty trained), the relationship must become more disengaged in order to allow the baby to become an individual. It is also important to note that the high level of enmeshment expected in mother–newborn relationships is important for infant attachment and development. This degree of investment is considered healthy and necessary at this point of the life cycle, where it would not be later on. That is, the degree of enmeshment and disengagement in relationships are not in and of themselves indicators of health or dysfunction, but rather ways of describing relationships. How relationships manage their interpersonal boundaries is of greater significance to understanding problems in relationships.

### *Disengagement*

A disengaged interpersonal boundary describes a relationship in which minimal investment of emotional energy and little information is shared or known. Not much time is spent considering the other and there is *low reactivity* to what other does or feels. For example, a brother has little information and seems unconcerned about his sister's recent breakup. Or a friend says, "I heard your brother was suspended from school," to which the brother replies, "Really? I had no idea. Want to catch a movie later?" Such relationships involve the provision of little support, warmth, or closeness. Sibling disengagement at certain points of the life cycle is expected. For example, as individuals become more invested in love interests and in pursuing separate activities associated with adulthood such as raising one's children, siblings may become quite disengaged. Interestingly, a fairly large subset of students in my sibling courses claim to become less disengaged with their siblings in adulthood, a dynamic that may be explained by the ability to interact without the intrusion of parents. Again, disengagement in and of itself does not suggest a problematic relationship, but rather describes the current state of affairs.

That said, the *cutoff* (Bowen, 1978), which entails intentionally ended relationships in which communication has been stopped and direct communication halted (e.g., "Those two haven't spoken in 20 years!"), represents an extreme and usually problematic level of high disengagement. In families, the cutoff is a superficial ending since the formal relational status remains, unlike with peers and romantic relationships that can be forever finished. That is, choosing to cut ties with a brother does not mean that this person is no longer a brother, and this relational status can be resumed at any time. He will forever be a brother.

Cutoffs represent unfinished relational business. Hurts, resentments, and lost affection remain even though communication has ended (Bowen, 1978). Indeed, it is a complex if not paradoxical concept in that actively maintaining a cutoff involves a degree of emotional investment and conviction. The cutoff is significant in sibling relationships because victims of sibling abuse may choose to end the relationship with the perpetrator sibling, expecting that this will bring an end to the relational issues. However, cutoffs do not resolve issues, which has implications for treatment. Even if the practitioner and client decide that stopping all contact with an abusive sibling is in the client's best interests, continued discussions of the abuse and the sibling are necessary.

As stated earlier, most relationships do not occur at these extremes but rather exist more toward the middle, which Minuchin (1974) refers to as the "normal range" (see Figure 2.1). That said, relational boundaries are fluid in that they change over time.

For example, a pair of strangers begins at the extreme end of disengagement. As they become friendlier, more trusting, and sharing of themselves, they will move toward the enmeshed side of the continuum. Should they become best friends, they will move even closer to enmeshment. But when one develops a relationship with a romantic partner, they will become more disengaged as one designates their attention elsewhere. The two best friends may remain close but their relationship will necessarily change and move more toward the middle of the continuum.

In short, enmeshment represents high connectedness while sacrificing autonomy, while disengagement is high autonomy while sacrificing connectedness (at the far ends of the continuum). Relationships in the middle of the continuum represent the balancing of connectedness and autonomy—a major challenge to most relationships.

### *Sibling interpersonal boundaries*

The interpersonal boundaries between siblings change over time as well, and are important for understanding the nature of the relationship. Children are often highly in tune with their siblings' relationships with their parents and notions of fairness. This level of emotional investment suggests enmeshment. Highly competitive, conflictual, and aggressive siblings are enmeshed, which is important for considering intervention strategies with aggressive siblings. For example, practitioners could take two courses of action related to managing siblings' interpersonal boundaries. Restructuring the relationship to become less enmeshed by refocusing interests and relational investments should decrease aggression. Alternately, assisting the siblings to refocus their negative involvement into positive involvement can represent an approach that may be most beneficial in the long run. The specifics of such interventions are taken up later in this book.

*Systems boundaries. Systems* or *external boundaries* describe the invisible filter that surrounds systems. This is illustrated in Figure 2.2 by the line around the family of four.

Similar to interpersonal boundaries, system boundaries represent the rules that regulate the flow of information between the system and external systems or individuals, and is also described on a permeability continuum with *open* or *closed* at its ends. Open boundaries involve high permeability, and closed suggest low. In open family systems, members are engaged with outsiders and are exposed to new information without much censorship. Conversely, in closed family systems, members have minimal involvement with outsiders, low investment in what occurs outside their family, and reveal little to those not part of the system. An inverse relationship occurs between system (external)

**FIGURE 2.2** System boundaries in a family of four.

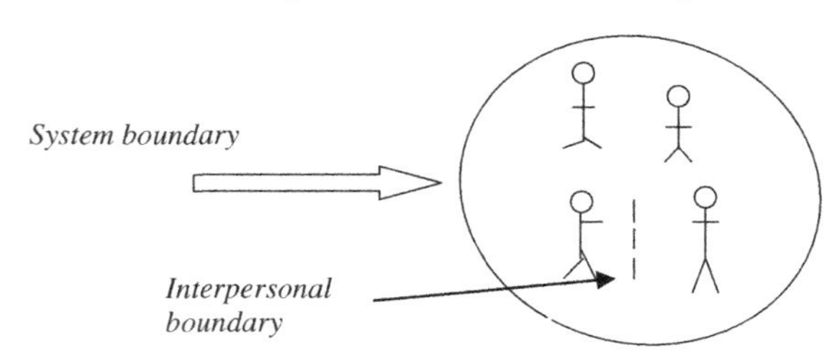

and interpersonal (internal) boundaries. The more closed the external boundary, the more enmeshed the internal boundaries. Stated in reverse, the more open the system boundary, the greater the disengagement between its members.

Family secrets such as abuses (e.g., parental, partner, sibling, substance) primarily occur in closed systems. Members often go to great lengths to avoid revealing the abuse to outsiders, fearing consequences (e.g., calls to child protective services, embarrassment). Accordingly, sibling abuse typically occurs within a closed sibling *system* boundary. System outsiders, such as parents, are often unaware of the violence. Perpetrators of abuse often use coerced secrecy to ensure that the system boundary remains closed. Typical strategies involve threats of further injury, harm to pets or other belongings, and public humiliation.

## SUBSYSTEMS

Sibling systems are subsystems of family systems. Subsystems are combinations of two or more individuals within a larger system. These combinations function as unique systems, each with its own relational rules and boundaries. In a family of three, three subsystems exist that include the parents, mother and child, father and child. The addition of a member to family size exponentially increases the number of family subsystems. For example, in a family of four (members A, B, C, D), there are 10 subsystems:

*Subsystem combinations of two members*:

**A–B   A–C   A–D   B–C   B–D   C–D**

*Subsystem combinations of three members*:

**A–B–C   A–B–D   A–C–D   B–C–D**

Traditionally, families have been understood in terms of three central subsystems; spousa, parental, and sibling (Minuchin, 1974). In families with children, the spousal subsystem consists of husband and wife, same-sex partners, unmarried couples, or other combinations of adult caretakers. It is also referred to as the executive subsystem because this is the unit that should be in charge of and work collaboratively to ensure productive, family operations. The parental subsystem describes relationships between parents and children. Parental subsystem combinations include a father and his oldest son, a mother and her middle daughter, a single mother with two of her three children, or two parents and their child. The sibling subsystem is comprised of the children in the family. When there are more than two siblings, there are multiple sibling subsystems.

Each subsystem has to maintain rules about the external boundary. For example, when a child tries to participate in parents' conversation, the adults can either permit the child to enter the spousa subsystem or tell the child to "stay out of it." Parents who allow their child to enter demonstrate a more permeable and open boundary than adults who restrict their child's involvement. If one thinks of a bedroom as a physical representation of an external boundary, when the parents are in the room they can have a policy that allows the children to come in (or enter their relationship) as they wish, or one that dictates that the child must knock first. It may be obvious that it is easier to have a one-on-one relationship when the door is closed. When the child enters the room, it becomes more complicated to sustain the one-on-one conversation. Simply the child's being there alters the way the parents talk to each other—for example, avoiding certain topics, censoring language. As soon as the boundary is open, the child can interfere, mediate, and greatly influence the parents' relationship. For example, a child may enter the room every time she hears her parents arguing, bringing the conflict to an immediate and unresolved halt. Of course, it is not always possible to keep the door, or the boundary, closed—particularly when children are very young.

Sibling subsystem boundaries represent rules for interacting with others (e.g., parents, peers, strangers). For example, a sibling pair must decide whether or not to share certain information with a parent. Such decisions define the boundary permeability of subsystem relationships. Of course, siblings cannot completely define their boundary. Parents can and often do involve themselves in their children's relationships, helping and teaching them how to behave with each other. However, parents involved in every aspect of their children's relationships interfere with their children's opportunities to learn how to autonomously function, how to resolve conflict independently, and how to develop closeness.

A challenge all subsystems face is agreeing on the external boundary. If one feels it should be more open than the other, there is often conflict between its members. For example, a wife decides to share an embarrassing story about her husband to a group of friends. The husband becomes angry with his wife because she told the story, but his anger is also because she violated their subsystem boundary—that is, agreement to keep that information within the spousal subsystem. Anger and hurt are frequently about boundary disagreements.

Subsystem boundaries shift in permeability over time, according to location, and in response to who is also present. It is impossible for subsystem members to have working agreements about all that can and cannot be permitted to cross the external boundary in every circumstance. As such, there is always a risk that subsystem boundaries will be accidentally violated by one of its members. Boundary violations, however, can be intentional and are aggressive acts meant to injure or demonstrate power over other members in the subsystem. For example, a child who promised to keep his sister's secret may decide to reveal it to their parents when he is angry with her or is looking to establish a more favorable position.

In practice, sibling subsystem boundary assessments can provide unique understandings of sibling relationships and frustrations. Intentional subsystem boundary violations can be framed as hostile acts that undermine the relationship, as opposed to "normal sibling rivalry." Of course, in cases where an individual's safety is at risk (e.g., a sibling knows his sister is boyfriend, or a brother is taking drugs, or sibling abuse), int violations are necessary and encouraged. Accidental violatio by developing an agreement to check with each other prior to larly important personal information with outsiders (e.g., parents, friends).

## TRIANGLES

A major family systems concept is the triangle that, at its most basic, views family relationships in groups of three people at a time. The triangle is the basic unit of interaction by which family systems professionals view family and individual behavior. Triangulation refers to a process in which a conflict between two individuals becomes too overwhelming and a third person (or issue) becomes a new focus of attention in order to lessen the immediate stress (Titelman, 2008)—forming the shape of a triangle. The third person is "triangled in" by entering or being invited into the conflicting dyad's relationship. By distracting the dyad from each other, the third person serves a stabilizing force.

In addition to lessening the intensity in the fighting pair, triangulation serves a second function: to gain power in the relationship to overpower the rival by having another person take one's side. For example, when an individual is caught in a room with two friends who are in a serious argument, at some point the fighting pair will turn to the individual and ask, "Who is right?" They are not, however, truly asking for a neutral judge but rather for the person to choose a side. A more accurate version of the "Who is right?" question is "You are on my side, right?" Side-taking, or alliance building, is a power move as well as a way of distracting from the immediate stress of discord.

The classic triangle involves a conflictual couple and their child. The child responds to the stress in the household by acting unusually, such as becoming sillier, more defiant, more aggressive, or engaging in bedwetting or school problems. The parents notice the child's change in behavior and refocus their fighting with each other to their child. The result is that the household stress quickly reduces as the parents attend to the child. As the child's behavior improves and stops being a distraction for the parents, they return to their conflict, which was put on hold by the diversion but not resolved. The household stress and discomfort return and the child reengages in the distracting behavior. The parents turn their focus to the child, the conflict abates, and the stress reduces. The child's behavior then improves, the couple returns to their unresolved conflict and the household tension resurfaces. The child's misbehavior then reemerges and so on. This repetitive pattern continues until the child "learns" that as long as he misbehaves his parents do not fight. In brief, the child's behavior becomes a function of the parents' relationship—that is, they need it for stability. In other words, the relationship would fall apart without it, and paradoxically, the couple cannot resolve their disagreements while focused on the child.

√hen such rigid triangulation exists, the child is unable to grow to be inde-endent as he is dependent upon the parents' relational status (Minuchin, 1974). Triangulation involving spousal conflict is recognized as a potent risk factor for child maladjustment (Fosco & Grych, 2010). Moreover, it is important to note that the third person is not triangled in neutrally. That is, triangles are about side-taking or *coalitions* or *alliances*, in which there is a two-against-one pattern involving two insiders and an outsider. In the classic triangle described above, one parent usually becomes more invested in the child while the other parent becomes more disengaged. Or, alternatively, the two parents disagree on how to address the child's behavior with one parent defending the child against the parent's expressing that punishment is in order. In both scenarios, a parent–child coalition is formed in which the child becomes an ally with one parent against the other. To illustrate variations of parent–child triangles, vignettes are provided here.

### *Vignette #1: "I did it all for the cookie"*

Doug, age 5, asked his mother for a cookie, who responded "No." Doug then went to his father who said, "Sure!" Doug then walked back into the living room with the cookie, where his mother was sitting. She yelled, "I said, 'No cookies!'" Doug responded, "Dad told me I could."

At first read, Doug may appear to be a manipulative child who has played his parents well. Instead, however, if this dynamic represents a repetitive interaction pattern, it can be viewed as a triangle in which the adults are in conflict about parenting, and which involves a father–child coalition against the mother. The intensity of the parents' conflict is diffused by fighting through Doug. That is, the mother and the father do not communicate directly and avoid confrontation regarding their differences. As noted earlier, coalitions are about power. The father–child coalition undermines the mother's power to parent. To put it bluntly, Doug does not have to abide by his mother's rules because he knows his father will usually take his side. In short, Doug has more power than his mother, because he is supported by his father. With regard to the parent's conflict, it is a win–win situation for the father to support his son. He gets to be the "good parent" in his son's eyes and wins an ally, while injuring his wife—all indirectly. This tactic, of course, comes at the Doug's expense. Although he may enjoy the power, he loses a close relationship with his mother.

It is not uncommon in families for parent–child coalitions to exist with siblings. One child, often the younger, knows she will be protected from the older child by the parent. The effect is to make an outsider of the older child and to undermine his power. The younger child learns she can do what she wants with the older child (e.g., have access to his toys, enter his room, call him names) because she knows that her parent will take her side. Being an outsider in triangle builds resentment and hostility.

*Vignette #2: "You are always at work!"*

Mary, a 10-year-old, lives with her mother and father. Her mother is depressed and often tells Mary how lonely she feels. Her father spends many hours at his workplace. When he comes home, Mary angrily yells at him, "You are always at work! You don't care about us. Mom is lonely and sad because of you." Her father then explains that he has to work to support the family and that her mother "always had issues." Mary defends her mother by repeating that he does not really care about them.

Similar to the family in Vignette #1, Mary's family involves a triangle with a parent–child coalition. In such structures, it is common for children to become the spokesperson for the allied parent and engage in the parents' conflict as the ally's representative. Mary voices her mother's frustrations *for her mother*. In this arrangement, the family avoids the stress of direct confrontation; the parents focus their attention on the child instead of each other, and the child is given power by one parent to undermine the other.

A similar pattern occurs in parent–child coalitions with siblings. The allied child becomes the mouthpiece for the parent, expressing the parent's unspoken frustrations and resentments. For example, a child may say to his similar-age sibling, "You always make trouble and disappoint the family. Don't you ever think before you act?!" Or, "How many times do you have to be told to put your dishes away?!" Such statements demonstrate the power shift accorded by coalitions and how children are moved into roles that are reflective of adult power. As suggested earlier, children in such positions often enjoy such power but it comes at the expense of poor relationships with the family members who are the perceived enemies, such as a sibling. The triangle with Mary and her parents precludes Mary from having a close relationship with her father, and she will not experience being fathered as long as she is operating like a spouse substitute. Similarly, Doug cannot be close to his mother and loses the experience of being mothered.

## Triangulation and Siblings

A few triangulation variations that involve sibling relationships are common. Two are discussed here: parental differential treatment and sibling coalitions.

Parental differential treatment refers to how parents interact with their children. When a parent provides more favorable treatment to one child than another, it represents a triangle with a coalition between the parent and the favored child. Such differential treatment supports perceived favoritism.

Despite social pressures to treat children the same, identical treatment is essentially impossible. Each child differs with varying individual needs, strengths, and temperaments, and parents adjust their behaviors accordingly. In this regard, differential treatment represents reactive parenting and is normative and expected. Additionally, parents themselves change over time. Parents of firstborns are typically more anxious than with laterborns. For example, they are more likely to call the pediatrician when the child has a cough, they went to pre-birth classes, and they bought books on milestone achievement to assess their child's development. They also closely document the firstborn's growth with multitudes of photographs and videos. By comparison, secondborns have parents who are more relaxed about parenting. They are less quick to call pediatricians, are unlikely to go to birthing classes, and have diminished interest in consulting parenting books. They also take fewer photos and videos (as most laterborns will attest). Parents change as they age. Laterborn children enter into families with parents who may be more mature, more stressed, or have more income than their older siblings. In short, parents do not treat their children in the same ways, and research has shown that parents and children both perceive differential treatment (Brody, Stoneman, & McCoy, 1992; Daniels & Plomin, 1985).

Parental differential treatment has been linked to an array of negative outcomes, particularly for the disfavored child, but also for sibling and parent–child relationships (Suitor, Sechrist, Plikuhn, Pardo, & Pillemer, 2008) for both the favored and the disfavored child (Brody et al., 1994; McHale, Crouter, McGuire, & Updegraff, 1995). It seems, however, that differential treatment is not problematic when children, even in adulthood, understand and perceive the reasons for the disparity to be fair (Boll, Ferring, & Filipp, 2005; Kowal & Kramer, 1997; Kowal, Krull, & Kramer, 2006). When injustice is perceived, children often resent and are motivated to act aggressively toward their siblings. Parental differential treatment that is problematically unequal is perceived as favoritism and is a risk factor for sibling aggression.

A type of parental differential treatment that may be particularly potent for perceived favoritism and injustice regards how parents intervene in their children's sibling conflicts. It is common for parents to protect their younger children from their older siblings (Felson & Russo, 1988), using statements such as, "You're older, you should know better," or "He's littler than you, let him have the toy." Such statements typically serve to increase sibling resentment and hostility because they reflect triangles in which the older child is the outsider to a parent–younger child coalition. In these triangles, younger children are empowered and older children disempowered, by the parent's protective position. In short, younger children are given the authority to engage, challenge, and disrupt older children because they know that a parent will protect them. This type of one-sided parental intervention likely serves to support and perpetuate sibling aggression.

### *Sibling coalitions*

In sibships of three or more, alliances between two against a third are common. It is not uncommon for an individual in conflict with a sibling to turn to another sibling for support against the rival. Sibling triangulation serves the same function as triangles in other relationships. It serves to overpower another in a conflict, avoid direct confrontation, undermine the outsider's authority, and win a favorable position with the allied individual. A sibling conflict dynamic that I have frequently noted entails a fairly fixed first–thirdborn coalition against the secondborn (i.e., middle child), which I refer to as a "leap pair." The firstborn uses their larger size and higher cognitive sophistication to pick on the secondborn. The secondborn then uses the same tactics on the thirdborn. When the secondborn aggresses toward the third, the firstborn comes to the rescue and serves as the thirdborn's protector. The middleborn child is the outsider in this form of sibling triangle and has less power in the family than the lastborn who is supported by the firstborn.

## An Important Triangulation Aside: Outsiders Act Like Outsiders

It is important to note that outsiders act like outsiders. It is difficult, hurtful, and isolating to be the "odd man out" in triangles. Outsiders frequently make attempts to become insiders (or disrupt coalitions) using aggression. For example, fathers who are on the outside of mother–child coalitions experience being both excluded and powerless. The mother's alliance with the child undermines the father's authority over the child. Responding to lack of power to parent, and perhaps to being disfavored, the father may turn to overly harsh and aggressive discipline strategies. The father's behavior, although seriously problematic, makes sense in this context.

It is similarly important to understand child behavior in the sibling context. Children who are on the outside of a parent–sibling coalition may behave in ways that appear odd or disturbed, but may be ways of expressing affect related to being an outsider—efforts to disrupt coalitions, become an insider, express hurt related to perceived unfairness and favoritism, and so on. Practitioners must be careful to avoid jumping to conclusions that aggressive children are inherently pathological and requiring diagnosis (e.g., oppositional defiant disorder, conduct disorder). Doing so reinforces the outsider experience. The family thinks of themselves as "us" and the "defiant one." In such cases, practitioners may be colluding in family scapegoating and triangulation, and serve to perpetuate the aggression. Taking a family systems view, outsiders no longer need to act aggressively when all feel included and fairly treated. Changing relational patterns in this regard can be highly effective in addressing problematic behavior.

### *Not all triangles are bad*

It is also important to note that triangles emerge in all relationships and are not inherently problematic. They are typically transient and may take many shapes, with alternating alliances. Patterns of triangulation in families can shift rapidly or they can become fixed, maintaining rigid structural alliances for long periods.

Families are constantly changing and adapting to both internal and external forces. Children grow older and require different parenting behaviors and rule sets. New members join through birth and marriage and others leave through death and divorce. Families can experience shifts in economic prosperity. Flexibility to make shifts as time moves forward is required for families to function well. Rigidity in relationships, inflexible rules, and fixed manners of interaction increase the likelihood of problems emerging. Families typically start treatment feeling stuck and the practitioner helps them to move forward by addressing rigidity.

Problem triangles are those that are fixed reflecting repetitive patterns of behavior—that is, two individuals rigidly, unwaveringly, and blindly supporting each other against a third. They can obstruct resolution of conflict, promote resentments, be injurious to the health and functioning of individuals (particular to outsiders), and impede emotional development. Structural flexibility is important to healthy family functioning. Families that can realign themselves when necessary and that can adjust to developmental demands without becoming disorganized or overwhelmed tend to function better than families that are inflexible.

### *Quadrangle*

Triangles are interlocking in that people who are outsiders of coalitions often find other individuals to ally with against those in the coalition. A common pattern involves a parent who is the outsider of a spouse–child coalition developing an alliance with a second child. The result is two parent–child alliances that form the shape of a quadrangle (Schachter, 1985) (see Figure 2.3).

As suggested earlier, a typical triangle in families involves one parent who systematically protects a child from the sterner parent. Feeling the child has been claimed by the spouse, the outsider parent then may develop a coalition with a second child, who also feels excluded from his or her sibling's

**FIGURE 2.3** Two parent-child alliances in a quadrangle.

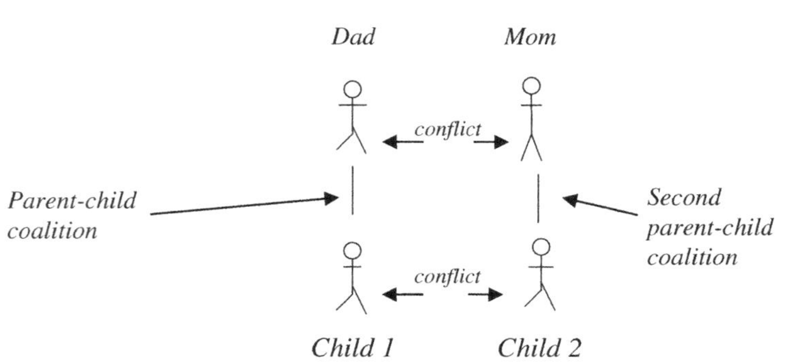

parent–child coalition. In the quadrangle view, sibling conflict is likely the acting out of marital problems, each voicing the (often unspoken) sentiments of their allied parent. Marital and sibling conflicts have been linked in research (e.g., Noller, Feeney, Peterson, & Sheehan, 1995). Moreover, children who perceive responsibility for their parents' conflict have more psychological adjustment and problematic externalizing behaviors than children who experience less self-blame (Noller, Feeney, Peterson, & Sheehan, 2000; Richmond & Stocker, 2003). The dynamics of rigid triangles, coalitions, and quadrangles require children to act as participants, as side-takers, and as mouthpieces of discontent, in their parents' marital conflicts. Such dynamics likely increase children's feelings of responsibility and self-blame.

## CONCLUSION

This chapter provided an in-depth review of family systems theory as a lens for considering sibling relational behavior. Similarly, the sibling relationship provides a helpful lens for understanding family systems theory. The presentation of an emergent and integrated sibling theory is continued in the next chapter that focuses on processes of influence and how they shape sibling relationships and aggression.

# 3

# A Theoretical Framework for Siblings: Part 2

This chapter continues the discussion of an emerging sibling theory to provide an integrated and unique way of viewing sibling behavior and to inform practice decisions. Specifically, I consider processes of sibling influence that shape individual identities, interests, and interaction. Siblings are quite different from each other and the processes that influence sibling difference are considered. The role of sibling comparison and resulting complementarity is highlighted as a potent force in sibling difference. This is followed by an in-depth discussion of the application of Darwinian principles to sibling relationships. I build upon and extend these concepts, offering new related and interdependent principles. I conclude by considering the role of siblings as models in expressions of aggression and support.

## SIBLING DIFFERENCE

Children from the same family are surprisingly different from each other. This likely comes as no surprise as many individuals refer to their siblings as "complete opposites." A compelling finding that kick-started closer examination of sibling differences stated that pairs of siblings are no more alike than random pairs of random strangers in regard to personality and psychological development (Daniels & Plomin, 1987; Dunn & Plomin, 1991). Such a finding may initially seem improbable as siblings typically share both genetics and environment. Both influences should explain greater similarity. The role of nonshared environments has been put forth as the primary explanation for sibling difference, but are not yet well understood (e.g., Plomin, Asbury, & Dunn, 2001). It is possible that few experiences are truly shared as individuals perceive events in idiosyncratic ways. Even shared experiences may influence greater difference.

One major source of nonshared influence is the sibling relationship itself. In a sibling pair, each experiences living with the other, and neither can truly understand what it must be like living with himself or herself. For example, Jennifer and Alison are sisters. Alison experiences and is influenced by Jennifer and conversely, Jennifer experiences life with Alison. But, Alison does not know what it is like to be her own sister. She is not influenced by an external Alison. Individuals develop in reaction and in contrast to their siblings in processes of deidentification, individuation, and differentiation (Bowen, 1978; Satir, 1983; Schachter, Shore, Feldman-Rotman, Marquis, & Campbell, 1976). They make efforts to be different from each other, even when trying to model the others' successes. Indeed, sibling differences are frequently noted and reinforced by interactions with each other and by family members, peers, and others who compare them.

## COMPARISON AND COMPLEMENTARITY

There are no groups of individuals who are compared more closely or often than siblings. Comparisons are being made even prior to the birth of the second child. It is not uncommon for a pregnant mother to hold her stomach and comment on perceived differences, saying something like, "This child is more active than the first." In families that add children through birth, the comparisons become exceptionally frequent and intimate immediately after the new infant is born. First observations are often relative to the older sibling—for example, "The baby looks more like his mother, and the older child looks more like his father." Even if the latter half of the statement was not made, it suggests a comparison. For example, if the observer were to only say, "The baby looks more like his mother," the unstated "*than his sibling*" is still implied. Sibling comparisons exist even when only commenting on one child.

In addition to appearance, siblings' actions are also closely observed and compared and subjectively couched to imply personality traits. For example, a parent may observe that a child is afraid to enter a dark room. This behavior can be described as "fearful," "timid," "careful," or even "sensible"—all subjective takes that have consequences for how the parent treats the child. Such descriptions also have implications for the child's siblings who are likely to be ascribed opposite traits such as "brave," "outgoing," or "careless," without doing anything (but be a sibling). The most common and potentially powerful comparative environment for children is the sibling relationship. One sibling cannot be described as "fearful" without inherently suggesting that another is "brave." These are not benign comparisons. Designated labels become expectations, internalized as identities, and cues for how others are to relate to them. Parents will treat their fearful child differently from the brave one, perhaps providing more encouragement or expressions of frustration.

Sibling comparisons typically emphasize differences rather than similarities (Saudino, Wertz, Gagne, & Chawla, 2004). In addition, individuals define each other in opposing ways as they initiate and respond to each other in their relationships (Heatherington & Friedlander, 1990). This pattern of comparing and defining individuals in shared systems as opposites can be understood using the principle of complementarity.

### Complementarity

The principle of complementarity suggests that a relational position or trait is only understood in regard to the interplay with its opposite (Minuchin &

Fishman, 1981). Opposites are inherently interdependent with each side defining itself in reaction to the other. In other words, a trait cannot be defined without referring to its opposite.

Complementarity has been most often used to describe unequal relational power arrangements (e.g., doctor–patient; teacher–student), where each person's power in a shared system is interdependently defined by the other. An increase in one's power is proportionally related and connected to the other's diminished power, and vice versa. As the person with less power gains authority, the individual with higher power has less. This interactive principle has important application for other relational dynamics, such as with personality descriptors.

In interpersonal theory, complementarity has been used to describe how members work together in productive relationships (Tracey & Rohlfing, 2010), and learning to be complementary is an important part. Similarly, the concept has been applied to the role of birth order pairings in marital adjustment (Birtchnell & Mayhew, 1977; Ortiz, 1981; Toman, 1959). While adapting to brothers and sisters in complementary ways is part of sibling life, complementarity is also a function of comparison by both siblings and others. I extend the concept of complementarity in this book and elsewhere (e.g., Caspi, 2011c) to describe the interdependent polarization of traits in relational systems through both interpersonal negotiation and comparative judgments. I offer it as a helpful principle for understanding and explaining sibling behavior.

The central thrust of complementarity is that every personality trait has an implied opposite. For example, a child cannot be labeled *fast* without another in their comparative environment (e.g., sibling subsystem) being *slow*; one cannot be *irresponsible* without others being *overresponsible*. There is no *bad* without the existence of *good*. When traits are overtly expressed, the opposite characteristic is ascribed to whoever is in the same comparative environment. For example, a mother cannot call her son *smart* without it being a comment on his sibling's intelligence. The sibling will likely understand it this way even if it is not the mother's intention.

It is helpful to consider each trait as existing on a complementary continuum with opposite traits at the ends. Here are just a few examples:

Neat________________________Sloppy

Outgoing____________________Shy

Serious______________________Silly

Uptight______________________Relaxed

Overresponsible______________Irresponsible

Smart________________________Dumb

Athletic______________________Unathletic

Each continuum represents the full range of behavior that could occur within its descriptors. That is, the reference group for comparison includes the general population. It is unlikely that two being compared truly engage in the extreme behaviors, but instead fall somewhere in the middle of the continua, such as illustrated here:

Neat__X______Y____________Sloppy

Because they share the same comparative environment, siblings are each other's reference points, not the general population. As such, they use descriptors that reflect extreme positions—that is, the neat one and the sloppy one—rather than "really neat" and "sort of neat," which are more accurate. To illustrate, consider the sisters, Jessica and Judy. Neither played any sports. In a family therapy session, Jessica jokingly shared that she was the athletic one (and Judy the unathletic one) in their family because she once attended a 1-week tennis camp when she was 9 years old. She added that since then her parents buy her running suits at Christmas while Judy is given jewelry and books.

### *The complementarity process*

As noted earlier, complementary reflects an interdependent process in which traits are interdependent and defined through mutual interaction. To demonstrate the process, I will use the neat–sloppy continuum as an example. A romantic couple (X and Y) has recently started sharing an apartment together. The two are both neat compared to most individuals as illustrated by this continuum:

Neat_____X_____Y_____________________Sloppy

At the start of the relationship they both define each other as neat people. However, X believes the apartment should be vacuumed twice a week while Y feels that once a week is sufficient. X likes the dishes to be washed immediately after dinner but Y prefers to relax first and do them half an hour later. As the couple spends their first week together, X gets to the vacuuming first. Similarly, X washes the dishes before Y moves to do them. In their relationship, X takes increasing responsibility for the cleaning activities and Y takes less effort. After some time their neat–sloppy continuum looks like this:

Neat__X_______________________Y____Sloppy

X increasingly beats Y to cleaning and becomes "the neat one." As Y does less, she becomes "the sloppy one." Conversely stated, the less Y cleans, the more X needs to. X has helped Y become sloppier, and Y has helped X become neater. Y could not be sloppy without X being neat, and X could not be neat without Y being sloppier. They interdependently define themselves and each other through their interactions and direct comparison of their behaviors.

The complementary definitions work when both find this cleaning arrangement acceptable. However, if a problem should arise regarding keeping the apartment clean, it is likely that each will view the other as the root of the problem. Y will see X as controlling, a clean freak, and anal retentive, or some other unflattering description that reflects *overly neat*. In short, X should "lighten up." Similarly, X will view Y as pig-like, dirty, and messy. In short, Y needs to "grow up." Yet, they do the dance together in interdependent fashion.

### *Complementarity process with siblings*

Sibling complementarity occurs in a process similar to the one outlined in the above example of the couple that recently began sharing the same apartment. As siblings act and interact, they are defined in comparison to each other in opposing ways by each other, parents, and other observers. Parents may label two children as neat and sloppy. Neither represents the true extremes of neat and sloppy, but falls somewhere in the middle of this complementary continuum. Their positions and labels are reinforced through their cleaning behaviors and how they are interpreted by observers. Parents and practitioners should be careful about labeling as it often informs children how to behave. For example, the child who is labeled sloppy may be fairly neat in comparison to other children. After hearing he is sloppy, he may "learn" that it is expected he act that way and that efforts to be neat will not be interpreted as such. The power of labeling is particularly significant when referring to children as violent when consequences and alternatives for hostility are not present.

To further illustrate the sibling complementarity process, consider the following example of a pair of siblings in early childhood. Kate and Daniel challenge each other to a footrace in which Kate wins. Descriptive labels begin to be applied by the siblings and perhaps by peers. Kate becomes the fast one and Daniel, the other slow one. Kate may actually be a slow runner in comparison to same-aged peers, and certainly in comparison to Olympic runners, but the primary comparative group for children and many adults is siblings. For many, siblings are the litmus test for success across the life span. Similarly, the child who excels at math may have a sibling who describes himself as "bad at math" although he does well in the subject. By comparison, he is less skilled than his brother. Parents, in conversations with friends and teachers, may describe and introduce their children as "my little mathematician" and "my good reader"—conveying powerful messages about identity and influencing, if not forecasting, the course of their development. In the same interdependent process outlined above, the reader may make increasingly less efforts with mathematics, while the sibling develops increasing interest in mathematics. They each reinforce the other's position.

As children grow and experiment with different activities and behaviors there, they begin to develop or discover talents in some areas and not in others. These talents are often associated with traits that define siblings in complementary fashion. If one child excels at a musical instrument and her sibling does not, she will be labeled as *musically talented* and her sibling as *without musical talent*. The process is closely linked to niche picking, which is discussed in depth later in this chapter.

Since siblings are our earliest, longest-lasting, and most powerful comparative environment, it is likely that much of who we are as individuals is in reference to our siblings. Only children are defined by sibling-like people in their lives (e.g., cousins, best friends) as well as parental expectations of behavior. It is important to reiterate that when people describe themselves, even without intending a complementary comparison, they do so in absolutist language involving labels, which has considerable implications for identity, behavioral expectations, and sense of self.

### *Labels*

Complementarity labeling of siblings is common in families. For example, a mother talking about her sons may describe one as overemotional. This label instructs how people should interact with the boy. Labels represent relational rules for behavior. Family members may be extra careful about sharing feedback with the boy, fearing that the he will be easily injured. They may also dismiss his expressions of emotion believing that they are not genuine, overblown, or histrionic. The label also informs the boy about how to behave. Because he is viewed as overemotional, he is likely to act according to his label and actively express himself emotionally. Indeed, the label may provide license to act out. He may also see himself as emotional, vulnerable, and deeply feeling. Conversely, and in a complementary fashion, his brother is likely to view himself as unemotional and see emotional expression as weak or unnecessary.

Labels are frequently internalized as part of one's self-image and identity. Harsh, negative, or hurtful labels are particularly problematic and often a form of psychological maltreatment. Children who were called belittling names (e.g., fatty, stupid, ugly) by siblings often experience long-term negative consequences (Mackey et al., 2010; Whipple & Finton, 1995; Wiehe, 1997).

### *Translocation*

Translocation is a concept that I introduce to describe the process of "being located" on a particular spot on a complementary trait continuum by the presence of a sibling. A firstborn may be labeled with a trait but the description has no implications for others. She does not define nor is defined by siblings. For example, parents may see their firstborn daughter as easygoing. As the second child enters the picture, the firstborn then becomes *located* by the presence of the new sibling via comparisons. If the second child is described as "more easygoing than the first," the firstborn has been relocated to the "more uptight" end of this continuum and is now considered that way. The firstborn has been redefined in a process of translocation. Translocation involves being recharacterized by the presence of a new sibling. With each new sibling born into the family, older children may be "moved around" to accommodate the new sibling's descriptions. Of course, siblings also locate themselves and are not just located by others. Here is a visual example using the serious–silly trait continuum (1 = firstborn; 2 = secondborn):

This firstborn (now the only child) is considered by his parents to have a serious disposition:

Serious______(1)______________Silly

The second child enters in and is described as "very serious":

Serious__(2)____(1)______________Silly

Even though the firstborn's actual behavior has not changed, they are now located as "silly" (in their family) compared with the more serious secondborn. With the entrance of a third child (3), we can see how the first is again translocated, redefining the firstborn once more:

Serious__(2)____(1)______________(3)____Silly

This third child is perceived to be sillier than her siblings and takes on this description. The behavior of the firstborn, again, is unchanged but he is no longer labeled as silly. He is neither serious nor silly in this family. Trait descriptions are not applied to children who fall between siblings on a given continuum, only those representing the far ends. The firstborn will not be thought of in terms of serious or silly in this family, but by other characteristics.

Consider this variation in which the third in this family is considered to be the exceptionally serious:

Serious__(3)__(2)__________(1)____________Silly

In this scenario, the first remains the silly one, but the second has been translocated into the middle position and no longer the serious one.

### *Changing labels*

Once siblings realize that their identity is associated with how they are located, they may attempt to redefine themselves. The conflict and competition that emerges in "vying for position" is often described as "sibling rivalry," and efforts to occupy labels are perceived to be more favorable to parents. Certain positions may yield better parental investment (e.g., attention, finances, time) than others. For example, in some families, being silly is highly supported by parents. They enjoy their children's comical performances and give them much attention, which conveys to the siblings that being silly is a high-reward behavior. In such families, it is likely that the siblings will begin acting even sillier, attempting to win the silly position on the family continuum. Of course, other families do not value or reward comical behavior and their children are unlikely to compete for the silly title.

It is difficult for individuals to redefine complementary sibling labels. It requires a significant change in behavior that involves outdoing the sibling in a particular area. A *sloppy* sibling wanting to become known as *the neat one* would have to outdo the *neat* sibling in this area. This, of course, has implications for the neat one who may not want to give up the position to occupy the sloppy location, particularly if being neat is rewarding. The neat one has much invested in, and practice with, being neat, is already more skilled and consistent in this area, and is likely to be able to outdo the sibling's new efforts at tidiness.

Further complicating efforts at redefinition is that parents and others are invested in the labels and their perceptions of others. They are unlikely to modify their interpretations, even when observing new or out-of-character behaviors. Consider siblings labeled *the bad one* and *the good one*. Once parents, teachers, and others hold these perceptions, it is almost impossible to change them as they interpret behavior through the lens of the labels. Should the bad one make efforts to behave, observations of this good behavior would be dismissed as a fluke. For example, the good behavior might be interpreted as suspicions (i.e., the child is planning something bad), temporary (e.g., the child is having a good day), or try to explain the new behavior through the "bad lens" (e.g., "Perhaps his father finally set him straight!"; "They must have upped his medication"). Each of these interpretations of the good behavior reinforce the perception that the child is bad. To put it succinctly, once individuals have a theory of others (i.e., label), they interpret all behavior through that lens. Data that confirm their theory are used to support it. Data that contradict their theory are used to support it, as is illustrated in the following case.

Katie is Jim's older sister. She is considered the bad child and Jim the good one. At the age of 16, Jim went to a party, got drunk, and on the way home he crashed into a tree. He was uninjured but the family car was totaled. Katie, age 18, was home watching television the night this took place. In response to discovering what had happened, their parents yelled at Katie, blaming her for the incident, saying that she had been a bad role model. Jim's accident was considered an "out-of-character accident" and he retained his position as the good one, not because of his behavior but because of his well-established label that guided how others interpreted his actions. Indeed, the parents' perception of Jim as good was reinforced, rather than challenged, by their interpretation of the events.

### Reframing

It is important to note that observations of behavior can be interpreted in multiple ways. While in and of themselves are difficult to change, all labels can be *reframed* using different descriptors to provide alternate understandings of behaviors. For example, a teen may label her mother's behavior as "smothering" and "overinvolved." However, the same behavior can be interpreted and reframed as "concerned" or "interested." The labels families choose to use with children are important because they become internalized as part of one's identity, and influence family expectations and interpretations of behavior. As will be taken up in depth later, complementary labels are often rigidly applied that can serve to keep families stuck in problematic interactions that support sibling aggression. Practitioners can reframe sibling complementarity to mobilize families in positive directions.

### Complementarity labels and quadrangles

The family quadrangle, described in the previous chapter, involves an interactional pattern of two parent–child alliances. This dynamic is commonly characterized by coparenting conflict that is reproduced by the sibling subsystem. That is, the siblings express their allied parent's discontents and see each other as enemies. It is common for complementary labels used to describe the coparenting (e.g., spousal) subsystem to be reproduced by the siblings as well. This can be observed in statements like, "You are just like your father, unemotional!" In general, comparisons to spouses are rarely favorable. In quadrangle families, they are particularly meaningful as they reflect betrayals, alliances, and labeling that emphasizes sibling difference. There is evidence that sibling difference is greater when coparents (e.g., spouses) are conflictual (Feinberg, Reiss, Neiderhiser, & Hetherington, 2005).

### Complementarity and sibling aggression

Little research on sibling complementarity exists, particularly in regard to how the term is used in this book. Anecdotally, however, when I informally ask the university students in my classes how many would describe their siblings as "opposites," a majority usually agree with this statement. It seems that most find their complementary definitions acceptable, many taking pride in their differences. But, expressions of frustration related to their considerable differences are also voiced. Practitioners may find it useful to inquire with client families about whether or not and how sibling differences and complementarity might be linked to aggressive relationships.

One complementary definition that may be particularly problematic and seems to be linked to sibling aggression are the labels, *the good one* and *the bad one*—that is, *angel* and *devil*. In a study of sibling deidentification using complementary (or "bipolar") personality scales, Schachter (1985) found that bad/good definitions of sibling pairs were more prevalent in a psychiatric clinic sample than in a nonclinic comparison group. The nonclinic group made less evaluative comparisons. She suggested that some deidentification may be pathological.

It makes sense that siblings labeled as bad and good would have more problematic, and perhaps more aggressive, relationships. Bad children are likely to resent good children for making them look bad, and are likely to perceive parental favoritism—that is, the "angel" receives preferential treatment such as less harsh discipline, more permissions, and greater trust. By comparison, the good one often resents the bad one for causing family disruption and parental emotional upset. The good one may also perceive favoritism as the bad one often receives a great amount of parental attention and investment of time. Parental differential treatment, a common source of resentment in children, is likely reinforced through good/bad labeling.

As noted earlier, it is difficult to change labels once they are assigned. Practitioners working with good/bad complementarity must focus attention both on the bad child's behavior and on how families reinforce misbehavior through labels. Working with complementarity in aggressive sibling relationships is taken up in greater depth in the following chapters on treatment.

## NICHE PICKING

In the past 15 years, Darwinian principles have been put forth to explain the processes that underlie sibling "rivalry" (i.e., competition). Using an evolutionary theoretical framework, Sulloway (1996) explains sibling rivalry as a natural conflict between offspring over parental resources such as time, money, and affection. Reflecting the evolutionary emphasis of organisms' self-interest in preserving their genetic line, children compete to win more resources than their siblings in order to develop into the best possible adult (e.g., strongest, prettiest, richest, most self-actualized), in order to attract the best possible mate, to have the best possible offspring, and to best promote the survival of the genetic line. It is not that young children are actively thinking about mates or their genetic line, or are aware of mating motivations, but that humans are wired to compete with their siblings for this purpose.

There are many ways in which children access environmental and parental resources. They can compete directly or choose divergent methods. *Niche picking* (Feinberg et al., 2005; Scarr & McCartney, 1983) or *niche partitioning* (Sulloway, 1996) refers to a process in which animals and humans diversify their strategies for acquiring resources. The concept comes from the Darwinian principles of adaptation and divergence (Sulloway, 1996). Siblings commonly choose different areas of interest and develop unique skills and areas of expertise as a means of adapting to their environment to garner resources. One child discovers that playing soccer will win the parents' attention and investment of resources, while another does this through artistic projects. One becomes known as "the athlete" and the other "the artist"—each garnering resources without competing on the same turf.

The function of diversification is to maximize opportunities for resources while minimizing direct competition (Sulloway, 1996). When children choose varied activities, they compete less, and are compared less. This enables accomplishments to be viewed as unique and to take place without the burden of measuring up to, or being outshone by, a sibling. When siblings choose the same niche, they must compete directly for resources and greater direct comparison of their abilities in the area. Same-niche competition raises the stakes as it produces winners and losers—that is, the one that is best in the niche receives more resources. The higher stakes of shared niches, greater direct competition, and fear of losing may all support sibling aggression, particularly efforts to undermine the others' successes. Alternatively, diversification can produce multiple winners. One child can succeed in baseball and the second as a musician, avoiding direct competition and comparison, and as such avoid conflict and being labeled as "losers." It is possible for both to win parental and other environmental resources without outdoing the other. That said, as one wins resources for their unique area of expertise, available resources for siblings are affected, but indirectly through a process called *niche construction*.

Niche construction refers to a process in which individuals alter the environmental pressures (e.g., ability to access resources) of others via their niche choices and successes (Odling-Smee, Laland, & Feldman, 2003). The concept has fairly recently emerged in the evolutionary literatures and is still being developed. I use it to extend the niche construct as applied to human sibling relationships by considering the effects of diversification on siblings' immediate environments and adaptive constraints, and those inherited by future generations. Niche construction argues that the impact of niche activity is significant whether or not individuals have diversified their interests because they exist in interdependent systems (Carpenter, 2001; Odling-Smee et al., 2003). A sibling's choices change the environment for others, and individuals' available choices are continually modified by the behavior of their siblings.

Moreover, the ways in which individuals adapt to their siblings' influences has implications for future generations. For example, a girl who chose to avoid athletics because she had a brother who excelled at all sports, instead selected to focus her energies on computer programming. Because of her brother's active sports life, her parents were often away although supportive of her niche. Feeling the environmental constraints of her sibling's niche construction, she adapted by finding an activity she could do independently. Her skill in this area led to a highly successful and lucrative career, affording her children a wide variety of financial access to varied interests. Following in her footsteps her son joined her company as a computer engineer.

## The Niche Picking Process

The process of niche picking occurs over time and involves multiple factors. Individuals end up in particular niches partly due to their own choosing, partly due to parental, sibling, and other influences, partly due to genetic fit, and partly due to what activities are reasonably accessible in the environment. For example,

Michael Jordon's primary niche was basketball. He had success in this endeavor because he wanted to play, because his parents and others supported this endeavor, and because he had the physique (largely the influence of genetics) that supported accomplishment in this niche. Basketball was also an available and feasible activity in his environment growing up. There are surely other individuals who are of similar build to Michael Jordon, but did not have the interest, interpersonal support, or accessibility to succeed in basketball.

The niche partitioning process commonly involves an older child becoming involved with an activity with parental enthusiasm and support. A younger sibling observes the excitement and makes efforts to do the same thing. To illustrate, Paula, an older sister to Julia, joins a youth basketball league and enjoys playing. Paula's interest in basketball deepens and she talks about it often. Julia observes Paula's excitement and newfound pride as well as her parents' support and interest. She also sees her parents and others cheering for Paula and giving her praise. Julia takes note that playing basketball looks like fun but also comes with rewards. Soon, she asks her parents to join a team too.

As Julia starts playing basketball, the niche partitioning process begins to take place. Although a variety of dynamics can unfold, three processes are common. In the first, Julia is not as good as Paula. She is younger, still developing her coordination, and begins to get frustrated. Her parents do not get as excited about her games and offer more critique and guidance than praise. Julia is not given as much time on the court as her sister, giving her parents and others less opportunity to cheer for her. She does not find basketball to be a source of pride, but rather a frustration. Julia is not likely to remain in the basketball niche, and is likely to ask to do something else, a niche in which Paula has not distinguished herself. This process may be quick or may occur over many years.

However, a second alternative process may also occur. Julia begins playing basketball and is exceptionally adept at the sport. Her parents and coaches take notice and she begins being recognized as one of the best on the team. When discussing their children, their parents make statements like, "Both girls are good at basketball, but Julia really seems to have a talent for the sport." Paula starts to observe that she is being compared unfavorably and feels that her sister has moved in on her turf. Her enthusiasm for basketball wanes and she begins investing in a different niche.

In the third process, both remain in basketball and compete for niche dominance. They are each motivated by their own achievements and to outperform the other, even if they are supportive of each other's efforts. Such families often take on the identity of the niche (e.g., "We are a basketball family") and parental investment, enthusiasm, and other resources target the success of both daughters. Of course, the competition may not be one of mutual support but of resentment. In such cases the wish to outdo often involves attempts to undermine the other's achievements, injure the other's sense of self, and/or gain parental favor. Viewing each other as rivals rather than as supports is common in problematic sibling aggression.

### *My turf!*

Siblings often view their niches as their turf. They have invested in their niche and tied their identities to it. As such, individuals may choose to avoid entering siblings' niches out of respect for their turf or for fear of conflict. Accordingly, the concept of niche picking challenges notions of independence and free choice. For example, one person's "independent" decision to enroll in a teacher education program may influence the sibling's choice not to become a schoolteacher. This type of independent decision is often made without consulting one's sibling despite its impact. Also, siblings usually want to be different from each other, to carve out their own identities, and make efforts to be different. The process of trying to be different from one's sibling is known as *deidentification* (Schacter et al., 1976).

### *Niche fields*

I introduce the concept of *niche fields* to refer to the range of possible niches available to individuals. The range, or field, of potential activities can be few or many across sibling environments, and it shapes the niche picking process. Families range widely in size, income, geographic residence, and cultural expectations. Families with high incomes offer different possibilities than poor families. For example, niches in wealthy families may include horseback riding and yachting, where families with fewer resources do not have these options. Suburban and rural families have more opportunities for golf and agricultural pursuits than urban ones. Cultural expectations also constrain choice. Niches are influenced by gendered pressures for girls to do female activities (e.g., dance, cheerleading) and boys to engage in male endeavors (e.g., football, tending to cars). Niche fields are constrained for all children but the range of possibilities varies across families.

Some parents attempt to make available or permit as many niche choices as they can. The parents tell their children they can do whatever they want to do. In these families, the niche fields are broad. Other families place high value on only a few niches and attempt to prohibit or minimize exploration in other areas. In these families, niche fields are narrow. For example, football is of high import to some families, and parents expect all their children to either play or engage in a football-related niche (e.g., boys play football, girls cheerlead). Narrow niche fields promote greater competition to distinguish oneself from siblings, to gain favorable comparisons and resources. Siblings commonly diversify and find microniches within narrow niche fields. For example, one sibling may play an offensive position while the other chooses defense. A practice consideration for working with sibling aggression is to help families either broaden their niche fields or assist with diversification within niches (i.e., microniches) to lessen immediate competition. However, team building is a preferable choice to solely niche-related modification because even in wide niche fields, as noted in the next discussion on practice, not all niches are viewed as having equal value. Parents may tell their children that they can select from a wide range of activities but to be more excited by and invested in some niches than others. Genetic endowments also influence niche fields. Some children may be more "naturally" suited for certain activities than their siblings.

### *Siblings provide resources too*

The classic understanding of niche processes focuses primarily on children vying for resources from parents (Sulloway, 1996). How parents influence their children's vying behavior has been minimized. As I suggested earlier, parents are not neutral or benign players in the niche-picking process but shape niche fields, favor some niches over others, and have varying degrees of ability to provide resources across niches. Also, the traditional view of children's niche selection focuses on parental resources, and other sources are generally overlooked or minimized. While it is true that parents provide the primary set of resources, siblings themselves offer important and powerful resources such as emotional support and investment, instruction, modeling, and often access (e.g., personal connections, financial support). The role of siblings as resources is an important consideration for practice as it alters the focus from competing for parental investment to sibling relationships that are about support. Sibling support has many positive developmental associations (Kramer, 2011), and development of sibling positivity is one part of the two-pronged sibling aggression treatment approach described in the following chapters.

## Niches and Practice

Sibling niche diversification offers a strategy to address sibling aggression in practice. Practitioners can encourage highly competitive and hostile siblings to select differing interests, to develop their own areas of expertise and identity, as a way to ameliorate aggressive relationships. However, niche construction suggests that simply diversifying may not be effective as competition for resources continue to exist. Children may compare how invested each parent is in their respective niche, and who is getting more from whom.

All niches are not created equal. Parents get more excited about certain activities their children undertake than others. A mother who used to be a dancer may invest more time and energy with her daughter who is learning dance than the daughter who is playing soccer. As such, some niches are more rewarding than others and children play close attention to the degree interests are supported. Children may also be misled by their parents about what niches have the best payoff. For example, children are commonly told that being good is what parents want, but observe that their misbehaving sibling gets much more attention and investment of time. I frequently hear students make comments such as, "I did everything my parents wanted. I got good grades, never got into trouble, helped around the house, but all they ever want to talk about is my brother who never did anything they asked!" The bad niche is one with the greater payoff.

Encouraging niche diversification may reduce direct competition but does not in itself offer a way to halt aggression. It also may separate siblings who are close and conflictual, resulting in distant relationships, each in their own niche. In practice, steps to build sibling support while halting problematic aggression are preferable. Siblings in the same niche who are close but highly competitive and aggressive may be better assisted by helping them learn to support each other—that is, as a team. Competing in the same niche has benefits such as the development of increased skill level gained by trying to outdo one's sibling. The Williams sisters, the tennis stars, may not have been as successful had one diversified and chosen another endeavor to invest in. Competing against each other likely made them better players than they would have been without this special sibling experience. They are also close. Had they selected different niches, they would have likely been more distant.

Siblings can be in the same niche and compete without the intent to injure the other. They can be taught to work together, be supportive and close, and work as a team. For example, during a karate tournament, identical twin sister Liz exclaimed, "You stink! I could have easily won that contest," right after Maureen had lost the match. Maureen responded by calling her names and telling her parents that Liz had stolen money from them a few days earlier. The conflict quickly became physically violent that included kicking and hair-pulling. These two see each other as enemies, each intending to harm the other emotionally and physically, as well as in regard to their social status with their parents.

In treatment, the practitioner reframed their experience as teammates rather than enemies. They and their parents were taught to reinforce positive and supportive interactions, and to view others in the competition as true rivals. Insults, name calling, tattling, and intent to hurt were no longer tolerated. At a more recent match, Maureen was eliminated in a tough match. As she left the mat, Liz said to Maureen, "You were so good out there. You landed a great kick. If the referee had caught it you would have won the match. You'll win next time." The parents praised this demonstration of support, and Maureen hugged Liz in return. Maureen cheered Liz on in her match, which the parents also praised. At home, Liz and Maureen would practice *with* each other rather than *against* each other, frequently praising the other for well-executed maneuvers. They continued to share the same niche, each winning parental resources, but also discovered that siblings can represent an important environmental resource (as noted earlier).

## COMPARISON

Because both complementarity and niche selection are functions of comparison, it is important to include a brief statement about the power and dangers of comparison. The more siblings are compared the more they are likely to compete and engage in aggression. Comparisons, particularly by parents, are potent, conveying sentiments of value, motivations to invest, and much about the relationships themselves. For example, parental comparisons result in perceptions of winners and losers and favoritism. Comparisons that place one child in higher regard than others generate resentment and distance in sibling relationships. For example, statements such as, "Why can't you be more like your brother?" indicate parental preference and disfavor.

Comparisons should be minimized and evaluative statements should be individualized and focus on discrete behaviors, not global labels. For example, it is preferable for a parent to say to a child, "I really like your painting. You seem to really enjoy it and be good at it!" than employing labels such as, "You are my little artist!" Siblings will hear this as that they are less talented as painters and likely to be less motivated to engage in artistic endeavors.

In practice, how comparisons are made and interpreted and how they constrain relationships should be evaluated and addressed. My recommendation is to help parents and siblings halt and avoid direct comparisons altogether, since it typically promotes aggression. Assisting families engaged in labeling to take less myopic and more flexible views of its members' behaviors is also recommended.

## SIBLINGS AS MODELS AND BEHAVIORAL REINFORCEMENT

The sibling relationship is a powerful learning environment. Living with siblings is instructive about how to behave. Siblings share advice, teach, challenge, and imitate each other. They serve as models for behavior. They observe each other's actions and associated consequences that inform future behavioral choices through a process of observational learning (Bandura, 1977). It is not uncommon for brothers and sisters to try to emulate successful behaviors that they observe; to "follow in their siblings' footsteps." Successful actions are those that bring about wanted outcomes, which includes both good and bad behavior's (e.g., smoking cigarettes to look cool). Older siblings are usually the models, but children also learn by watching their younger brothers and sisters. Siblings also serve as sources of direct reinforcement (Whiteman, Bernard, & Jensen, 2011).

While siblings are quite different from each other, they are also similar in various ways, particularly in regard to deviance, including drug, alcohol, and cigarette use (Begun & Berger, 2011; Rende, Slomkowski, Lloyd-Richardson, & Niaura, 2005), sexual activity (East & Khoo, 2005; East, Slonim, Horn, Trinh, & Reyes, 2009), and antisocial behavior (Lauritsen, 1993; Patterson, 1984; Slomkowski, Rende, Conger, Simons, & Conger, 2001). Modeling and patterns of direct and vicarious reinforcement may serve in the development of ongoing aggression (Patterson, 1984, 1986; Patterson, Dishion, & Bank, 1984). Sibling aggression may be learned by copying each other's behavior and by reinforcement rewards, such as feeling powerful, adrenaline rushes, and distraction from other stresses. Sibling aggression may also be reinforced by feelings of connectedness and engagement gained through physical conflict (Bank & Kahn, 1997; Gnaulati, 2002). Hostile opposition between siblings may represent efforts at differentiation and deidentification (Raffaelli, 1992). The rewards of creating unique identities, particularly in adolescence, also likely reinforce aggression.

Siblings also model and imitate positive behavior, which is also reinforcing. Older sibling's prosocial behavior has been linked to younger sibling's sharing, cooperation, and greater peer competence (Stocker, 1994), and better psychological adjustment (Dunn & Munn, 1986; Kim, McHale, Crouter, & Osgood, 2007). Considering the many benefits of prosocial sibling relationships (Kramer, 2011), practitioners engaged in sibling aggression treatment should evaluate and change patterns of modeling and reinforcement that support aggression to patterns that promote prosocial engagement.

## CONCLUSION

This chapter continued the presentation of an emerging sibling theory. The theory offered here draws upon existing theories and principles, many of which have been further developed and extended to include new principles and constructs. Most aspects of the framework have empirical support, with some yet to be adequately examined. Theoretical frameworks are important and useful for guiding practice. The framework presented here suggests that relationships between brothers and sisters are highly interdependent, greatly influential, and central to processes of sibling aggression and support.

The practice of both stopping problematic aggression and building support in sibling relationships is taken up in depth in the following chapters. The concepts of complementarity, niches, and niche fields, as well as processes of sibling influence, support, and resentment, are active parts of the assessment and intervention process of the task-centered sibling aggression treatment approach presented in this book.

# 4

# The Task-Centered Sibling Aggression Treatment Approach

This chapter will provide an overview of sibling aggression treatment informed by the theoretical principles discussed in the previous chapter. A two-pronged intervention that aims to both halt negativity and promote supportive sibling relationships will be emphasized. An overview of task-centered practice (Reid, 1992) is provided as the foundational model for the development of the two-pronged approach put forth in this book: the task-centered sibling aggression (TCSA) treatment approach. Task-centered practice provides an open framework and promotes integration of strategies from other approaches. Since the family is the primary context for sibling behavior, structural family therapy (SFT) techniques (Minuchin, 1974) are incorporated, as well as behavioral methods (Leitenberg, Burchard, Burchard, Fuller, & Lysaght, 1977; Reid, 2004). Overviews of both SFT and behavioral strategies are provided followed by the presentation of the TCSA treatment approach.

## A TWO-PRONGED APPROACH

Treatment of sibling aggression should target two areas: (1) eliminating harmful aggression and (2) building supportive relationships. Addressing only one is problematic. Interventions focused solely on stopping troublesome interaction may teach siblings to avoid or stop communicating with each other (Kramer, 2004), resulting in apathetic sibling relationships. Distant siblings are concerning since supportive relationships seem to have so many important benefits (Kramer, 2011).

Alternatively, sibling aggression treatment that solely focuses on building positive relationships may fail to address the dynamics that support the hostilities. For example, prosocial relational skill development is not likely to address problematic resentments due to overt but dismissed parental favoritism. Moreover, positive relationships may also include dangerous violence and neglecting direct efforts to stop it risks client safety. Direct efforts may include creating safety plans and actions to bring harmful aggression to an immediate halt.

There are other pragmatic reasons for addressing aggression. Families will expect the practitioner to directly address aggressive sibling behavior, particularly if it is the presenting complaint. Also, it may take some time to teach and integrate prosocial behavior, whereas strategies to halt violence can be done more rapidly (e.g., creating separate daily routines to keep siblings from shared space). From a temporal standpoint, it makes sense to first stop dangerous aggression and then to develop prosocial behavior for warm and supportive relationships (e.g., after formulating separate routines, create safe space to work on building positivity). In cases where sibling aggression does not pose an immediate danger (but may be irritating), a focus on prosocial skill development may take center stage. In most cases, simultaneous attention to both approaches should occur. Task-centered procedures lend themselves to a two-pronged treatment approach in which activities to both halt negativity and enhance positivity can be formulated and employed.

## TASK-CENTERED PRACTICE

Task-centered practice is a well-known and widely adopted social service treatment model (Fortune & Reid, 2011). The model has received continued empirical development, and has been empirically validated for a wide range of psychosocial issues. It is an open and integrative approach that provides a core framework for incorporating theoretical, research, and practice contributions that work best for ameliorating the problem at hand. As such, it is not wedded to any particular theory, but instead offers a series of steps for practitioners and clients to carry out together for problem alleviation. The model can be used as a stand-alone treatment approach but is frequently combined with other approaches, with a preference for empirically validated interventions. Task-centered practice is also a brief, time-limited treatment approach where explicit contracts that frame clear objectives and end dates are utilized.

The task-centered model is a sensible framework for treating sibling aggression and incorporates into practice the research and theoretical discussions presented in the previous chapters. There has been some preliminary empirical support for task-centered practice for sibling aggression (Caspi, 2008; Reid & Donovan, 1990).

A condensed history and overview of task-centered practice will be provided, followed by a presentation of its principles and procedures. The development of TCSA will be reviewed, and the incorporation of family systems theory and SFT will be discussed in the context of the model. Specific assessment and treatment procedures for sibling aggression and implementation of TCSA are taken up in subsequent chapters.

## A BRIEF HISTORY OF TASK-CENTERED PRACTICE

This approach was developed in the late 1960s and formally introduced in the early 1970s after research on case management interventions demonstrated that short-term structured approaches were as efficacious, and sometimes more so, than traditional long-term or indefinite time treatments (Reid &

Shyne, 1969). With these findings in hand, and drawing upon Perlman's (1957) problem-solving paradigm, Reid and Epstein (1972) developed the task-centered approach. Since then, the approach has experienced major expansion and has become well known to researchers and practitioners around the world. It has been the focus of a substantial number of books, texts, and research studies, which have consistently demonstrated its efficacy (Fortune & Reid, 2011; Ramos & Tolson, 2008). Task-centered practice is the foundation for social service provision in three countries (England, Netherlands, and Norway) (Eriksen, 2010; Marsh, 2010; Trotter, 2010), utilized by practitioners as a treatment approach around the globe (Fortune & Reid, 2011), and is generally considered one of the major approaches in the social work profession (Coady & Lehmann, 2008; Hepworth, Rooney, & Larsen, 2002; Kanter, 1983; Reid & Fortune, 2003; Turner, 2011).

In the past 35 years, the task-centered approach has evolved tremendously. It has been adapted and empirically validated for an impressively wide variety of individual, family, group, and community problems, as well as for educational and administrative purposes (Fortune & Reid, 2011). Much of the model's development, adaptation, and improvement was done using the design & development (D&D) research paradigm (Thomas & Rothman, 1994) (for in-depth review, see Fortune, in press). A partial list of problems and populations with which the approach has been successfully implemented includes "suicide and depression, AIDS, addictions, sexual abuse, child neglect, frail elderly, sex offenders, juvenile delinquents, maladaptive youth in treatment centers, homeless persons with psychiatric difficulties, immigrants, loss and grief, parent–child conflict, pregnant adolescents, families of children with developmental disabilities, and aggressive siblings" (Fortune & Reid, 2011, p. 515). The development of task-centered sibling aggression treatment (Caspi, 2008; Reid & Donovan, 1990) reflects one of its many valuable adaptations.

## OVERVIEW OF TASK-CENTERED PROCESS

The task-centered model is an "action-oriented" approach in which the client and practitioner implement tasks both within and outside the treatment setting to solve problems. The hallmarks of the approach are its structured client-directed problem-solving process, empirical orientation, and focus on client task implementation to ameliorate situations. Problems are addressed in an incremental fashion, where clients direct much of the problem and task selection process. This differs from many other approaches that rely on practitioner directives. In this way, the task-centered approach is client centered and empowering. Clients often learn and integrate the structured problem-solving process, which they are then able to implement with other and future problems, and without the necessary assistance of a professional practitioner.

The centerpiece of the approach is the task planning and implementation sequence (TPIS), an empirically supported sequence of problem-solving steps

(Ramos & Tolson, 2008; Reid, 1997). It is the central activity of the treatment meeting and involves clients, with practitioner guidance, in prioritizing and selecting problems to address, and formulating the actions or *tasks* to resolve them. Problems selected for immediate work, *target problems*, are quantitatively assessed usually in terms of frequency and severity. Tasks to address target problems are identified and considered, including potential obstacles that could be encountered during implementation. Selected tasks are then typically implemented outside the treatment meeting in the real world, directly within selected problematic relationships and situations. At the start of each clinical session, client task implementations and target problems are empirically evaluated. This process continues until target problems have been successfully ameliorated, usually according to the client or the treatment plan.

Two central features of task-centered practice regard how problems are viewed and the use of tasks to address them. Each is taken up in more depth here.

## Problems

Psychosocial problems are generally viewed as temporary breakdowns in problem management (Reid, 1992). Families continuously and successfully handle many problems throughout time, but occasionally difficulties arise that seem irresolvable. In task-centered work, practitioners will ask about prior problem-solving efforts regarding the issue that brought them to treatment in order to avoid repetition of failed strategies and to identify what has worked in the past and to develop more efficacious tactics. Identification of new strategies is a collaborative process that emerges from an understanding of client perceptions of problems and particularly how they interact with them. The process of considering fresh approaches to handling frustrations motivates clients to change and often quickly alleviates distress, which in itself can be paralyzing. Additionally, the time-encapsulated nature of the model suggests that problems are seen as practical matters that are transitory and solvable, rather than symptoms of serious dysfunction that require a long course of treatment.

Problems occur in various environments and exploration of contextual considerations is important in understanding the obstacles clients encounter when attempting to solve their problems. The context is also evaluated for existing opportunities for change and resources that can be brought to bear to improve circumstances. In the case of sibling aggression, parents and other family members are seen as the first and most immediate context. Problems between siblings may involve parents who engage in differential treatment, interfere in sibling relationships, or have marital conflict. More distant systems also influence sibling relationships. For example, comparisons by athletic coaches and teachers may heighten sibling competitiveness and conflict. Societal understandings of sibling violence as normal constitute a contextual obstacle to amelioration. Also, ethnic and cultural variations in regard to sibling hierarchies and role expectations may serve as both obstacles and resources to problem-solving efforts.

Problems are understood as *wants* rather than *needs* (Reid, 1992). Needs are what practitioners perceive clients to have (e.g., Beth needs to learn to control her temper in order to improve her sibling relationship), as opposed to wants that are client-defined (e.g., Beth wants her sister to stop borrowing her clothes to improve their relationship). Clients are inherently more motivated to work on self-defined and initiated objectives. The approach focuses on the problem at hand, immediate wants, and the obstacles and resources to achieving them, not the remote or historical origins of a problem. In other words, detailed descriptions of early childhood experiences and multigenerational family assessments (e.g., using genograms) are not generally part of the treatment process. It may be mutually decided, however, that such exploration is needed if historical considerations emerge as obstacles to alleviating the presenting problem—although such work is generally not seen as required for problem resolution.

### *Target problem formulation*

Families often begin treatment with multiple problems. A step of the target problem formulation process is *problem identification*. Each family member is asked to share their perception of problems. The practitioner asks clients to list and prioritize problems to identify the most pressing areas for immediate work. Each family member may describe problems in unique ways—that is, from their individual points of views. The practitioner helps frame target problems so that they address varying perspectives and so that they advance problem-solving actions. For example, a younger brother who is frequently picked on by an older sister may describe the problem in a number of ways—for example, the sister's annoying behavior, her hatred for him, or his own difficulty coping with her. The last description is preferable as it allows more opportunity for problem-solving action. The boy cannot control his sister's behavior, but can control his own and may consider options for interacting with her differently. The sister's perspective of the problem may be quite different. She may describe the problem as being located in her brother—that is, he is a "pest" and is "always in her business." The practitioner helps families frame target problems in ways that account for multiple perspectives by highlighting interdependent processes that are best for taking control of the situation and for taking action. For example, the practitioner may describe both the brother's and sister's perspectives as sibling conflict, a view they can both relate to, agree upon, and take action.

Target problems are typically formulated as part of an assessment process and represent a beginning to intervention. That is, framing problems in a new way—one that is action oriented and addresses multiple perspectives—sets the course for task development. A powerful assessment strategy and one that helps illustrate the interdependence of problems is identifying sequences of family interaction. In the task-centered sibling aggression model presented in this book, identifying transactional sequences is a practitioner-led strategy that is primarily utilized during problem exploration and formulation processes. See the section "Identifying Transaction Patterns" later in this chapter for an in-depth description of this process.

It is common in task-centered practice to select three problems to address at the same time. Problems are often linked and success in one area fosters progress with other issues. Accordingly, obstacles to amelioration of one problem may be tied to another area requiring attention. Commonly, up to three tasks are chosen for each of the three selected problems; a total of nine tasks to be implemented among treatment meetings.

### *Problem review*

Task-centered practice empirically tracks problem change during the treatment process. Clients are asked to report the frequency and severity of target problems at each treatment meeting. This process is called *problem review*. At the start of treatment, clients may need to actively count how often problems take place in order to establish a baseline. This may entail making a note of each problem occurrence when it happens. For example, a mother may be instructed to place an "X" on a sheet each time her son and daughter squabble. Additionally, she is asked to record the severity of each altercation on a scale from 1 to 10; 1 = not severe, 5 = moderately severe, 10 = extremely severe.

Tracking problem severity and frequency is useful in empirically evaluating interventions. If severity and frequency diminish, it suggests that treatment strategies are working. Conversely, no changes or increases in severity and frequency indicate that different interventions and tasks are needed.

## Tasks

In task-centered practice, the process of problem solving is done by taking action, compared to other (usually time unlimited) approaches that focus on developing insight or creating empathic environments (e.g., psychodynamic, humanistic). Action is taken in the form of planned tasks that are implemented by clients and practitioners within and between meetings. A central function of the treatment meeting is to prepare for task implementation. Tasks are identified and formulated by both clients and practitioners in a mutual process, with preference given to those raised by clients because they are most expert on their realities. Practitioners work with clients to generate their own tasks, particularly ones that fall within their existing repertoire of strategies. The more they represent exciting possibilities, the more likely they will be carried out with success.

Tasks represent incremental work toward problem resolution. Problems are not addressed "all at once" but rather in a stepwise fashion. As the old quote goes, "You walk a mile one step at a time." Or as a ranch owner puts it, "You can eat a whole steer, just one steak at a time." Problems are broken down into smaller parts, which are more easily addressed and create less anxiety. For example, the idea of cleaning a bedroom in terrible disarray may be experienced as overwhelming. However, selecting only a small portion of the room to clean seems doable, causes less stress, and heightens motivation. A second small part of the bedroom is selected once the client has had success with the first.

### *Types of tasks*

The range of tasks is broad and can involve behavioral, cognitive, affective, and even insight-oriented activities. As an example, an obese client struggling to lose weight may select tasks involving exercise (behavioral), self-restraint (cognitive "self-talk"), tuning into emotions that may trigger binges (affective) or, if determined to be psychological, activities designed to uncover potential underlying reasons for overeating (insight-oriented). The task-centered perspective might suggest that knowing why (i.e., possessing insight) one overeats does not necessarily cause changes in one's eating to solve an obesity problem. It is taking action, whether or not the underlying psychological reasons are known to the individual that will bring about the change to solve the problem. In short, as a father told his son who was complaining about being overwhelmed by homework, "You can either complain about it, or do something about it. Let's talk about what you can do, and then do it." Difficulty taking action because of "underlying issues" is viewed as emotional obstacles to amelioration. As such, developing insight is about overcoming an obstacle and not the primary mode of intervention. Anticipating and identifying obstacles to successful task implementation is a formal step of the task-centered process. A more in-depth discussion of obstacle-related activities is taken up later, in the overview of the model's steps.

In situations that involve two or more participants, such as families or sibling subsystems, client tasks are often *shared* or *reciprocal* and reflect interdependent processes (Reid, 1992). Shared tasks involve cooperatively carrying out an action. For example, a husband and wife may both select to be more restrained in their individual spending habits in order to stick to family budget, or two siblings taking turns possessing control of the television remote control. By comparison, reciprocal tasks address relational interactions. For example, one sibling may take on the task to stop calling his sister hurtful names, and his sister will agree to knock on his bedroom door before entering.

When shared and reciprocal tasks go well, it builds a sense of cohesiveness in the relationship and can go far in generating goodwill for future positive interaction. However, such tasks require more of clients than individual-oriented actions, as they involve committing to the relationship. If one sibling should decide not to share the remote, the other is less likely to be willing to continue taking turns. It is important for practitioners to help clients that make shared and reciprocal agreements to be able to regain commitment to the task, even after one (or both) of the participants has failed to implement it on one occasion.

In other words, if the task fails once, clients should be helped to avoid an "all bets are off" reaction that involves completely abandoning responsibility for task implementation. Rather, it is helpful to prepare clients to consider what will happen when one does not follow through and to "reset" (i.e., start over) and agree to try the task again. One study reported that reciprocal tasks are more likely to succeed when carefully planned during treatment sessions (Reid, 1987), including trying them out using enactments or role play.

### Task complexity

Tasks range in their level of sophistication and ambition. At the start of treatment, simple tasks are formulated and with implementation success the level of complexity and challenge is increased. For example, a client who is fearful of dental visits may select the task of identifying a dentist to contact, with a second task of calling to schedule an appointment. These activities are simple and straightforward. Once these are completed, future tasks may be more complex such as using cognitive behavior worksheets to identify internal dialogues that support fear. Task complexity is also dependent upon the skill level and motivation of the client. For some, a task to make a phone call may be too simplistic, and more complex tasks are selected. For others, this task may be too challenging. Practitioners and clients mutually evaluate and formulate tasks so that they are challenging but attainable. Practitioners should avoid setting their clients up for failure by selecting overly difficult tasks. Failure to complete treatment activities can result in diminished motivation and expectations of success.

### Task specificity

Clients and practitioners focus much attention on the formulation of tasks, and together define where, when, and how they will be carried out. The better the tasks are defined, the more likely they will be carried out with success. Tasks often sound good but are plagued by ambiguity that leads to poor implementation. For example, in a case involving an older brother who used violent tactics during babysitting to control his much younger siblings, it became clear that he was unaware of alternative child control and discipline strategies. When yelling did not work, he hit. After his mother learned this she said when they got home she was going to teach her son different ways to care for his siblings when they were misbehaving. At the subsequent session, the practitioner asked how the teaching task went and the mother reported that she had not done it because "it was a very busy week." Although the task idea was excellent, its specificity was inadequate.

By comparison, an approach more likely to result in success would involve specifying in great detail where, when, and how the task of "teaching different ways to address misbehaving siblings" would be done. The improved, detailed task might be stated as "mother will teach her son about redirecting and time-outs at 4 p.m. on Wednesday." The mother and son are then asked to write down their meeting on the family calendar located on the pantry bulletin board. In formulating this task it is clear that the practitioner asked the mother to be specific about which child care strategies she was going to teach, when and where she was going to teach it (with great specificity), and reinforce the importance of completing the task by formally recording it (e.g., on the family calendar). This type of specificity increases the likelihood that the task will be implemented successfully. Having families try out and rehearse tasks during treatment meetings helps promote clarity about task expectations and also raises the likelihood they will be completed outside sessions. Task success is reinforcing and increases client investment and confidence in taking on subsequent and more complex tasks. As clients experience task success and observe lessening problems, motivation increases.

### *Rehearsal*

It is helpful to try out (e.g., rehearsal, role play, guided practice) tasks with clients prior to asking them to implement them outside the treatment relationship. Rehearsal can serve to clarify tasks and identify obstacles to implementation. For example, in my role as a practitioner, I suggested to a teenage boy that he invite his father to join us at the next treatment meeting. The boy agreed to the task but returned without his father. Upon inquiry, the teenager said he had completed the task but that his father did not want to come. I asked him how he invited his father, to which he replied, "I said, 'Hey, Dad, you want to go hang out at Jon's?'" His answer was a lesson to me that future tasks of this type needed to be rehearsed. His father may have thought his son had asked him to spend time with him at another teenager's house. Had we rehearsed his invitation task prior during our meeting, it is likely that this unclear way of inviting his father would have been identified and more appropriate behaviors selected.

In a similar example, a pair of sisters engaged in continuous insult giving agreed on a task to give each other just one compliment when at home. When asked how the task went they explained that the attempt to give a compliment turned into "huge fights" because each interpreted the other as disingenuous. The practitioner asked them to describe to him what happened and the older sister said, "I told her that I like her hair and she freaked out!" To which the younger sister responded, "My hair didn't look nice. I hadn't done anything to my hair. I had just gotten out of bed. She was being sarcastic and mean!" Defending herself, the older said, "I did mean it. She honestly looked nice." Had the complimenting task been rehearsed prior to implementation, it would like have become clear that discussion of how to give and receive compliments was needed if this task were to be adopted.

## Task Review

As suggested above, task-centered practice empirically monitors task implementation. Task performance is systematically reviewed, typically at the start of each treatment meeting. Task success is evaluated by asking the client to numerically rate their perceived success, usually directly after implementation on the TCSA Task Review Form (see Appendix D). The following scale is used to rate task performance: 1 = not completed; 2 = partly completed; 3 = mostly completed; 4 = fully completed; N = no opportunity to complete. Often, each family member is given their own Task Review Form to complete.

At the start of each session (starting from the second), task performance is discussed by reviewing completed Task Review Forms. Tasks that are effective or show promise may be selected or updated for continued implementation, and those that are not are abandoned so that new ones can be devised. The task review focuses on task efficacy and its fit for client implementation. It is done concurrently with the *problem review* process in which clients keep numerical track of the severity and frequency of their problems (discussed earlier in this chapter). By doing both reviews together, practitioners and clients can observe connections between task selection and implementation and its impact on problem amelioration.

Exploring *how* individuals came to a score rather than the chosen number often illuminates how clients think about tasks. I have found that it is not uncommon for clients and practitioners to have different understandings of task implementation processes, even after substantial discussion. A strategy for asking about task implementation is to ask the client to provide an example of what they did. For example, an adolescent girl who selected a task of sharing her clothes with her younger sister gave herself the score of "4" (i.e., fully completed). When I asked her to give me an example of sharing, she said that she picked out old clothes that she no longer wore and gave them to her sister. My perspective was that such behavior was more akin to "donating" or even "unloading" unwanted clothing than sharing that involves turn-taking and borrowing. The girl's description of how she carried out the task provided an opportunity to clarify understandings and expectations. When client examples of implementation match practitioner understandings, opportunities for praise or refining tasks are present.

## BASIC PRINCIPLES OF TASK-CENTERED PRACTICE

Reid (1992) described eight central principles that underlie the task-centered approach. I add a ninth feature that is unique to task-centered practice: its active attention to identifying potential obstacles to planned interventions. Each principle is briefly presented here with a special focus on its relationship to sibling aggression considerations.

### Empirical Orientation

A central thrust of task-centered practice is its empirical orientation, which is enacted in four ways: (1) development and formal testing of the approach through programs of research; (2) integration of research-validated interventions; (3) monitoring target problem treatment progress; and (4) assessing task implementation success.

As noted earlier, the task-centered approach has an extensive history of empirical development and evaluation, and research has demonstrated the model's effectiveness for a wide array of social problems and across an impressive range of social and practice settings (Reid, 1997). It is frequently noted as a model of evidence-based practice (e.g., Gorey, Thyer, & Pawluck, 1998; Reid & Fortune, 2003; Rzepnicki, McCracken, & Briggs, in press). Few, if any, practice approaches have been systematically developed through such widespread programs of research. Historically, treatment models are conceptually formulated and then disseminated to the public before testing or refining them for efficacy, without the input of treatment "receivers" (i.e., clients), without evaluating practitioner fidelity, and without recording practical implementation or "ease of use" concerns (Caspi & Reid, 1998, 2002). By comparison, task-centered practice has been formulated for a variety of specific practice concerns using research-derived knowledge, client and practitioner feedback, and initial testing (e.g., Bailey-Dempsey & Reid, 1996; Caspi, 2008; Caspi & Reid, 1998; Naleppa & Reid, 2003). One such specific practice concern includes task-centered treatment of sibling aggression (Caspi, 2008; Reid & Donovan, 1990).

In addition to its own empirical development, task-centered practice also draws upon other existing empirically validated interventions. It directs practitioners to integrate tested methods and research-based knowledge in treatment formulations. Treatments that have been shown to be more efficacious for certain problems than others are preferred (representing "best practices") for integration and application in practice (Briggs & Rzepnicki, 2004). For example, research has demonstrated cognitive behavioral interventions as most effective for clinical depression (e.g., David-Ferdon & Kaslow, 2008). As such, the task-centered practitioner working with a depressed client would incorporate cognitive behavioral strategies as tasks (e.g., writing down negative thoughts, rehearsing positive self-talk). When effective interventions do not exist for a particular treatment concern, practitioners should consult the research literature and identify findings to inform assessment and intervention decisions (Mullen & Bacon, 2003). For example, few treatment approaches for sibling aggression exist and none have yet been established as most efficacious. However, the developmental and family research literature provides practitioners with findings that can inform treatment—for *empirically derived* practice (Caspi, 2011a). For example, parents' lack of intervention in their children's conflicts is linked with subsequent sibling aggression (Kramer, Perozynski, & Chung, 1999). Such information helps direct practitioners to assess for passive, hands-off, parenting approaches when working with sibling aggression cases.

Task-centered practice's empirical orientation also involves active evaluation of its own individual treatment effectiveness by measuring target problems and progress toward alleviating them. Quantitative evaluation of target problems is done at each treatment meeting session so that clients and practitioners can empirically assess the success of their work together. For example, a parent reports at the first treatment meeting that her children are fighting 10 times a day. After 6 weeks the parent observes that fighting is down to three times a day. It is easy to see that there has been significant improvement and that interventions have been effective (although more work may be warranted). If fights were not explicitly counted, neither the parent nor the practitioner would be sure that treatment was working since the siblings continue fighting multiple times each day. The parent may become frustrated and even exclaim that the counseling sessions have not greatly improved the situation. By comparison, if each week the parent reported that sibling fighting had remained the same or increased, the practitioner and family would clearly know that treatment and task selection are not working and that different interventions are in order.

Rapid assessment instruments (RAIs) are recommended as an alternative or supplemental strategy for empirically tracking problem change (Levitt & Reid, 1981). RAIs are empirically validated surveys, inventories, or scales that provide scores for evaluating psychosocial problems. They can be employed throughout treatment to monitor progress. For example, a depressed individual may be given the Beck Depression Inventory (BDI) (Beck, Steer, & Garbin, 1988). The initial score is considered a starting point or baseline for treatment evaluation. Weekly score tracking provides insight into intervention effectiveness. If the client scores lower on subsequent BDIs, selected tasks are working. Unchanged or increased scores indicate that treatment strategies are ineffective and should be modified.

Many inventories that measure sibling relationships and aggression exist and each can be used as an RAI for practice. Some examples include the Sibling Relationship Inventory (Stocker & McHale, 1992), the Conflict Tactics Scale revised for sibling aggression (e.g., Kettrey & Emery, 2006), the Lifespan Sibling Relationship Scale (Riggio, 2000), the Brother–Sister Questionnaire (Graham-Bermann & Cutler, 1994), and the Scale of Negative Family Interactions (Simonelli et al., 2005), a comprehensive instrument that includes measures of sibling, parental, and sexual aggression. Practitioners working with sibling aggression work can consult available inventory compilations that include a wide range of practice scales and instruments for use as RAIs (e.g., Corcoran & Fischer, 2000; Johnson, 2009).

The task-centered approach of continual tracking of progress essentially operationalizes the single-systems design research methodology (e.g., Nugent, 2010; Reid, 1993; Thyer & Myers, 2007). Practitioners can empirically demonstrate the effectiveness of their work by quantitatively recording treatment progress to clients, themselves, employers, and third-party payers. Successful treatment innovations should be disseminated as research findings in academic journals and other practice resources.

Finally, task-centered practice involves systematic tracking of the effectiveness of discrete strategies via the task review process. At the start of each clinical session, practitioners and clients review task performance ratings, mutually identifying what actions worked, which encountered obstacles, and which were ineffective. By monitoring task performance, clients and practitioners can identify and utilize interventions that work, based upon client successes, and avoid repeated attempts at actions that bear little fruit and are ultimately frustrating.

## Integrative Stance

Task-centered practice focuses largely on client-defined problems in which treatment goals are not predetermined. The approach takes an integrative stance by selectively drawing upon "empirically based theories and methods" (Reid, 1992, p. 3) for most empirically potent or "best practices." For example, task-centered treatment for depression integrates cognitive behavioral methods, which has frequently been identified as the most efficacious for such problems (e.g., David-Ferdon & Kaslow, 2008). Task-centered practice has been empirically supported for a range of family problems (Benbenishty, 1988; Reid, 1992), including for treatment of sibling aggression (Caspi, 2008; Reid & Donovan, 1990). Because sibling issues have been systematically shown to be tied to family considerations (Caspi, 2008; Hoffman & Edwards, 2004), family systems make sense for many if not most sibling aggression concerns. SFT (Minuchin, 1974) has been successfully combined with task-centered treatment for working with families (Reid, 1985). The task-centered sibling aggression treatment approach put forth in this book draws upon family systems theory, SFT techniques, as well as behavioral strategies.

## Problem-Solving Actions (Tasks)

As noted earlier, task-centered practice believes that change is best effected by taking action in the form of well-articulated tasks. Planning task implementation constitutes the main activity and function of sessions.

## Systems and Context

Task-centered practice takes the view that problems do not occur in isolation but are rather situated and often connected to multiple systems and contexts. As such, interventions may focus on multiple systems and contextual change. For example, sibling aggression has been linked to peer bullying (Duncan, 1999). A child bullied at school may in turn pick on a younger sibling. Interventions will likely need to target extrafamilial (e.g., school, peer) systems in order to assist with reducing sibling hostility. Similarly, sibling relationships differ across cultures and attending to the sociohistorical contexts is important for understanding and facilitating change (e.g., see Watson & McGoldrick, 2011).

## Focus on Client-Acknowledged Problems

Problems in task-centered practice are mutually defined by clients and practitioners, but derived from the clients' expressed concerns rather than the practitioner's assessments. In this approach "the client's priorities become the practitioner's" (Reid, 1992, p. 4). The primary objective is ameliorating the problem that brought the client to treatment. Practitioners, however, may identify challenges and pathways for problem resolution of which clients are unaware. For example, sibling conflict has been linked to marital conflict (Stocker & Youngblade, 1999). A practitioner may quickly identify that marital discord exists in a family that has sought treatment to reduce sibling hostility. During the course of treatment the practitioner can share the observation of marital problems and connect it to the sibling fighting, for the purpose of resolving the client's complaint of sibling aggression. Once the marital conflict is acknowledged and its link to sibling aggression understood, their marital discord can be formally addressed as a target problem. Problems are client-directed but mutually defined in task-centered practice.

Families frequently seek help for issues without recognizing that there is also a sibling aggression issue at hand, and that it may be aggravating or causing the problem that brought them to treatment. For example, school behavior problems have been linked in research to sibling aggression (Garcia et al., 2000). A family may not recognize that their child's academic troubles are connected to sibling issues. The practitioner who is knowledgeable about siblings can make this link for the family, who are then more likely to agree to address sibling conflict as a target problem in order to help ameliorate school difficulties.

## Practitioner–Client Relationship

In the task-centered approach, the practitioner–client relationship focuses on identifying and agreeing upon problem-solving actions, and is not the primary medium for change. Problem-solving is facilitated by relationships in which clients feel respected, valued, and validated. Moreover, clients appreciate having their view of problems taken seriously. A positive working alliance is built through respect, but is also propelled by the experience of taking action and experiencing progress.

The practitioner–client relationship is collaborative, where practitioners share observations and clinical assessments, and avoid hidden agendas (Reid, 1992). Both problems and ideas for resolving them (i.e., tasks) come from client input. By asking clients what they have tried and their thoughts on best approaches to ameliorate problems avoids repetition of actions they have already attempted (e.g., "I've already tried that and it didn't work"), and is responsive to client's problem-solving abilities. Practitioner-defined directives sometimes fall outside the client's capabilities. Task-centered procedures include client evaluations of their abilities to complete problem-solving endeavors, and to overcome potential task implementation obstacles. Finally, motivation for completing tasks is increased when clients participate in their formulation. When created and dictated by the practitioner, clients may not fully understand assigned tasks, view them as overly difficult, or may even be culturally incongruent—all of which will decrease motivation.

In regard to combative siblings, a parent who is told by the practitioner to stop intervening in their children's arguments may find it impossible to resist at the time fighting occurs. In task-centered practice, a practitioner may suggest this task, and if after discussion the parent believes that it is appropriate and doable, they may agree that it is worth carrying out.

## Planned Brevity

The task-centered approach is a time-limited, brief-treatment model and contracts for service are typically for 6–12 weekly sessions. This is based upon extensive research that has consistently demonstrated that short-term treatments have outcomes as good, and sometimes better, than indefinite arrangements (Koss & Butcher, 1986). Having a clear deadline seems to motivate client and practitioner action, whereas indefinite arrangements sometimes lose focus on target problems and clear markers that determine an end to treatment are usually absent. In brief treatment approaches, treatment concludes when the problem that brought the client to treatment has been resolved to the client's satisfaction. Knowing that treatment will come to an end also minimizes the potential of clients becoming dependent on practitioners for support and problem solving.

Although task-centered procedures emphasize time-limited arrangements, short-term contracts need not be rigidly followed. Client situations may require extended arrangements—for example, family reunification in foster care (Rooney, 1981). Practitioners and clients can recontract to work on new target problems, but there is a formal recognition of achievement and the resolution of problems. Task-centered treatment of sibling aggression has been shown to be effective using time-limited arrangements (Caspi, 2008; Reid & Donovan, 1990).

Target problems and selected tasks implementation and treatment are formally agreed upon using contracts. Written contracts also include checks to ensure that potential obstacles were discussed and that tasks were rehearsed during sessions. Written contracts are preferable to verbal ones as they increase accountability and can serve as reminders of what was agreed to. Contracting is done at the end of each session. Agreements made during the session are reviewed and formally recorded.

## Structure

Task-centered practice provides a well-articulated structure with a clear sequence of problem-solving steps for both individual treatment sessions and the overall intervention program. Clients are educated about task-centered procedures and participate as collaborators in addressing their problems. There is little mystery for clients about the problem-solving process. Practitioners do not have hidden agendas. Receivers of the approach (e.g., clients) report appreciating the structure and knowing what to expect during treatment (Caspi, 2008). Task-centered practice is organized into three phases of treatment. The sequence of steps carried out during each phase is similar, but with minor variations.

### Phases of treatment

The task-centered approach is organized into three phases: initial, middle, and ending. The sequence of steps that make up sessions are employed throughout but each phase is characterized by unique differences. During the initial phase, the primary focus is on problem exploration and formulation, and is usually completed during the first two meetings, marked by the development of the first set of selected tasks. The middle phase constitutes the bulk of treatment and is characterized by active problem and task evaluations, continued selection of tasks, and ongoing implementation. This is done following a well-articulated series of steps carried out at each meeting (see "The Task-Centered Meeting" for a detailed description). The ending phase, often referred to as "termination," refers to a process that marks the end of treatment. It is characterized by a review of the problems and evaluation of the current situation, emphasizing accomplishments. Successful problem-solving strategies are mutually highlighted so that clients can draw upon them in future situations. Noting successes is often positively reinforcing. Although the final meeting constitutes the ending phase, discussion of the contracted duration of treatment occurs from the first session when contracting occurs, and throughout treatment that includes reminders of "how much time is left." If the client wishes to continue treatment to address other target problems, a new contract is formulated and the phases are repeated.

### The task-centered meeting

Each task-centered meeting is organized by a well-defined series of steps. The task planning and implementation sequence is employed throughout the treatment, but slight variations exist in each phase. The initial phase begins with the first meeting that focuses on introducing clients to the task-centered approach and procedures and involves initial problem identification, target problem formulation, and the selection of initial tasks to be implemented in between the first two meetings. The middle phase represents the bulk of treatment and its ordered sequence is outlined in Figure 4.1. Meetings at this phase begin with the task review and end with contracting. Each of these steps has been described in depth earlier in this chapter, except for the identifying and resolving obstacles process, which is presented at the end of this section.

Clients generally implement tasks in between clinical sessions and repeat the above sequence at each meeting, beginning with the task review. This process continues until target problems have been successfully ameliorated. This sequence is intended to provide direction and structure for meetings with clients. It is meant to be used flexibly and not in a rigid fashion. The practitioner

**FIGURE 4.1** The task-centered meeting sequence.

- *Task Review*: Review success of implementation of tasks selected at prior meeting
- *Problem Review*: Mutually evaluate frequency and severity of target problems
- *Target Problem Formulation*: Identify, prioritize and select up to three as target problems for immediate work. This step includes problem identification and specification
- *Task Selection*: Identify, evaluate and select up to three tasks for each target problem
- *Identifying and Resolving Obstacles*: Identify potential obstacles to successful task implementation, modify tasks accordingly
- *Contracting*: Clarify agreements about target problems and planned tasks to be implemented between meetings

and clients may find it necessary to dedicate time to activities that may be important for problem solving but not explicitly part of the task planning and implementation sequence (e.g., venting emotional experiences). Additionally, the sequence can be adjusted to incorporate strategies from other approaches. For example, family therapy techniques such as enactments, which may involve having clients recreate a recent argument, can be added into the meeting sequence as part of the problem identification process.

In the ending phase, the meeting sequence includes three steps. First, target problems and the client's situation in general are reviewed. Second, successful problem-solving strategies employed by clients are identified, and, third, discussion takes place that considers handling of any remaining problems and whether or not further work is needed. In cases where continued work is identified as necessary, the practitioner and client recontract. Because task-centered practice emphasizes client-centered problem-solving efforts, there is usually little need for intense emotional discussions related to "saying goodbyes" (e.g., exploration of abandonment issues).

## Anticipating Obstacles

A ninth unique feature of task-centered practice, one that separates it from other problem-solving models, is its active attention to maximizing client success by anticipating potential obstacles to task implementation before they are carried out. Clients often believe during clinical meetings that tasks sound doable or are easy, but find them difficult to complete when they attempt them. For example, a pair of sisters engages in frequent and intense fights related to borrowing clothing without permission. During task-centered work, they agree to the task of asking permission prior to taking the others' clothes. When they try it at home, they discover that when one denies the other permission, the same intense fighting erupts. They also discover that there are not always opportunities to ask for permission. One sister wanted to borrow a sweater but her sister was not at home. She decided to take the sweater because the sister was not around to ask for consent. Obstacles identified during implementation are helpful for refining tasks for reimplementation.

Anticipating obstacles prior to implementation is particularly useful in maximizing task success. In this step, the practitioner asks clients to imagine carrying out the selected tasks and to identify possible challenges that could be encountered (Reid, 1992). If clients are unable to identify obstacles, practitioners may use prompts such as asking "*What if?*" questions. To continue the example of the clothes-borrowing sisters, the practitioner may ask each sibling "*What if* your sister is not at home and you want a piece of her clothing? How would you handle this so that a fight would not take place?" and, "What if your sister tells you 'no'—that she does not want you to borrow a piece of clothing?" Such questions help clients anticipate behaviors of others, how they may respond to others, and the possible consequences of their actions. By identifying the obstacle prior to implementation, clients are more prepared to handle them if they arise. Contingency or "backup" plans can be made for when obstacles arise so that clients have strategies for working past them to maximize task success. For example, the sisters decide that if they cannot ask permission from the other because she is away or unavailable, then they must wait until the sister has returned before taking the clothing. When clients struggle to identify obstacles, the practitioner's initial ideas can serve to "prime the pump" and clients often are then able to generate their own. For example, after answering the initial "What if?" questions, one sister asked, "But what if when she's away I really need to take one of her shirts because the only one that will match my outfit is in the dirty laundry?" Anticipating such problems enables discussion of what to do when such challenges arise.

A common obstacle to successful task implementation is client ambivalence about a task, which fosters low motivation or even resistance. Frequently, tasks are new behaviors for clients that raise anxiety, or may be viewed as unlikely to create positive change. The step of anticipating potential obstacles should include questions about client confidence and motivation to complete a task (Reid, 1992). Clients may openly agree to tasks to please the practitioner but internally believe that they will not implement them successfully. Sharing that ambivalent feelings is common and opens the door for discussion and problem-solving obstacles related to motivation.

## TASK-CENTERED PRACTICE AND STRUCTURAL FAMILY THERAPY

Since the beginning of its development, the task-centered model was designed to incorporate theory and technologies (e.g., treatment strategies) from varied sources (Fortune & Reid, 2011). The approach can be improved by drawing upon other approaches, particularly strategies that have demonstrated empirical effectiveness or promise. As noted earlier, task-centered practice has successfully utilized SFT techniques (Reid, 1985). Because sibling relationships and dynamics are embedded in families, a family treatment approach makes sense. When possible, task-centered family practice, like SFT, prefers work with all family members. A brief overview of SFT and its integration with task-centered process is provided prior to presentation of the model of TCSA.

## Structural Family Therapy

Structural family therapy was developed and introduced by Salvador Minuchin in the 1960s and 1970s and has grown into a well-known and widely used psychotherapeutic approach. Drawing upon family systems and communications theories, SFT focuses on identifying and addressing the unspoken rules that direct interaction and operations. Because family relationships are rule-governed, interaction patterns are repetitive. Family "structure" refers to how families organize themselves according to invisible and often idiosyncratic rules that guide the ways members behave with each other (Minuchin, 1974). Problems are not viewed as located within individuals, but within the family system's rules, transactional patterns, and organization. The way relationships are organized can serve to support an ongoing problem despite family efforts to resolve it. Reorganizing or *restructuring* the family is the central intervention of SFT. Assessment of transactional patterns is done by identifying repeating sequences of behavior (i.e., process) through observation of the family in action, and by using active inquiry—to map the family's structure. Learning about family interactional processes enables practitioners to identify patterns of rigid triangulation and coalitions, and poorly defined boundaries. Once family structure is identified, restructuring interventions, such as modifying triangulation, disrupting alliances, clarifying and adjusting boundaries (including subsystem boundaries), and identifying new parenting behaviors, are employed.

### *Identifying transaction patterns*

Identifying sequences of family interaction is part of the assessment process. Transactional pattern identification is usually done using observation and active inquiry.

*Sequences of behavior: Observation.* Structural family therapists observe interactions to identify how families are organized, and specifically to note problematic triangulation, coalitions, communication, boundary definitions, and hierarchy. This is done beginning with the first meeting. Practitioners note how the family interacts, such as how closely they sit in proximity to each other (e.g., who sits closest to whom, who sits between whom), nonverbal behaviors (e.g., how one person may become withdrawn when another speaks), and side-taking behavior (e.g., who defends whom against whom).

Because interaction patterns repeat across time and circumstances, what the family says (i.e., content) is usually considered less important than how they communicate (i.e., process).

The SFT practitioner makes note of transactional patterns during conversations with the family. Families may also be given activities to do (e.g., play a game, plan an imaginary trip) in order to observe them in action. A powerful SFT technique is the *enactment*, which involves asking family members to discuss a conflict or engage in a familiar challenging situation (e.g., getting a child to behave) during the treatment session—that is, "to dance in (the practitioner's) presence" (Minuchin & Fishman, 1981, p. 79). For example, conflictual siblings may be told to select a topic that causes them to argue, and then discuss it. The discussion typically turns into an authentic argument enabling the practitioner to observe how the siblings behave with each other, how the conflict escalates, and how the parents manage the fighting. It may be observed that the mother jumps in to protect the younger child while the father barks occasional and half-hearted demands to "stop fighting," which are ignored. Observing this, the practitioner quickly identifies (1) a triangle with a mother–younger child coalition in which the older child is the outsider, (2) a sibling subsystem boundary in which the mother, but not the father, can easily enter the sibling's relationship, disrupting their ability to interact autonomously, and (3) a spousal subsystem that does not act as a unified parenting team, which undermines the father's hierarchal position.

Families also spontaneously offer practitioners opportunities to observe structure. For example, during a family meeting, a 10-year-old boy sitting next to his 12-year-old sister started poking her in the cheek. She first slapped away his hand, which did not make him stop, but instead seemed to encourage him to do it more forcefully. In response, she stood up and kicked him in the shin. Neither parent reacted directly to the physical violence. Instead, they looked at the practitioner and shrugged, the father added, "We told you he was a problem." In this case, the spontaneous enactment enabled the practitioner to see how sibling violence is handled by this family, noting a sibling subsystem boundary that was overly autonomous and parents who were perhaps too disengaged and inadvertently giving permission to the children to act this way. Of course, a single interaction does not necessarily convey an accurate understanding of the family. It instead suggests possibilities that practitioners can either verify or reject as they continue to observe. Initial impressions can also be explored by asking about them through active inquiry.

*Sequences of behavior: Active inquiry.* Practitioners can also learn about transactional sequences by asking about them in great detail. In a process called "tracking," practitioners use clarifying questions to learn about family structure (Minuchin, 1974). One approach is to have a family describe a recent incident. The practitioner inquires about when and where the event took place, who else was present, and how each person behaved at each moment during the encounter. Questions such as "*What happened next?*"; "*Then what did you do?*"; and "*Who else was there?*" are used to elicit and formulate a refined understanding of the family's process.

Practitioners avoid asking why incidents occurred or why individuals behaved in a particular manner. "Why?" questions are avoided because they usually provide global insults that are not useful for problem solving. For example, during one family meeting, Tom (14-year-old boy) said that he frequently hits his 9-year-old brother Jake. When asked why he does this, Tom replied, "Because he is a jerk." When pressed for elaboration, he says, "Jake thinks he is God's gift to the world and can do whatever he wants. His attitude makes me mad and he deserves to be brought down a couple notches." While Tom's explanation may provide some insight into his thought process, it does not provide helpful information in regard to how family interactions may support his hitting behavior. Moreover, it suggests the problem is solely located in Tom, and will fail to identify how Jake, his mother, and his father are also involved. From an SFT perspective, identifying how fighting starts, escalates, and resolves is more useful for both assessing family structure and devising interventions to disrupt processes that support ongoing sibling. Chapter 7 provides a complete case example using Tom and Jake's family and illustrates the use of active inquiry to identify sequences and how the problem is not Tom's, but one located in family interaction.

*Boundary clarification.* Another focus of SFT involves identifying and clarifying boundary relationships. Transactional sequences often illuminate poorly defined boundaries, which may be too open, closed, or inconsistent. Siblings benefit from having autonomous relationships in that they can experience each other directly, without intrusion. This enables opportunities for closeness and learning how to resolve their own conflicts. In order for siblings to have autonomous relationships, their subsystem boundary must not be overly permeable and open to high parental involvement. Parents can easily interfere in their children's sibling relationships in the name of "keeping the peace." Many parents enter into their children's relationships and conflicts by communicating for them (e.g., speaking to one child on behalf of the sibling) and trying to manage them (e.g., telling the children to go to separate rooms to stop fighting). Such efforts, while well intended, can serve to create distance and further hostilities, particularly if a parent systematically favors one child over the other.

Children also invite their parents into their subsystem. During conflicts, children frequently call for the aid of a parent. Parents who are quick to enter run the risk of interfering rather than helping. How parents involve themselves in sibling subsystems makes a difference. Entering as a neutral party with the aim of helping children develop problem-solving skills is typically helpful, whereas mechanical and autocratic methods (e.g., reflexive punishment, yelling) is usually problematic. Of course, parents must become involved in cases of sibling violence. Once dangerous aggression has been successfully halted, efforts to make the sibling subsystem less permeable to parental involvement can promote sibling closeness and positivity.

Sibling subsystem boundaries may also be too close to parental involvement. Parents have long been advised to stay out of their children's conflicts, and purposely restrain their involvement. They may also believe that children should know how to behave with each other and fail to teach communication and problem-solving skills. In the case of violent and abusive sibling relationships, children are unlikely to share their violent experiences with parents for fear of further abuse, retribution, or family disruption. Additionally, minimal parental involvement suggests that parents are unaware of positive and supportive sibling interactions and therefore are unable to reinforce such behaviors. Practitioner attention to family interpersonal and subsystem boundaries can be helpful in devising interventions to balance parental involvement to promote sibling autonomy and safety.

## Integrating Task-Centered Practice and Structural Family Therapy

As discussed earlier, task-centered practice is an open model that promotes integration of other treatment technologies. Here, the task-centered (TC) approach provides the framework for intervention, and SFT assessment and treatment strategies are integrated. For example, the SFT strategies that include identification of transactional sequences, triangulation, coalitions, and boundaries are identified and shared with clients to inform the TC process of formulating target problems and generating tasks to ameliorate problematic patterns.

Integration of SFT strategies is fairly straightforward; however, the two approaches do differ in how they view the role of the practitioner and how the problem is solved. In task-centered practice, the practitioner is a collaborative partner who guides clients through an explicitly shared problem-solving process in which clients' ideas direct the process (Reid, 1992). In comparison, the structural family therapist largely directs the process, including assigning tasks. Assessment and intervention is typically done by the therapist, and clients are not always aware of the therapist's objectives or how change is going to be brought about. SFT therapists also function as change agents in which they enter into family systems to reshape interactional patterns (Minuchin, 1974). They may take sides, promote confrontation, and restrict participation of some family members while promoting involvement of others. The task-centered approach provides less direction for practitioner involvement in family systems. Practitioners typically act as outsiders who focus on identifying problem-solving efforts with families.

The two approaches also differ in their problem-solving emphases. In general, TC sees taking *direct* action on a client-identified problem as the focus of intervention, whereas SFT attacks the problem *indirectly* and views alteration of family interaction as the primary mechanism of change. In SFT, the client's view of the problem is redefined as a family issue. TC practitioners start with the clients' definition of their problems, but problems are often mutually redefined during a collaborative problem exploration process. Practitioners may offer clients new ways to think about their problems and ways to go about solving them, but ultimately the actions taken to resolve challenges are client-directed. As an example of direct versus indirect approaches, consider a family with a lashing-out (i.e., angry) teenager. In SFT, the whole family is seen together and the target of intervention is family process, which is assumed to be creating the environment for sustained lashing out—that is, the problem is addressed indirectly. In TC work, the teenager's lashing out is treated using a combination of perspectives, including the teenager, the family, and the practitioner. Lashing out may be addressed directly using behavioral methods such as anger management, and at the same time the teenager's perspective that his parents are overly restrictive may require them to modify their behavior. The TC practitioner may also integrate SFT concepts by introducing the family to the concept of triangulation and how it may be contributing to the teenager's frustrations. As this example illustrates, the differences between SFT and TC intervention targets are not contradictory, and SFT can be somewhat seamlessly integrated into the TC framework.

In addition, the differences between TC and SFT regarding practitioner stance are not irreconcilable. SFT practitioners alter their stance depending upon the treatment activities being undertaken at a particular time. For example, therapists act as outsiders during data collection and insiders (i.e., act as a member of the system) during interventions (Minuchin, 1974). In an integrated task-centered/SFT approach, practitioners can similarly move in and out of family systems, although most efforts will be from the outsider stance. Task-centered procedures, such as problem identification, task planning and implementation, and task review, are done as mutual endeavors with clients. When employing SFT strategies, such as enactments, tracking, and observation of transactional sequences, practitioners also use the outsider stance but give increased direction. However, in the integrated approach there may be occasions when the practitioner may find it necessary to take sides, share emotional reactions, and unbalance the system in order to highlight dynamics for the purpose of informing target problem formulation and corresponding task selection. Families with highly inflexible structures may be difficult to engage in task-planning activities aimed at undoing transactional patterns such as rigid triangulation. Taking an insider stance may help unbalance and move the system by illustrating resistance and adherence to rigidity (i.e., relational rules that sustain problem behaviors).

## Integration of Behavioral Methods for Parenting

The primary objectives of the two-pronged sibling aggression treatment approach are to simultaneously halt antagonism and enhance sibling relationship quality. Behavioral interventions can play an important part of meeting these goals and are integrated into the task-centered sibling aggression treatment approach. The inclusion of behavioral methods in task-centered practice is common. In the TCSA model presented here, behavioral methods are offered primarily as a way to assist parenting practices. For example in Chapter 6, I offer a *Positive Behavior Approach* to share with parents/guardians for the purpose of promoting positive sibling relationships. It offers a series of steps to productively manage problem behavior in children by focusing on prosocial skill development.

Parents often struggle with their children's sibling aggression and in their frustration engage in ineffective parenting strategies that frequently involve yelling and punishment. Parents may look to family practitioners for alternative discipline methods. Behavioral strategies can be taught, rehearsed, and selected as parenting tasks. Strategies to suppress sibling aggression are effective but risk emotionally apathetic and disengaged relationships (Leitenberg et al., 1977). As noted earlier, sibling warmth and support are linked to beneficial outcomes (Kramer, 2011), and therefore, disinterest in one's siblings is a problematic treatment outcome. Behavioral methods, however, can also be used to effectively increase prosocial interaction between siblings. In particular, reinforcing good sibling behavior *when it occurs* can be an effective way of building sibling positivity. Negative reinforcement strategies are effective for stopping bad behavior when it occurs by offering choices of consequences and rewards (e.g., "You can either continue poking your sister and lose permission to play your video game tonight or share your crayons with her and be able to play your games later." TCSA integrates active parental reinforcement of wanted behaviors, both when they occur and as a strategy to modify unwanted activity.

It is important to note that parents often reactively punish their children for misbehaviors such as sibling aggression. Punishment is not recommended for a few reasons. First, while it may foster immediate compliance, it is generally ineffective as a long-term solution; second, it frequently although inadvertently "teaches" individuals to avoid being caught rather than engaging in good behavior; third, it generates negativity in the parent–child relationship; fourth, it may escalate to physical aggression that is generally regarded as detrimental to children's health (e.g., Deater-Deckard, Ivy, & Petrill, 2006; Gershoff, 2002) and models violence; and fifth, it does not teach new, expected, or prosocial behaviors. On this last point, children's misbehavior should be regarded as teachable moments that include the provision of alternative, prosocial, and expected behavior. When wanted behaviors are not articulated, children only learn that they are punishable and do not enhance their relational skill set. Punishment differs from negative consequences in that the consequence is generally unknown to the child. It does not provide the child an opportunity to self-correct or try it again.

## THE TASK-CENTERED SIBLING AGGRESSION TREATMENT APPROACH

The TCSA treatment approach was developed using D&D (Thomas & Rothman, 1994), a research methodology focused on systematic building of treatment models. D&D is particularly useful for psychosocial problems for which few intervention technologies exist, such as sibling aggression treatment.

The D&D process involves formulating a preliminary set of guidelines (i.e., model) to inform practice based primarily on empirically derived knowledge. The model is then implemented in a pilot test and systematic data are collected to identify which aspects of the guidelines work and which do not. This feedback is used to revise the model, which occurs prior to formal dissemination, evaluation testing, and practitioner use. While outcome data are often included in the pilot testing, the primary focus is on the model's implementation for the purpose of improving the internal workings (i.e., guidelines). Outcome data from TCSA's pilot testing step of the D&D process indicated tentative empirical support (see Caspi, 2008). "Support for TCSA is bolstered by prior studies that have used task-centered procedures for family problems (Reid, 1985, 1992) and sibling violence (Reid & Donovan, 1990)" (Caspi, 2008, p. 583). Models that have demonstrated some effectiveness are better choices than untested approaches or ones that have not received systematic development. The following presentation of TCSA is a revised and improved model drawn from application of D&D.

## The TCSA Approach

TCSA is organized into the three phases reviewed earlier in this chapter: initial, middle, and ending. The steps for TCSA meetings follow a slightly modified sequence from the task-centered approach but the core problem-solving process remains the same. New and modified steps are in bold typeface and discussed in depth following the outline of the TCSA sequence presented here (the central steps were presented earlier). For quick reference, the TCSA sequence of steps is included in Appendix E.

## Outline of the TCSA Sequence

*Initial phase* (from the first meeting until completion of the first contract)

1. **Social Stage**
2. **Provide TCSA Overview and Sibling Education**
3. Target Problem Formulation
   a. Problem Identification and Specification
   b. Identification of Transactional Sequences
4. Task Selection
5. Identifying and Resolving Obstacles
6. **Rehearsal**
7. **Contracting**

*Middle phase* (from completion of the first contract through the final meeting)

1. **Social Stage**
2. Task Review

3. Target Problem Review
4. Target Problem Formulation and/or Reformulation
5. Task Selection
6. Identifying and Resolving Obstacles
7. **Rehearsal**
8. **Contracting**

*Ending phase* (the final meeting)

1. Target Problem Review
2. **Identification of Successful Problem-Solving Strategies**
3. **Review of Client Problem Situation in General**
4. **Discussion of Future Work and Possible Recontracting**

## Description of New and Modified Steps for TCSA

### *Social stage*

The social stage was introduced to task-centered practice as a way to ease the transition to, and focus on, the formal work of treatment (Caspi & Reid, 2002). Clients are welcomed and conversation is relatively informal and may include discussions of locating the agency, parking, or topics triggered spontaneously such as noting a client's sports shirt and talking about the client's interest in the game. Often, such conversations provide opportunities to quickly transition into problem-solving efforts. For example, twin sisters Theresa and Yvonne each wore opposing jerseys from opposing baseball teams, the Yankees and the Red Sox. This observation first led to a friendly, social stage and discussion about how they both enjoy baseball, but their loyalty to their teams caused an actual argument. The relationship between team and sibling rivalry made for a natural transition to the problem identification stage.

### *Provide overview of TCSA and sibling education*

The purpose of this step is twofold. First, clients are introduced to task-centered practice and its problem-solving sequence of steps. Copies of the TCSA guidelines are often shared with clients. Second, practitioners introduce clients to the Five Family Dynamics associated with sibling aggression, which are presented in depth in the next chapter. Formal attention to education about sibling relationships is provided during this step, although explicit information about sibling aggression is incorporated throughout the TCSA treatment process.

D & D research on TCSA indicated that families wanted education about sibling relationships during the treatment process as a formal step of the model (Caspi, 2008). Families expressed appreciation for practitioner explanations of what dynamics might be causing their sibling conflicts. For example, one mother shared that when the practitioner mentioned that perceptions of parental favoritism often caused siblings to be antagonistic, she suddenly realized that her dismissal of her youngest child's claims of unfairness might be part of the problem. She cited that piece of information as central to the problem-solving process. She added that if the practitioner had not stated this overtly, she may have not understood how she was part of her children's frequent squabbles. One family suggested that sharing research or handouts on sibling aggression was helpful, and TCSA practitioners are encouraged to do so.

### *Rehearsal*

In TCSA, trying out planned tasks during the treatment meeting is a formal step of approach. It occurs after tasks have been selected and potential obstacles have been anticipated. The purpose of having the family rehearse their tasks is to clarify implementation and to identify obstacles that may not have been anticipated. It is not uncommon to discover during rehearsal that seemingly well-planned tasks were more difficult to implement than anticipated. Trying them out in the meeting with the practitioner present allows for tasks to be additionally structured, modified, or further practiced prior to implementation in the "real world." An in-depth discussion of the benefits of rehearsal is taken up earlier in this chapter.

### *Contracting*

As noted earlier, formal contracts are used at the end of each treatment meeting (for examples of blank and completed contracts, see Appendices B and C). The purpose is to clarify what was agreed upon during the meeting and to confirm expectations of planned tasks. Target problems, anticipated obstacles to successful implementation, and rehearsal are also included in contracts. Preference is given to written contracts over verbal ones for their ability to serve as physical reminders of what was agreed to and increasing accountability. Clients occasionally report that they forgot what was discussed during the prior treatment meeting and so did not do what they agreed to. Using written contracts reduces such forgetting.

Contracts also provide continuity between treatment meetings and help maintain the focus on selected target problems. They are utilized at the start of treatment meetings to assist with task implementation review, providing a link between meetings. Treatment, particularly with chaotic or multiproblem families, risks jumping from one issue to another (e.g., the crisis of the week). Contracts help minimize haphazard and unfocused treatment. That said, contracts are not meant to be used as rigid prescriptions for clients to follow. Rather, they should be used flexibly to guide treatment work. Clients often creatively modify tasks when outside the treatment session and in their "real" environments.

During the contract step of the model, selected tasks are reviewed. It often becomes necessary to revise these tasks or develop new ones after the steps of considering potential obstacles and rehearsing planned tasks. The contracting step often focuses on formulating modified and better versions of planned tasks.

At the end of the treatment meeting, a copy of the contract is given to the client family and one remains with the practitioner. Clients frequently report that they were grateful to have contracts in hand when they were about to implement tasks. As one client put it, "I knew we agreed to have a discussion about coming up with rules for watching television, but could not remember the specifics. So, I looked at the contract and it reminded me of what we were supposed to do during that conversation. I think if I didn't have the contract we would have forgotten the tasks we agreed to and ended up fighting the same way we always do."

### *Identification of successful problem-solving strategies*

Practitioners and clients mutually review the task-centered problem-solving process and identify which tasks were effective for selected target problems. These tasks are framed as potential solutions to similar future problems should they arise. Moreover, the problem-solving process is highlighted as a general strategy for solving problems in general.

### *Review of client problem situation in general*

Practitioners and clients explore the clients' current situations in regard to current problems and mutually assess client capacity and motivation to address them independently.

### *Discussion of future work and possible recontracting*

In cases where problems are manageable and the target problems are resolved to satisfaction, discussion of future work focuses on maintaining success and family harmony, and how to manage problems should they reemerge, which includes implementation of identified effective tasks. In situations where problems continue or new problems are present, practitioners and clients should discuss whether or not recontracting is warranted.

## CONCLUSION

In this chapter, the TCSA treatment approach was introduced. Specific assessment and intervention considerations for TCSA implementation are reviewed in the next chapters.

# 5

# Assessment and Target Problem Formulation

This chapter will present sibling aggression assessment areas and strategies. The two primary ways in which sibling hostility emerges in treatment is discussed. This is followed by a discussion related to the various facets of sibling aggression to be assessed. These include evaluations of behavior, intent, harm, frequency, severity, and fear. A simple strategy related to fear evaluation is introduced for sibling abuse assessment. Unique considerations for each of the types of sibling aggression presented in the first chapter are presented. These include sibling competition, conflict, physical violence and abuse, sexual abuse, psychological maltreatment, and relational aggression. Child welfare considerations for formal reporting are then considered. This is followed by presentation of the assessment strategy of identifying family transactional sequences to discover dynamics that are likely supporting ongoing sibling hostility. The chapter concludes with an overview of the Task-Centered Sibling Aggression (TCSA) treatment approach's target problem formulation process, an assessment framework that provides an in-depth and empirical understanding of sibling aggression behaviors. This chapter provides an in-depth overview of sibling aggression assessment before presentation of the Five Family Dynamics (FFD) treatment modules in the next chapter, which offer more targeted assessment and intervention strategies.

## THE WAYS SIBLING AGGRESSION EMERGES IN PRACTICE

Sibling aggression will present itself in practice in one of two ways. First, sibling aggression may be the identified or *overt* problem that brings families to treatment. Second, it may not be identified as a problem but be linked as an underlying or related issue. It may also be present and be problematic, but not connected to the reason the family sought treatment. Such *covert* sibling aggression should be identified by the practitioner as an issue needing attention. Additionally, sibling aggression can be a primary or secondary issue. For example, a family seeking treatment to assist with negotiating a divorce may also have sibling hostility. Practitioners and families may prioritize coping with family dissolution issues over sibling aggression, but simultaneously attend to both.

## Overt Sibling Aggression

Families occasionally seek professional help for sibling aggression. Parents may seek help after becoming frustrated and feeling unable to manage their children's seemingly constant fighting. Pediatricians often hear such complaints (Pakula, 1992) and may refer the family to a mental health professional. The timing of initiating treatment is usually meaningful and it is helpful to ask why clients decided to seek help at this particular time. Families may report that sibling fighting has been occurring for many years. Asking "Why now?" is important. An aggressive event, such as physical injury, broken household items, or a larger than normal fight, often precipitates the call for counseling or consultation. In violent and abusive situations, referrals may come from child protective services, schools, or hospital staff.

## Covert Sibling Aggression

Perhaps more often, sibling aggression is not the expressed reason for treatment, but is present and may be linked to the presenting problem. Covert sibling aggression can emerge in two ways. First, systematical inquiry into sibling relationships at intake may reveal sibling tensions. Asking about various types of sibling aggression, the frequency and intensity of hostile encounters, the intent to harm, and whether any of the participants experience the relationship as distressing is important to develop a clear understanding of whether or not sibling aggression exists and to the extent that it is problematic. Identification of sibling hostility should lead practitioners to question possible relationships to the problems that brought the client to treatment. For example, peer bullying is linked to sibling abuse (Duncan, 1999). A child referred for bullying his peers may also be the victim of sibling bullying. Attending to sibling aggression directs the practitioner to consider a different treatment approach than if it were not identified. That is, addressing sibling aggression may reduce the child's peer aggression and help protect the child's safety.

The second way a practitioner may identify sibling aggression is by knowing the consequences and factors associated with it, as outlined in Chapter 1 (and listed in Appendix A). These can be used as risk factors to aid the identification of sibling hostility. A practitioner who notes that a client possesses a number of these known links to sibling aggression should ask about it. For example, a practitioner working with a teenage client with a history of delinquency, substance abuse, and depression, all risk factors for sibling violence (Button & Gealt, 2010; Hoffman & Edwards, 2004), should assess for it. If identified, practitioners should work with families to include sibling aggression intervention as part of treatment.

Finally, if harmful sibling aggression is identified but is unrelated to the identified target problem for treatment, practitioners are advised to raise the aggression as problematic and offer to recontract to address or to take it up after the initial presenting problem has been adequately ameliorated. If the sibling aggression threatens client safety, then it must be addressed as any abuse identified in treatment and protecting the victim becomes the immediate focus of work.

## UNIQUE ASSESSMENT CONSIDERATIONS: FACETS OF AGGRESSION

Sibling aggression assessment should be part of every intake and be systematically included in assessment as it is with other forms of interpersonal violence. It is widespread, has many known deleterious effects, and is linked to a variety of other social problems. Inquiry should proceed from the broad to the specific, beginning with questions about the quality of the sibling relationship and if sibling aggression is or has been a feature of the client's experience. Because sibling hostility is often seen as normal, clients may not perceive aggression behaviors between siblings as problematic. As such, it is important to continue inquiry into sibling aggression even when clients initially deny its presence. I recommend asking about six facets of sibling aggression that include exploration of behavior, intent, harm, fear, frequency, and severity. Although many of these examples refer to children, these facets of inquiry can be used with adults, particularly retrospectively to understand their experiences of growing up with siblings. Note that the following does not include assessment for sexual abuse. Although some of the discussion applies, sexual abuse assessment requires additional considerations.

### Behavior

When conducting intakes or completing sibling aggression assessments, practitioners should ask about specific aggressive sibling behaviors such as name calling, hitting, shoving, and making threats (e.g., *Do you and your brother ever call each other names?* or *Does your sister ever tell you she is going to hurt you or your toys?*). Siblings and parents who initially denied sibling aggression may acknowledge name calling, hitting, and threats. Families, particularly those that view sibling hostility as normal, may be surprised by the practitioner's line of inquiry. Educating families about sibling aggression and its negative effects and links to other problems is important when challenging views that sibling hostility is harmless.

### Intent

Considering the prevalence of sibling aggression, most families will acknowledge that aggressive behavior between siblings occurs. A second area of inquiry is related to distinguishing rough play (e.g., wrestling, which often includes shoving and hitting) from problematic violence. Determining the intent behind aggressive behaviors is important in this regard. Questions such as, "When you hit your brother do you want to hurt him or is it just for fun?" are helpful. Recipients of hitting may not see it as playful sibling behavior, and "fun" rough play can turn quickly into attempts to inflict harm. It may help to identify if such escalation is in place because it suggests interventions to either stop children from engaging in rough play or to teach stopping on their own once it no longer becomes about fun. A developmental benefit of rough play is learning about one's own competitiveness, emotional self, and the limits of one's strengths. As such, simply stopping the play may be both disappointing to the siblings and developmentally limiting. Moreover, some have argued that rough play is a socially acceptable way for boys to physically engage with each other in a friendly and affectionate way (Gnaulati, 2002).

In addition to asking about intent to harm, it is important to ask about their perceptions of siblings' intents. A child may believe his sister intends to hurt him, whereas the older and stronger sister perceives her actions to be playful. The younger child may retaliate out of anger with the intent to cause harm. Interventions may include helping children learn about the impacts of their actions to learn self-regulating skills and perspective taking. Older and younger siblings often experience the same interaction quite differently. For example, 9-year-old Tom has an earlier bedtime than his 12-year-old brother Bill. When Tom was lying in bed trying to fall asleep, Bill would silently enter his room and pull all his covers off and run out of the room laughing. Tom remade his bed and got in it to get back to sleep, at which point Bill would run back in to pull Tom's covers off again. Years later, Bill remembered this event as a "fun time between brothers," a bonding moment, whereas Tom recalled being annoyed and feeling negatively about the sibling relationship, a divisive moment.

Assessments that include violent sibling behavior with the intent to do harm are clear indications of problematic sibling aggression. Exploring actual harm, frequency and severity, and existence of fear provide important information about the seriousness and nature of sibling hostility.

## Actual Harm

Practitioners should inquire about whether intent to harm has resulted in the perpetration of actual harm. Questions such as, "Have you ever intentionally hurt your sibling?" or "Have you ever been intentionally hurt by your sibling?" will usually produce responses about physical harm. The nature of the harm caused will provide the practitioner with the understanding of about the severity of the sibling aggression, and whether or not it has become violent. Practitioners should also explore whether or not the violence is either mutually or individually perpetrated, with a clear aggressor and victim. This will help to distinguish between abuse (unidirectional aggression) and violence (mutual aggression). As a reminder, what may appear and even reported to be mutually violent interactions may upon closer inspection reveal a perpetrator and victim. The usually younger and weaker victims often rely on violent tactics to defend themselves or to retaliate. They may view the violence as frightening and debilitating whereas the older and stronger child enjoys the violence, often receiving rewards for engaging in it and "winning."

Practitioner questions about harm are often interpreted by clients to refer to physical injury. It is important to also ask explicitly about psychological assault—for example, "Did you ever try to make your sister cry by teasing her?" Both practitioners and clients are at risk of perceiving psychological assaults to be less problematic than physical ones, although emotional aggression can be quite harmful.

If serious harm is reported then practitioners must take immediate action to assess the likelihood of recurrence (i.e., was the injury a one-time accident or was it part of ongoing intent to harm) and create a safety plan with the family to prevent further harm. As with any abuse, serious injury perpetrated by siblings, with reasonable threat of reoccurrence, should be reported to state child protective services.

## Frequency and Severity

Identifying the frequency and severity of sibling aggressive encounters is important for learning about how entrenched the conflict is and the course of action required. Occasional but very severe aggression implies different interactional patterns than ongoing mild aggression. Severe but sporadic flare-ups indicate exploration into patterns of escalation—for example, What triggers the aggression? Who is present? When do they occur? How are they resolved? Frequent mild aggression suggests less immediate focus on triggers and greater attention to family dynamics and interactional rules.

Establishing the frequency and severity of problems is a central part of task-centered practice (Reid, 1992). It enables empirical evaluation of work with clients. Clients are frequently asked to keep count of how often problems occur by noting occurrences on a chart, sometimes kept on the kitchen refrigerator (Caspi, 2008). Each time a sibling fight takes place, a check is added to the chart and tallied at the end of the day or week. Similarly, the severity of problems is rated, often on the same chart. For example, siblings will rate the how bad (i.e., how severe) a conflict incident was for them on a scale from 1–10 (1 = mild; 5 = moderate; 10 = severe). Having this information provides practitioners and families with baseline information for the sibling conflict and can track the progress of interventions. Take, for example, a sibling pair that count their "fights" for 2 weeks and discover they average eight conflicts each day, with one child rating the severity of the fights as a 9 and the other child giving a rating of 7. At the first session, the practitioner asks them to try an alternative behavior to lashing out—that is, walking away. During the week between sessions the siblings both attempt this new behavior and continue charting the frequency and severity of their fights. At the second session they report that they averaged three fights per day and the severity dropped to scores of 4 and 5.

This indicates that the "walking away" intervention was initially effective. If instead the ratings remained the same or were higher at the second session, it would suggest that the intervention was not effective. Moreover, if no ratings were kept, the siblings would report that the walking away exercise did not work because they were still fighting, rather than noting that their fights were decreasing in both frequency and severity and that the intervention was working. Learning that one is heading in the right direction can in itself be reinforcing and encourage more productive work. Establishing an ongoing monitoring of frequency and severity ratings is important for evaluation of discrete interventions and overall practice.

## Fear

An important element of abusive sibling relationships is fear. I offer a powerful but simple and straightforward strategy to assess sibling abuse, called the "fear to be alone" question. This strategy entails asking clients individually *whether they are (or have been) afraid to be left alone with a sibling*. There are no other true compelling reasons for a child to be afraid to be alone with their sibling except the threat of psychological cruelty, or physical or sexual harm. Many individuals have reported being tormented by a sibling and living in fear of, as one client put it, "never knowing what will happen next." Fear of a sibling may also be related to sibling caretaking and neglect. Children who feel their caretakers fail to provide basic needs may be afraid about being left alone with them.

When clients answer that they are afraid to be left alone with a sibling, further assessment is indicated to determine whether they are experiencing serious maltreatment. It is important to add that client denials of sibling fear do not mean the absence of abuse. Clients may worry about disclosure or appearing weak. Also, sibling abuse is not restricted to unsupervised occasions and often occurs in the presence of parents and others. Some violent siblings may not experience fear, but rather experience hostility as stimulating, particularly when aggression is mutual. Some may also be numb to feelings of fear, or interpret their emotional reactions differently. The fear to be alone question should not be used as a stand-alone strategy for assessing abuse, but as a starting point to be followed by more discrete understandings of sibling dynamics.

It is important to distinguish between fear to be alone with a sibling and not wanting to be with a sibling. Siblings may feel great negativity toward each other but not be afraid to be with one another. The identification of fear is to be handled as abuse, with the likelihood that the perpetrator is using it to control the victim.

The "fear to be alone question" asks about fear rather than actual behavior, which clients may be more open to discussing. It bypasses protective stances to keep abusive behavior hidden. When using this strategy, practitioners should first introduce the notion of sibling aggression by asking about its lesser forms and in broad terms. For example, a practitioner may begin by asking if an individual feels a sibling has been mean to them, followed by questions of intent to harm. In cases where intent to harm is reported, clients should be met with separately in order to then implement the "fear to be alone" strategy. This is illustrated in the following case vignette.

### *Case vignette: Utilizing the "fear to be alone" question*

During a family meeting, a practitioner asked brothers, Doug (age 12) and Jimmie (age 8), if they were ever mean to each other. The practitioner asks this to open discussion about sibling hostility. Note that asking about it in the past provides emotional distance and may create a greater sense of safety for discussing unpleasant behaviors.

*Practitioner*: In many families I have worked with, I have found that siblings are often mean to each other. Have you boys ever been this way?

*Doug*: Sometimes.

*Jimmie*: Yes.

*Practitioner*: I see. How so?

*Doug*: We have called each other names. Broken each other's toys ... things like that.

*Jimmie*: He [Doug] likes to push my books off the table when I am doing homework.

*Practitioner (directed to both)*: Those do sound like mean things. When you do these things, like call each other names, do you ever do it because you want to hurt your brother ... or make him upset?

*Jimmie*: Yes.

*Doug*: Sometimes. Sometimes we are just kidding around.

*Jimmie*: Well, breaking my toys and calling me names is not just goofing around. I hate it!

*Practitioner (progressing to more serious aggression)*: Do you ever hurt each other physically? For example, do you ever hit each other?

*Jimmie*: Sometimes.

*Doug*: He's such a baby! I don't hit him hard.

*Practitioner*: Does he hit you too, Doug?

*Doug*: Not really. If he did, then I would really hurt him. But, I don't really hit him that hard now.

*Practitioner (exploring intent to harm)*: I see. When you hit him, do you try to hurt him?

*Doug*: Maybe a little, but like I said, I don't really hit him that hard.

*Practitioner*: OK, so you don't think it is a big deal, but it sounds like Jimmie might?

*Jimmie (looking downward)*: Well, I don't like it.

*Practitioner*: You would like it to stop.

*Jimmie*: Yes.

*Practitioner*: Doug . . . you would also like the name calling, hitting, breaking toys to stop?

*Doug*: It's really not a big deal. But I would like him to stop being so annoying.

*Practitioner*: I can understand that. So, you would like Jimmie to stop annoying you, and Jimmie, you would like Doug to stop doing mean things to you? (*Both nod their heads in agreement.*) As I mentioned when we first met, sometime we are going to meet all together and other times we will meet individually. I would like to meet with each of you individually to better understand your experience so I can help you both get what you want and need from our time together. Sound OK? (*Again, they both nod in agreement.*)

The practitioner asks if he can first meet with Doug. Meeting with the sibling who seems to be the perpetrator or initiator of violence is encouraged in order to reduce anxiety about practitioner motives (e.g., to get the victim to tattle). Practitioners can reduce client worry by framing it both as the normal course of treatment and according to their perceived strengths. For example, in this case, Doug is the older brother. The practitioner might say, "I usually start with the oldest child as they usually have a unique perspective about what is happening." Because client safety is a concern, deescalating perpetrator anxiety about individual meetings may lessen the possibility of using abusive tactics either as retribution for what the victim might have disclosed or to keep the victim silent.

The practitioner meets with Doug and asks him for more detailed accounts of what happens when Jimmie annoys him. Initially, the focus is on Jimmie's behaviors and Doug's frustrations. Doug shares that he feels he is being smothered by Jimmie, and unable to spend any time alone. He adds that when he complains to his parents about it they tell him that he and Jimmie should learn to handle it for themselves. Doug reports that this makes him frustrated and hate Jimmie.

*Practitioner*: Hate is a strong word.

*Doug*: It is. But we are so different. I don't like him. I never have.

*Practitioner*: That's quite sad.

*Doug*: I guess. It would be better if he were never born.

*Practitioner*: That's quite a statement. Sounds like you really would like to be the only child in the house.

*Doug*: That would be great!

*Practitioner*: What would be different?

*Doug*: I could have some privacy. Do the things I want to do.

*Practitioner*: What do you want to do?

*Doug*: I don't know ... like, after school I could go hang with my friends without having to take him along, or help him with his homework ...

*Practitioner*: Your folks want you to do those things?

*Doug*: Mostly my mom. It's so annoying. They always tell me that I am responsible for him. What about me? Who's responsible for me?!

*Practitioner*: You feel no one is looking out for you?

*Doug*: Exactly!

*Practitioner*: So it's not really all Jimmie's fault ... about being annoying?

*Doug*: No, but he should have gotten the message by now that I don't want him around.

*Practitioner*: I wonder if we found a way for you to have more alone time, without Jimmie, if you might be open to trying to have a different type of relationship with him—a more friendly relationship ... you know ... like brothers.

The practitioner intentionally used the expression "like brothers" to suggest that Doug is experiencing a loss. Doug indicates that he would be open to it.

*Practitioner*: Having a different type of relationship is one where you and Jimmie are nicer to each other and don't try to hurt each other on purpose. If I can help you have more alone time, do you think you can refrain from trying to hurt your brother ... either by hitting him or by calling him names, or threatening to break his toys?

*Doug*: Yes, I think I could. I only do it because he is annoying.

*Practitioner*: And I guess you know on some level that hurting Jimmie is not going to make your mother stop asking you to take care of him?

*Doug*: Yes, but sometimes I think that if I hurt him I am getting back at my mom.

*Practitioner*: Oh, that's interesting.

The practitioner continues with Doug, further exploring his experience, feelings about his mother and evaluating his openness to halting violence. The practitioner then asks to meet alone with Jimmie in order to further explore potential abuse, including utilizing the "fear to be alone question."

*Practitioner*: Jimmie, when we all were together earlier I was getting the feeling that you wish you had a nicer relationship with your brother?

*Jimmie*: Yes. He is mean to me.

*Practitioner (assessing fear and employing the strategy)*: I was wondering if you have ever been afraid to be left alone with Doug?

*Jimmie*: Well ... sometimes ... yes.

*Practitioner*: What do you mean?

*Jimmie*: I don't know ... well ... if he is in a bad mood he can be very mean ... he sometimes hits me hard for no reason, or tells me he is going to get me when I am not ready . . . THAT is scary. Then I spend all my time wondering, "What's he going to do? When is it going to happen?"

*Practitioner*: That does sound scary. Does he then "get you"?

*Jimmie*: No. He just tells me that so I will be scared. I think he thinks it's funny to do that to me.

*Practitioner*: But I can tell you don't think it's funny. What does he mean when he says he is going to "get you"?

*Jimmie*: I don't know . . . he doesn't always say. Once he said he was going to choke me when I was sleeping.

*Practitioner*: Well that is certainly frightening! Did you think he was going to kill you?

*Jimmie*: Well, not really . . . but you never know with Doug. Like I said, if he's in a bad mood, he's mean. When he's in a good mood I don't mind him . . . but I never know whether he will nice or mean.

*Practitioner*: It must be scary not knowing what will happen.

*Jimmie*: It is.

*Practitioner (empirically assessing fear)*: Let me ask you, how would you rate how scared you are of being along with Doug today . . . extremely, a lot, some, not that much or not at all (with an older child, the practitioner would likely use a 1–10 scale)?

*Jimmie*: I guess I would say, "some."

*Practitioner*: So you are really not that afraid he will do anything to you too bad right now?

*Jimmie*: No, not right now.

*Practitioner*: Have you ever told your parents about what Doug does to you and how you don't like being alone with him?

*Jimmie*: They know he hits me sometimes.

*Practitioner*: And what do they do?

*Jimmie*: Nothing. They tell him not to, but he just ignores them. He never gets in trouble or anything.

*Practitioner*: That must be frustrating for you. How about being alone . . . that he hurts you sometimes when you are alone?

*Jimmie*: No. A couple of times he told me that if I did tell Mom or Dad about something then I would really get it. So I didn't say anything. (*Jimmie gets a panicked look and adds*): You're not going to say anything are you?

*Practitioner*: Well, I don't think I have to at this point. Do you think he is going to seriously hurt you between now and the next time we meet? Or choke you in your sleep? I have to make sure nothing bad is going to happen to you and that you will be safe from harm.

*Jimmie*: I don't know. PLEASE, please, please don't say anything.

*Practitioner*: You sound really worried about it. What are you afraid will happen?

*Jimmie*: I don't know.

*Practitioner*: When I met with your brother he told me that he would stop hurting you if we found out a way for him to be alone more. He feels like he is with you a lot. Does that sound right to you?

*Jimmie*: Well, he complains about me a lot. I guess he might but my mother makes me go everywhere with him. Believe me; I don't want to be around him!

*Practitioner*: Oh, that's interesting. Your mother is pushing you to spend so much time together?

*Jimmie*: Yes.

*Practitioner*: So, if we figure out a way for both of you to have more separate time right now, you think you might be less likely to be hurt by your brother?

*Jimmie*: Yes.

*Practitioner*: OK, so when we go back into the family meeting I am going to talk about the fact that you both want to have more separate time. Because your parents already know that you are being hurt by your brother I will hold off on sharing the threats he makes when you are alone. But, I am going to talk about that violence between siblings is a bad thing and that your family needs a rule that brothers are not allowed to hurt or say mean things to each other, or break each other's stuff, and so on. We are going to keep track of when you are both mean to each other, but we are also going to focus on how to be nicer to each other, too. Does that sound OK?

*Jimmie*: Yes.

*Practitioner*: Good. But, I want to make sure that you are safe, too. So, we are going to make a family plan to try to make sure you are as safe as possible ... but I will not share the details about what you told me. Is that OK?

*Jimmie*: Yes, that sounds OK.

*Practitioner*: One more thing. As I said, we are going to be keeping track of the mean things Doug and you do to each other, so it won't be strange to talk about it ... but I want you to promise that if Doug does try to hurt you in a bad way that you will share that, too.

*Jimmie*: What do you mean? We'll be keeping track of the mean things?

The practitioner briefly explains the task-centered process of recording the frequency and severity of sibling aggression.

*Practitioner*: So, you see, your fights with Doug will be a normal part of our conversation. So, will you share the times you are really hurt by him too?

*Jimmie*: I guess so.

*Practitioner*: Even if he says you better not tell or you're going to get it?

*Jimmie*: I don't know.

*Practitioner*: I hope you will. I'll check in with you again next week to see how you are doing.

The practitioner recognizes that Doug has been abusive toward Jimmie but feels reasonably sure that Jimmie will not be seriously hurt in the immediate future. Both Doug and Jimmie expressed a desire for a better relationship and share similar ideas about how to accomplish this. Additionally, when the practitioner asked Jimmie for an assessment of the danger (assessing fear level), Jimmie indicated that the chances of being seriously harmed were not extreme. During the subsequent family meeting, the practitioner discussed the seriousness of sibling violence and created a plan with the family to bring it to a halt. The practitioner also focused on helping the mother be less involved in orchestrating her son's interaction, giving greater autonomy to the siblings (this included discussing greater involvement with her husband). The practitioner also raised the importance of talking about prosocial skill development.

## ASSESSING FOR AGGRESSION TYPES

There are a variety of types of sibling aggression, representing an array of behaviors and dynamics. Some forms are more problematic than others. The various types were presented in Chapter 1 and range in severity. These include nonviolent competition and conflict, mutual violence, unidirectional abuse, sexual abuse, psychological maltreatment, neglect, and relational aggression. Assessment considerations for each follow.

### Nonviolent Competition and Conflict

As discussed in Chapter 1, sibling competition has many benefits and should only be considered for intervention if it is psychologically injurious to one of the siblings. Intense competition often involves active and frequent comparison. It can create high stress related to winning and being viewed more favorably and feeling superior. Or to state conversely, siblings have high stakes in avoiding being seen as inferior and a loser. When competition results in one child consistently demonstrating superiority, it may be deleterious to the loser's self-esteem and psychological function. Moreover, if families place great value in "winning" at particular activities of high investment, losing may have consequences related to disfavoritism and feeling like an outsider.

Assessment of sibling competition and how it is enacted in families is indicated when evaluative comparisons are frequent, become quickly heated, and particularly if they involve gloating. Taking pride in one's accomplishments and skill level is important, but it not need come at the expense of one's brother or sister. Gloating involves conveying the message, "I am better than you." Parents who fail to address this behavior give tacit approval to problematic one-upping.

Practitioners are encouraged to help parents intervene in ways that support the winner's sense of pride, but prohibit gloating, insulting, and teasing. One method is to introduce the children to the concept of being a "good sport," which offers prosocial skills and behavioral rules for winning and losing. Winners can offer supportive comments like, "You did really well and I am sure you will get me next time" and "Thanks for playing, you make it hard for me to win." Losers can give "high fives" and say, "Nice job." Such interactions build connectedness and a sense that the siblings are in it together—that is, that they are a team. Parents must be encouraged to positively reinforce prosocial and supportive interactions around competition, and convey the notion of being teammates.

## Conflict

Two types of conflict are identified in the literature: constructive and destructive. Conflict is an expected part of life and learning how to productively engage in it is important. Similar to competition, assessment of conflict should identify destructive and constructive behaviors for the purpose of changing negative disagreements into ones that are handled positively.

Constant competitive bickering is annoying to both the children and their parents (Patterson, 1986) and is a form of destructive conflict. Individuals engage in repetitive behaviors when there is a payoff (i.e., reward). Frequent conflict suggests that one of the siblings has a stake in initiating disagreements. Examples of rewards include the initiating child feeling more powerful and superior, and knowing that parents will take their side. How parents manage their own stress and behaviors in regard to their children's repeated arguments must be included in assessments. Parents who reactively yell do not convey or teach their children methods for reducing conflict. Children may also enjoy the excitement of family discord and their parents' emotional reactivity. Children often engage in quarrelling when they are bored (e.g., imagine children on a long trip in the backseat of a car). Assessment should identify what rewards are associated with initiating bickering. Interventions can change the rewards to be given for prosocial behavior, including restraint, cooperation, perspective taking, and mutual problem-solving (Kramer, 2011).

## Mutual Physical Violence and Abuse

Violence and abuse are distinct from conflict because they involve the intent to harm physically and/or psychologically. Violence is distinct from abuse in that it involves mutual aggression, whereas abuse is unidirectional with an identifiable perpetrator and victim. The abuser's objective is to control and overpower victims.

Assessment considerations for violence and abuse were addressed in some depth earlier in this and previous chapters. It should be standard practice during intakes to complete sibling violence and abuse assessments in order to ensure client safety. This includes evaluation of whether or not formal reporting of child or elder maltreatment is indicated. In cases where violence cannot be quickly halted and the risk of ongoing serious abuse from a sibling remains, reporting is necessary.

Assessment includes asking about serious sibling aggression directly, and using the factors linked to sibling violence (presented in Chapter 1) to inform inquiry, particularly when violence and abuse have not been disclosed but are suspected. In addition, conducting a fear evaluation using the "fear to be alone" question presented earlier is encouraged for assessing the presence of abuse and torment.

Unlike other types of family violence, people are less fearful about discussing sibling aggression as they often think of it as normal behavior. That said, resistance to disclosure is not uncommon. Sibling violence frequently occurs outside parents' knowledge, and children may be reluctant to reveal it in their presence. Perpetrators often use threats of further violence and family disruption to keep victims silent. Assessment must be done carefully, taking cues from clients about how to proceed. Practitioners can move slowly by starting with "lighter" questions about sibling dynamics, proceeding to lesser forms of sibling aggression, before asking about more serious hostilities. Behaviors that suggest discomfort or efforts to keep a topic from being addressed (e.g., efforts to change the discussion, sudden fidgeting) should be noted and addressed in order to aid disclosure.

Assessment often involves interviewing families in multiple configurations. Generally, family practitioners begin with the whole family present, followed by individual meetings. Sometimes, sibling-only meetings are warranted, such as when parental involvement interferes with open discussion, or when children want to keep information from their parents. Although sibling violence questions are asked during family session, individual meetings are recommended in order to assess maltreatment in a private and safer setting. Some may have tried to report their victimization but their efforts were dismissed by parents or residential facility staff. Normalizing sibling violence and the reluctance to speak about it are helpful techniques. Statements such as, "Violence between siblings is exceptionally common," and "Many people are worried about talking about what their siblings have done to them," can be useful for opening discussion. Taking cues from clients, practitioners may then choose to conduct sibling-only interviews for the purpose of further aggression assessment; however, conjoint sibling work is not recommended if there are concerns about ongoing serious victimization. Conjoint sessions are more appropriate once violence has been ended, and the focus of work is on assault prevention and creating positivity.

Prior to client disclosure, practitioners must make clients aware of the consequences of revealing current violence and abuse, particularly in cases of sibling sexual abuse where the likelihood of child removal is high. Practitioners should make sure they are knowledgeable about their state's child and elder abuse and neglect policies, and the procedures for handling siblings as perpetrators. Most child protective agencies categorize sibling abuse cases as parental neglect. The implications of disclosure affect the whole family, not just the siblings. It is important to note that when discussing with families about the implications of disclosure, language should be adapted so that clients can understand what is being asked. For example, with young children, play therapy techniques (e.g., dolls and stuffed animals as metaphors) can be used for assessment (Caffaro, 2011).

Human services formal response to sibling violence has been highly inconsistent. Most instances have been handled by the child welfare system, but siblings represent a small proportion of reported cases (Jensen & Eriksen, 2002). Compared to the sibling violence prevalence rates found in research, the relatively low percentage of sibling cases suggests considerable underreporting or misidentification. Child welfare workers vary widely in their understandings of sibling violence (Kominkiewicz, 2004) and tend to underestimate its prevalence (Begun, 1995). Human service practitioners receive little if any training about siblings or sibling violence during their formal education or in postgraduate continuing education programs (Caspi, 2011b). Moreover, practitioners are generally unfamiliar with how children's sibling roles in family life vary across cultures, and risk misinterpretations of behavior (Hafford, 2010).

It is important to consider that after reports have been made, children who are sibling abuse perpetrators are more likely than adult offenders of child abuse to remain in the same home, school, and community as their victims (Caffaro, 2011). Children's risk of ongoing harm must be assessed, including eliciting information for developing safety plans to protect victims. Safety plans are common strategy in cases of partner battering and are particularly indicated when the perpetrator and victim continue to share the same residence. Even after a family member has been removed (usually the perpetrator in sibling cases), the likelihood of future unsupervised encounters with siblings suggests that safety plans should be standard practice for sibling aggression. Developing safety plans for siblings is taken up in the next chapter on intervention.

## Sexual Abuse

Sibling sexual abuse assessment entails unique challenges that include disclosure, safety, and making the distinction between age-appropriate sexual experimentation and exploitation. Although sexual abuse intervention is not addressed in depth in this book, assessing client safety is a critical aspect of practice. As such, considerations for sibling sexual abuse assessment are provided here. As noted prior, abuse assessment should be a standard part of most intake processes. In addition to asking about it directly, practitioners should also observe for behaviors that may indicate sibling sexual abuse. The "fear to be alone" questions is useful for identifying potential abuse; however, many victims of sexual abuse do not fear their victims and may believe that their perpetrators are benevolent and protective. Many children do not have the cognitive development or experience to understand either consent or coercion related to sexual behavior. Practitioners who suspect sexual abuse should perform a sexual history (Brewer, 1999). For young children, sexual behavior, knowledge, or language that is beyond what is expected for their developmental age is an indicator. For older children and adults, sexual histories can be beneficial in revealing a history of sexual victimization that was not originally understood this way by clients, or the first time they have had the forum to talk about it.

Sibling sexual abuse is complicated by having to make the distinction between abuse and age-appropriate sexual experimentation. An age-spacing criterion has been frequently raised as a consideration for making this distinction when siblings are or have been engaged in sexual interaction. It is assumed that closer-aged siblings are more likely to be involved in nonabusive sexual exploration, whereas wide-age-spacing is more indicative of abuse. Using age-spacing is a problematic strategy for assessment (Caffaro, 2011). For example, Laviola (1992) reported that over half her sample in a study of women sexually assaulted by an older brother were within 5 years of age of their abusers. Rather than age, practitioners should rely on other indicators such as power differentials (even if older than the perpetrator), coercion and secrecy, and consequences for psychological and emotional development (Canavan et al., 1992).

Although some nonabusive sexual activity may be part of normal psychosexual development, the extent to which this occurs and the types of behaviors involved are poorly understood (McVeigh, 2003). The idea that sexual exploration is normal has contributed to a myth of mutuality that has confounded understandings of probable abusive practices. I argue that the use of the word "incest" has perpetuated the mutuality myth and encourage the use of the term sibling sexual abuse when abuse has been identified.

In addition to indicators such as fear and coercion, family characteristics have been linked to sibling sexual abuse. These common features can be used to aid assessment and include high interpersonal and economic stress, substance abuse, punitive parenting, and exaggerated patriarchal norms (Haskins, 2003).

Sibling sexual abuse involves serious boundary transgressions and victimization has been linked to a host of negative consequences. A few include deep shame, guilt related to believing they were participants who could have but did not put a stop to it, difficulty in interpersonal relationships, affective and dissociative disorders, and posttraumatic stress responses (Caffaro, 2011; Wiehe, 1997), all inhibiting disclosure. Victims are often confused about the meaning of sexual encounters with siblings, which despite psychological disruption may be experienced as nurturing and physically pleasurable. Feeling guilt and shame raises assessment challenges regarding disclosure. Fear of being blamed for sibling sexual activity, as well as potential family disruption, further inhibits disclosure (Thompson, 2009). Normalizing these emotional responses, the experience of being abused, and highlighting power differentials in relationships can help provide a safer environment for disclosure. Disclosure of sibling sexual abuse in childhood is rare, occurring less than in cases of parent–child sexual abuse (Carlson et al., 2006).

From my professional experience it seems that individuals with intellectual disabilities may be at particular risk for sibling sexual abuse, particularly when they are socially isolated. In a case that came to the attention of child welfare services, an older brother (age 16) with cognitive impairment was systematically sexually abused by his younger, and much physically smaller, brother (age 12). Because the victim was physically much stronger than his younger brother, the court interviewer asked him why he did not resist or "put a stop" to his brother's abuse. The boy responded by saying that his younger brother is his "friend and the only person who pays any attention" to him. He added that he greatly disliked the things his brother made him do, but that without his brother, he would be completely alone.

This boy's frank explanation illustrates the complexity of coercive relationships and how his behavior could be misinterpreted as consensual by practitioners, by his family, and by himself. His explanation is also one that practitioners working in the field of sexual abuse frequently encounter: the trading of sex for attention. This trade-off is one tied to power differences, whether related to differences in age or intellectual development, and involves coercion and exploitation. The victim often holds the perpetrator in high regard and the prospect of being in a close and seemingly favored position seems rewarding. However, the victim is not a willing participant in these relationships, but a subservient partner who acquiesces because he or she sees no other solutions to emotional pain or lack of power to change the nature of these encounters.

Sibling sexual abuse is a serious interpersonal violation that is unique from other types of sibling aggression. One way in which it differs is in regard to formal reporting to authorities. Identification of active sibling sexual abuse must be reported. Interventions must attend to shame, guilt, self-blame, and other dynamics that are not typically associated with other sibling hostilities. For example, "cutting" (i.e., self-mutilation) and suicidal ideation are not uncommon in sexual abuse cases, but from my professional experience, these behaviors are rare in cases involving other forms of sibling aggression. Only a handful of intervention offerings for sibling sexual abuse are available and development in this area has been limited (Welfare, 2008). Examples include group (e.g., Thompson, 2009) and family (Caffaro & Conn-Caffaro, 1998; Haskins, 2003) approaches. Practitioners should also look to research to inform practice in this area (Welfare, 2008), and to aid in the prevention of sibling sexual abuse (Smallbone, Marshall, & Wortley, 2008).

## Psychological Abuse

Name calling and teasing are common in sibling relationships and are often considered normal and harmless by parents and practitioners. However, verbal assault can be damaging and often rises to the level of abuse when meant to torment, dominate, and injure. Perpetrators often deny their intentions and defend their behavior by saying they were being playful (e.g., "I was only joking"; "I was just teasing"). Teasing is potentially quite harmful (e.g., Keery et al., 2005; Martin et al., 1997), and should be treated as serious aggression. Psychological abuse also includes threats of physical assault and damage to personal property, and reflects dominance intentions.

Assessment of psychological abuse should include inquiry and observation of behaviors meant to dominate, control, and belittle, and include noting recurring hurtful themes, such as teasing, insulting, and making threats. The repetition of cruel statements is not intended to be playful. They are also not limited to moments of uncontrolled anger, which can also be abusive but often done out of spite or hurt, and not necessarily to dominate. Statements such as "you're ugly," "stupid," or "unlovable" are meant to injure and make the other feel small. Siblings may not recognize how much influence they possess, and hurtful comments are frequently internalized and have long-term consequences (Wiehe, 1997). The old saying, "Sticks and stones may break my bones but names will never hurt me" is incorrect. Broken bones and physical injury typically heal quickly, whereas emotional insults often hurt for many years. As I noted earlier, I recommend that practitioners and parents institute a "no name calling, insults, or threats" rule to create safety for children, and to create and model a nonviolent environment. Parents must intervene when their children are trying to injure each other, as nonintervention is perceived as tacit approval. Moreover, it is a form of parental neglect and failure to protect their children from maltreatment. This rule should be modeled by parents and instituted as early as is possible in children's relationships.

## Neglect

Child neglect is "a type of maltreatment that refers to the failure by the caregiver to provide needed, age-appropriate care although financially able to do so or offered financial or other means to do so" (USDHHS, 2007). It is generally organized into four types that include medical, educational, physical, and emotional deprivation of needs. Neglect also includes the failure to protect from imminent harm. Although it is the most common form of child maltreatment (www.childwelfare.gov), assessment of child neglect is generally not considered in regard to sibling behavior. It is, however, an important area of assessment in relation to both parenting siblings and sibling caregiving.

Parents are engaging in neglect when they fail to protect their children from sibling violence. It is a parent's responsibility to safeguard their children's welfare, even if this means shielding their children from their other offspring. Siblings occasionally expose their brothers and sisters to illegal and antisocial behavior, encouraging and sometimes coercing them to participate (Begun &

Berger, 2011; East et al., 2009; Rende et al., 2005). Parents may not be aware of how their children are being corrupted or exploited by their other kids. Assessment should also attend to parent involvement, supervision, and rules about sibling autonomy. Because of their influence, siblings may need to be kept separate from independent shared time when one child is involved in destructive activities.

Parents often rely on their older siblings to take care of their younger children. Sibling caretaking is widespread and takes many forms, from short-term baby-sitting to ongoing primary care provision. Parental reliance on siblings may be a function of economics, with the middle class using siblings for short-term functions, and more resource-poor families for long-term care arrangements (Burton, 2007). It is also a cultural function, where some groups see and value children as competent caregivers fulfilling a vital role in family life, while others see sibling caretaking as unsafe, unethical, and fostering unhealthy development. Leaving children in their older sibling's care may result in allegations of child neglect (Hafford, 2009) because it challenges Western child-rearing norms that emphasize adult supervision (Burton, 2007).

Sibling caretaking was a cultural norm and relied upon heavily in the United States through the mid-20th century (Weisner & Gallimore, 1977). Although it has declined since then, it remains prevalent, particularly in communities of color (Hafford, 2009). Siblings serve important socializing functions and most children do well under sibling care. However, children caring for children does pose some real risks and assessment must consider cultural practices and norms while also evaluating actual (rather than perceived) risk of neglect. Formal child welfare neglect indicators can help making this distinction (see, e.g., www.childwelfare.gov). For example, neglect involves behaviors such as the failure to provide nurturance, preventing children from normal social contact, and terrorizing, belittling, and encouraging destructive behavior. Practitioners should observe for and inquire about these behaviors in determining neglect, rather than assuming that a child caretaker is automatically problematic. That said, many adults are unprepared to meet the demands of childcare, and children may be less ready. Sibling caretaking and its implications for sibling aggression is again discussed later in this chapter as one of the FFD.

## Relational Aggression

Relational aggression involves actions that aim to socially injure, isolate, and reduce the social status of victims. These include public humiliation, spreading rumors, and actively preventing participation in social activities. The identity of the perpetrator is often unknown to the victim as these behaviors are typically done indirectly. Little investigation has been done regarding sibling relational aggression but it seems to be fairly common. School-aged children utilized it more frequently with their siblings than physical or verbal tactics (O'Brien &

Crick, 2003). It has been associated with poor sibling relationships (Updegraff et al., 2005b), and with peers it has been found to be associated with increased internalizing problems (Card et al., 2008).

As noted in Chapter 1, peer jealousy has been linked to greater relational aggression and prosocial behavior (Culotta & Goldstein, 2008), which poses interesting questions for sibling relationships and assessment. High sibling jealousy may be an indicator that relationally aggressive tactics are being employed, particularly if physical and verbal hostilities seem to be absent. It may also be that children in good sibling relationships, which involve higher prosocial behavior, use more relational methods than those in poor sibling relationships, who likely rely more on overt tactics such as physical assault. Observing a positive sibling relationship may not suggest the absence of aggression, but rather the use of relational methods.

Because many families may be unfamiliar with relational aggression, practitioners should explain the concept with families and inquire whether or not it occurs. They may provide a few examples to both normalize the behavior and help trigger examples from clients of actual relational aggression taking place. Positive families have less sibling relational aggression than negative ones (Yu & Gamble, 2008), and likely have less sibling hostility in general. Yu and Gamble (2008) found that perceived maternal psychological control (i.e., using behaviors such as shaming and conditional approval to manage children's behavior) has been linked to sibling relational aggression, and should be considered an indicator during assessment.

## Assessing Interactional Sequences

As discussed in the previous chapter, identifying interactional sequences is a central assessment strategy of family treatment models (e.g., Haley, 1976; Minuchin, 1974; Satir, 1983). Family members' interactions are repetitive. How conflicts are initiated, fought, resolved, and who sides with whom within a family are essentially the same in every disagreement. By observing and asking about how families interact provides insight into processes that support problems such as sibling aggression.

A variety of approaches are used to identify sequences. Practitioners may give families a task to complete (e.g., plan a vacation, play a board game, family sculpting) and then observe how they interact. Or, during intake, the practitioner may observe who is the family spokesperson, side-taking patterns, who speaks for whom, hierarchy, and how conflicts take place and are brought to an end. Enactments and tracking provide detailed information about family transactional patterns. A recent incident is selected and asked about in great detail from just before the conflict started to how it ended. The practitioner asks tracking questions like, "Then what happened?" "Then what did you do?" "How did your mother react?" "Who else was there?" to assist the family in providing a detailed description of the sequence involved in sibling conflicts. Once family patterns are understood, interventions to change behavioral sequences can be devised. To illustrate, the following example of a family of three is provided. A similar example of the enactment and tracking process is also provided in the full case example in Chapter 7.

### *Case example: Identifying sequences*

A mother sought family treatment for her sons' frequent fighting. During the first meeting, the practitioner asked them to describe a recent sibling conflict in order to understand the family's process and interactional sequences. The following excerpt from the meeting illustrates the practitioner's use of tracking with the mother and her sons, Bart (age 7) and Dexter (age 10). Note that during the tracking process the practitioner does not challenge perceptions or actions but rather acts neutrally and is interested in collecting information.

*Practitioner*: Think of a recent fight. Can you describe it to me how it happened and what happened?

*Dexter*: I was putting together a model airplane and he wouldn't leave me alone, so I twisted his arm really hard and shoved him to the floor, and told him to leave.

*Practitioner*: Start earlier. You were building the airplane and your brother approaches you . . .

*Dexter*: Yes.

*Practitioner*: OK, so what happened?

*Dexter*: He asked if he could see the directions.

*Bart*: I just wanted to see if the wing was on backwards. It looked backwards!

*Dexter*: It wasn't backwards!

*Mother*: Come on boys. Dexter, if you just let him look at the directions he would have seen you were right.

*Practitioner*: OK, hold on for a minute. Mom, were you there when this happened?

*Mother*: No, I came in later when I heard the yelling.

*Practitioner*: What were you doing at the time?

*Mother*: I was trying to do laundry. It's tough to get anything done in this house with the constant fighting.

*Practitioner*: I bet! Now Bart, you wanted to see the directions for the model and then what happened next?

*Bart*: He told me "No," I couldn't see it and I should just go away.

*Practitioner*: And then what happened?

*Bart*: I got mad so I just reached for the directions.

*Practitioner*: I am sure it did make you mad. So you reached over for the directions and then . . .?

*Bart*: He grabbed my arm really hard and twisted it. So I punched him and told him to stop.

*Dexter*: I told him not too and he still does it. That's what always happens! That's why I twisted his arm—to get him to stop.

*Practitioner*: OK, if I understand this, Dexter, you feel you told him he was not to look at the directions but he went and did it anyway. So, you got angry and chose to try to hurt him?

*Dexter*: Yes, he deserved it. He never listens!

*Practitioner*: That can be frustrating. OK, so what happened when Bart punched you?

*Bart*: He punched me back, hard! And then he shoved me to the floor.

*Dexter*: Yes, I did. As I said he deserved it!

*Mother*: Dexter, you shouldn't hit your brother—you're bigger than he is!

*Dexter*: That's what she always says. I'm bigger. But, what am I supposed to do, just let him touch my stuff or punch me and get away with that? No way!

*Practitioner*: OK, so what happened next?

*Dexter*: Bart started screaming like a baby—which he is—and Mom came running in.

*Practitioner*: And?

*Dexter*: And she immediately started yelling at ME! Telling me that I am bigger and should have just let him see the directions.

*Practitioner*: You felt she took Bart's side?

*Dexter*: Yes! She always does! No matter what happens. Whenever we fight, Mom always says (sarcastically imitating his mother's voice), "You're bigger, Dexter, you should know better."

*Practitioner*: What happens then? What happened when Mom yells at you?

*Dexter*: Nothing. I usually just go to my room.

*Mother*: He usually rolls his eyes and stomps off. He just can't seem to understand what it means to be a big brother.

*Practitioner*: And then what happened next . . . after he stomped off?

*Mother*: Well, later he'll come down for dinner. He loves to eat!

*Practitioner*: Is there any more conversation about the fight at dinner.

*Mother*: No, it's pretty much over.

*Practitioner (checking in with the boys)*: Is that right? Is it over then? [They both nod their heads in agreement.]

*Practitioner*: Is that the way other fights go? Is this sequence of events the usual?

*Mother*: Yes, it seems that way. Dexter prevents Bart from doing something and then it ends up with them punching each other.

*Practitioner*: It seems pretty straightforward.

*Mother*: Yes, I think it is . . . but what upsets me is that Dexter is always saying how much he hates his brother. It's upsetting. I want them to be best friends, but he seems to dislike Bart so much . . . and I think Bart looks up to him.

The above dialogue illustrates the practitioner's use of tracking to identify the typical sequence of interactions that characterize Bart and Dexter's aggressive encounters. Identifying the sequence highlights important dynamics that are useful for informing treatment. For example, the practitioner can easily see the pattern of triangulation and parental favor in the family's description. The mother consistently takes Bart's side, making an "outsider" of Dexter in his own family. She does this with good intentions, believing that because Bart is younger and smaller he needs protection. The mother also thinks she is encouraging her older child to become more mature. Its effect, however, is to make Dexter increasingly resentful of Bart who he experiences as favored. It also provides Bart with an incentive to challenge his older and stronger brother because he knows his mother will come to his defense. Because of potential safety risks, it is unusual for younger children to take on their more powerful siblings if there is no payoff, such as garnering a parent's favor.

The consequence of this family sequence is that Dexter is unable to protect himself, his belongings, or the activities he engages in, as Bart can intrude whenever he likes. This rigid triangle (i.e., Mother and Bart in a coalition against Dexter) serves to perpetuate the sibling aggression. Dexter feels he has no other recourse than to physically overpower his brother in order to express his needs for autonomy. Bart has been given permission by his mother (via her protection) to intrude at will, giving him more power in the sibling relationship than Dexter. Additionally, Bart is supported in his physical retaliation by his mother coming to his defense.

This family's pattern is a common one. Parents often come to their smaller child's defense in sibling conflicts (Felson & Russo, 1988), believing they are doing the right thing. Identifying such sequences through enactments and tracking provides powerful information for devising interventions that alter family interaction patterns. Moreover, families can take part in formulating strategies to alter sequences because the tracking process helps them become aware of their own actions in the conflict. Client participation in the formulation of assessment and treatment strategies is central to task-centered practice (Reid, 1992). Tracking enables a common language for formulating target problems.

## TARGET PROBLEM FORMULATION

In the task-centered approach, *target problems* are mutually identified by the practitioner and the family and are the concerns that become the focus of work. During the first step, *problem identification*, each family member is asked to share their perception of the problem. What begins with the initial, and often global, reason for treatment becomes a more refined list of issues for work. In sibling work, the initial phone call may be stated as a broad goal to "have my kids stop fighting all the time." After the *problem identification* process, the practitioner and family will have generated multiple understandings that include individual members' perceptions and wants. Using the example of Dexter and Bart from earlier, Dexter's wishes may include wanting his brother to "stop bothering him all the time," whereas Bart's might see the problem as "Dexter is always trying to hurt me," and among the mother's identified problems is that, "Dexter never lets Bart join him in any activities."

As you can see, the picture becomes more complex but also lends itself to more discrete treatment objectives that can address all the expressed problems and wants. For example, target goals can include: (a) having Bart decrease his intrusions on Dexter's autonomy by engaging more in his own activities and obtaining permission to join his older brother prior to involving himself; (b) methods to help Dexter develop nonviolent strategies for expressing his frustration with Bart such as seeking help from his mother prior to hitting; and (c) having the mother work with her children to determine joint and solitary activities and select activities that Dexter and Bart can both willingly do together.

The target problems usually include input from the practitioner who draws upon his or her expertise and observations. In the TCSA treatment approach, the practitioner makes use of the assessment considerations and strategies presented in this chapter. For example, having tracked the Bart and Dexter's family interactional sequence that supports the sibling aggression, the practitioner may offer side-taking as a problem, as well as the mother's focus on negative rather than positive behaviors and the lack of consequences for violent actions.

As noted earlier, an important step in the task-centered process is *problem specification* that involves getting details about the frequency and severity of occurrences of each target problem. Continuing the example of Dexter and Bart, the practitioner would ask each family member about how often the sibling fights occur and for each to rank them in regard to severity. Initially, Dexter, Bart, and their mother said that the fights occurred about two or three times each day and more on weekends, when they spent more time together. To gain a more accurate information, as one of the first week's tasks (an *assessment* task), the practitioner asked them to count the fights each day by writing the time and date on a chart each time one took place. It was decided that Dexter would be the one in charge of counting the fights, partly because the practitioner wanted Dexter to become more cognizant of his actions that were now more automatic. The mother was asked to support Dexter in his accounting, and Bart was asked to be the witness but allow his brother to have the final call. Another practitioner objective in structuring the task this way was to begin altering alliances and boundaries. In addition, the practitioner asked each family member to rank the severity of each fight on the same chart, which included a space for each member. The purpose of asking them to do this was

**FIGURE 5.1** Sample Chart for Recording Aggression Frequency & Severity

| **Number of Fights** (Write time and date of each fight) | **Severity of Fights (1 = mild; 5 = moderate; 10 = severe)** Mom | Dexter | Bart |
|---|---|---|---|
| | | | |
| | | | |
| | | | |

to establish a clear picture of how often the aggression took place and how severe the fights were. A sample of the chart can be seen in Figure 5.1.

The chart is reviewed at the beginning of the second family session. Discussion about ratings often follows. Sometimes family members disagree on what constitutes an aggressive act. Differing views of severity are also discussed and understood. That is, problem accounting is a process that initiates further explorations and understandings and does not end with attainment of tallies. As noted, a picture of how often and severe sibling aggression occurs is helpful for monitoring progress and the impact of interventions. It provides practitioners with a way to empirically measure their practice to engage in best practices. The process of evaluating changes in target problems is a central feature of task-centered practice. Weekly monitoring of problem frequency and severity, after establishing a baseline, constitutes a variation of a single system research design and promotes practitioner use of empirically based practice (Gellis & Reid, 2004; Rosen, 2003).

An alternative or supplement to client charting is the use of RAIs, the Sibling Relationship Inventory (Stocker & McHale, 1992), the Conflict Tactics Scale revised for sibling aggression (e.g., Kettrey & Emery, 2006), the Lifespan Sibling Relationship Scale (Riggio, 2000), the Brother–Sister Questionnaire (Graham-Bermann & Cutler, 1994), and the Scale of Negative Family Interactions (Simonelli et al., 2005), a comprehensive instrument that includes measures of sibling, parental, and sexual aggression.

The problem identification process also includes exploration of the assessment considerations put forth in this chapter. Practitioners should use this step to assess for intent to injure, to actually harm, to experience fear, and for the types of aggression present in the sibling relationship.

## CONCLUSION

This chapter provided practitioners with various assessment considerations and strategies for evaluation and empirical understanding of sibling aggression. Included was a quick method for identifying sibling abuse. The strategy of identifying transactional sequences was presented as a powerful method for discovering family patterns that likely support sibling hostility. Understanding sequences is important for interventions that include disrupting problematic interactional patterns, which is taken up in the next chapter and which includes presentation of the FFD common to sibling aggression.

# 6

# Intervention and Task Strategies: Five Family Dynamics

This chapter focuses on sibling aggression intervention. It begins with a discussion of safety plans as client welfare is a major concern of practice, particularly when aggression is a central feature. A presentation of enhancing prosocial sibling relationships follows. The treatment model presented in this book is two-pronged and focuses on both halting destructive sibling interaction and promoting positive relationships. Prosocial competencies are introduced to inform formulation of task strategies for increasing productive encounters. This is followed by presentation of the Five Family Dynamics (FFD) that support sibling hostilities. Each is offered as a module to guide assessment and intervention within the framework of the Task-Centered Sibling Aggression (TCSA) treatment approach. Research literature and practitioner experiences provided the direction for recommended task formulations for each of the FFD. It is important to note that the FFD presented in this chapter focus primarily on strategies to stop aggression. In order to carry out the two-pronged approach, it is recommended that each FFD be accompanied by sibling positivity efforts. The fifth FFD, *Focus on Negativity*, includes overt strategies for building positive relationships using the Positive Behavior Approach (PBA). PBA provides clear steps for managing negative interactions and can be implemented in concert with any of the FFD. The chapter concludes with the presentation of the PBA.

## SAFETY PLANS

As discussed in the previous chapter, client safety must be a focus of treatment for aggression, particularly in violence and abuse cases where the threat of immediate harm is high. Sibling hostility is unique from other forms of family violence because it exists in a social context that views it as normal, which serves to minimize consideration of its real potential to result in serious harm. That said, sibling violence is also unique because siblings can be violent to each other in ways that do not necessitate child welfare services reporting. For example, if a father were to frequently punch his child, a report is mandated. By comparison, if a brother regularly punches his brother, many may believe that an immediate report is not indicated. Practitioners should evaluate the degree of harm, fear, intent, and severity of sibling violence in making this determination. Additionally, the potential to bring sibling aggression to a quick halt should be considered. Once the seriousness of sibling aggression is addressed directly with families, many will take action to stop it. If it is determined that aggression can be brought to an end, it should be accompanied by a safety plan. Safety plans are an outline of specific activities to be implemented to protect individuals from future victimization. In cases where quickly halting violence is not possible and the threat of present danger persists, child welfare reports should be made and a safety plan completed until social services determines formal case management. Safety plans are particularly important in sibling abuse cases, a unidirectional form of violence with a clear perpetrator and victim.

Safety plans are common tools used in partner battering (i.e., domestic violence) cases. In partner battering, plans are completed with the victim and usually outside the perpetrator's knowledge. By contrast, sibling violence safety plans are completed in collaboration with the family, unless it is assessed that they are unable or unwilling to take steps to stop the violence. In such cases, reports are made to social services and safety plans are made only with the victim.

Safety plans should list behaviors that victims, parents, and perpetrators will undertake. The action list should also be done collaboratively when possible. Families are usually most expert about their situations and can best identify available resources and potential tasks. Once danger is identified, the focus of the session should become the safety plan. The task-centered process of identifying tasks can be used to formulate the action plan.

The development of safety skills is part of completing a safety plan. This may include teaching children the meanings of abuse and violence, as well as rehearsing new skills and learning to anticipate the consequences of personal actions. Learning to implement a safety plan is typically an incremental process and practitioners must be careful to assume that once one has been completed victims and their families have the tools to carry out the steps. Additionally, safety plans must include steps to protect victims in any location where individuals may be unsafe (e.g., schools, transportation to day treatment).

For victims, plans usually include actions to prevent further violence and to address abuse when it is happening. Victim prevention tasks may include telling a parent or other authority figure when they feel they are in danger, avoiding perpetrators when supervision is absent, and identifying a predetermined place to go, such as a neighbor's residence (for older children). Helping perpetrators identify, learn, and rehearse strategies for avoiding hostile externalizing behaviors should be part of safety plan development. A list of emergency phone calls, including 911, neighbors, and other supports, should be created for both perpetrators and victims. Safety plans also commonly include prevention tasks for parents that include taking steps to provide increased supervision, restrict sibling alone time, and supporting victims reporting of threats.

Victim tasks to be undertaken during violent interactions may include telling parents, calling emergency numbers, going to a prearranged safe place, and walking away. Perpetrator actions may consist of walking away, breathing exercises, implementing alternative prosocial behaviors rehearsed during meetings, voicing anger to parents, and calling on supports (e.g., friends) to vent or to use as distractions. Parental tasks may include reminding perpetrators of alternative behaviors, demanding that violence cease, enforcing prediscussed consequences, and separating the children.

Many parents find it difficult to stop violent sibling interactions. They feel powerless and commonly also find themselves victims of the child perpetrator. Parent abuse (i.e., child-to-parent violence) is both prevalent and dangerous (Walsh & Krienert, 2007), particularly to mothers. In my professional experience, sibling violence cases have commonly included violence against parents. Child-to-parent violence research has been exceptionally underrepresented in the literature and empirical links to sibling violence have yet to be established. However, practitioners, particularly those working with adolescents, should assess for parental abuse when working with sibling violence cases. If identified, safety plans should also include steps to protect parents from harm.

## PROMOTING PROSOCIAL BEHAVIOR

As presented in Chapter 4, the sibling aggression treatment offered here is a two-pronged approach that aims to both halt problematic aggression and promote prosocial behavior. The benefits of positive, warm, and supportive sibling relationships are many and important (Kramer, 2011). A major concern about solely halting aggressive behaviors is the creation of distant relationships in which siblings simply avoid interacting (Leitenberg et al., 1977). Efforts to promote sibling support via prosocial skill development should be included in all sibling aggression cases.

Kramer (2010, 2011) has distilled prosocial sibling behavior into an "emerging list of essential competencies," which can be used to guide practitioners and parents in the promotion of positive sibling relationships. These are outlined here (Kramer, 2011, p. 53):

1. Positive engagement (e.g., play, conversation, the promotion of mutual interests among siblings).
2. Cohesion (e.g., recognizing and valuing instances of help, support, protectiveness, cooperation, loyalty, trust, and pride).
3. Shared experiences that build support (e.g., appreciating siblings' unique knowledge of one another and of their family to strengthen bonds).
4. Social and emotional understanding (e.g., perspective taking, decentering, learning to assess and respect siblings' unique views, needs, goals, and interests as legitimate in their own right).
5. Emotion regulation (e.g., identifying and managing emotions and behaviors in emotionally challenging and frustrating situations).

6. Behavioral control (e.g., refraining from undesirable sibling-directed behaviors such as bossiness, teasing, and failing to respect personal boundaries and space).
7. Forming neutral or positive attributions regarding the sibling's intent (e.g., learning to check or correct faulty attributions that may falsely impute negative or hostile intent).
8. Conflict management and problem-solving (e.g., learning to consider conflicts as social problems and then using collaborative methods to solve these problems).
9. Evaluating parental differential treatment (PDT) practices (e.g., openly discussing the impact of PDT perceived as unfair, and adjusting parental behaviors so that children's unique needs are met).

The above list of prosocial behaviors can be utilized to guide task selection for developing positive sibling relationships during treatment. Many approaches to drawing from this list can be taken, including working in incremental fashion, starting with the first area and working through the remaining eight, addressing each in the listed order. Each area can be viewed as a target goal broken down into discrete tasks. As examples, utilizing the first area, *positive engagement*, practitioners may explore formulating tasks that promote shared interests and increasing mutual play. For the second area, *cohesion*, parent tasks could include creating a family environment that promotes sibling loyalty (e.g., "family comes first") and positively reinforcing moments when siblings come to each other's protection.

Kramer's list of prosocial sibling behaviors can be shared with clients in order to open discussion and mutual exploration of task possibilities. The benefits of sibling support should be discussed and encouraged to be adopted as a mutually agreed-upon treatment objective. Becoming a socially competent participant in sibling relationships takes time and practice. Practitioners should offer ample opportunity to try out new behaviors through rehearsals, role plays, and multiple chances to implement them outside treatment sessions.

## THE FIVE FAMILY DYNAMICS

Family life, sibling relationships, and aggression are complex, and disruptions raise a broad array of practice considerations. As Reid notes, families produce "a range of issues whose diversity defies simple classification. However, some groupings can be made" (Reid, 1992, p. 96). In the case of sibling aggression, I have organized common themes into the Five Family Dynamics (FFD), each of which can be considered a module with its own assessment areas and intervention tasks. These crude and sometimes overlapping classifications provide practitioners and families with a relatively quick and straightforward way to identify target problems for focused treatment.

Reid (1992) reminds us that the target problem, rather than theory or practice technologies, should direct treatment. Practitioners should therefore use FFD classifications as points of inquiry, rather than having them direct the process, because although the modules are neat, dynamics are often messy. As will be seen in the discussion of one of the FFD, parental favoritism, multiple understandings of favoritism exist in families—often with two children, each defining it very differently with both feeling the other is favored. Without developing a clear understanding of family definitions and the processes that underlie these understandings, the imposition of empirical findings or theoretical frameworks can serve to complicate rather than aid the process.

This being said, having an organizing conceptual model is a powerful aid for guiding practice. It helps practitioners identify and alter the processes that support target problems. FFD is offered as a guiding framework for identifying and modifying features that exacerbate sibling aggression. FFD assessment and task strategies should be implemented flexibly, as empirically and/or theoretically based suggestions, to be used in combination with emergent solutions and other relevant treatment modalities, not as rigid prescriptions. The FFD are organized around target problems that support sibling aggression. Each dynamic is addressed with its own menu of possible tasks. It is important to note that the FFD are also not mutually exclusive and cases frequently involve multiple categories. All or any combination of the presented FFD may be present in a sibling aggression case. Accordingly, task selection may reflect multiple dynamics and is not restricted to only one of the FFD. The features and dynamics of aggression are complex and the FFD do not cover the full range of considerations that emerge in sibling aggression cases. Finally, it is important to note that the FFD reflect *indirect* intervention strategies in which sibling aggression is addressed by altering family dynamics and not by attending directly and only to sibling behaviors. *Direct* interventions represent strategies that explicitly target sibling behavior and interaction. TCSA relies primarily on direct strategies mutually formulated between the practitioner and client family. Sharing the FFD with clients helps to facilitate consideration of family dynamics for direct intervention. This process is illustrated in a case study in the next chapter.

The FFD for assessing and treating sibling aggression are:

1. PDT and Favoritism
2. Direct Comparison
3. Parental Support for Aggressive Behavior
4. Ineffective Supervision
5. Focus on Negativity

## PARENTAL DIFFERENTIAL TREATMENT AND FAVORITISM

As discussed in Chapter 1, PDT and favoritism have been linked to sibling aggression and less warmth (McHale et al., 1995; Singer & Weinstein, 2000).

Using family systems concepts, this dynamic can be understood as triangles involving parent–child coalitions with the second child as an outsider and as disfavored. Favoritism, PDT, and parent–child coalitions are often identified during the assessment processes of problem identification and tracking transactional sequences. Children may make claims of unfair treatment, or practitioners may make note of parents supporting one child over another (as in the Dexter and Bart case presented earlier). Practitioners should listen and observe for signs of favoritism or parent–child coalitions that make outsiders of children in their own families. Outsiders behave like outsiders, and often respond to feelings of exclusion by lashing out.

Favoritism and PDT represent overlapping but different constructs, which have not been systematically distinguished in the literature. They are often used interchangeably, complicating understanding and application of research findings. Suitor et al. (2008) have attempted to differentiate the two constructs by viewing favoritism as related to parent affect and PDT to parent behavior. In an attempt to further and perhaps more clearly differentiate the concepts for their practical utility in clinical treatment, favoritism is used here to refer to *perceptions* of parental preference, whereas PDT refers to differences in *actual behaviors* employed by parents. Frequently, PDT and favoritism are simultaneously present in families with sibling aggression.

It is important to note that despite parents' best efforts to be fair, children may still believe favoritism exists. It is the *perception* of unfairness that is distressing and alienating, and causes resentment. Practitioners must be careful to not dismiss accusations of unequal treatment. It is also important that when actual differential treatment is observed practitioners share their observation and ask about it. However, differential treatment itself does not necessarily generate favoritism perceptions. Children seem to accept differential treatment when they understand why it exists and find the reasons to be sensible (Kowal et al., 2006). It is a problem when the causes are unclear, which results in perceptions of injustice. Parents frequently dismiss children's claims of being treated less favorably, which can serve to promote sibling hostility. As such, assessing for ignored claims of injustice is an important part of evaluating favoritism and differential treatment processes.

As suggested earlier, favoritism can have several interpretations and result in each child believing a sibling is their parents' favorite. For example, favoritism can refer to both *privileges* (e.g., "He's allowed to do things I am not"), and *time* ("They spend almost all of their time with him"). This dynamic can occur in families that ascribe complementary labels of good and bad to their children. "Bad" children perceive "good" ones to be favored because their parents give more privileges, are less strict, and generally express more warmth toward the good children. At the same time, good children believe that the bad ones are favored because their parents focus more time and energy worrying about and interacting with them. In regard to treatment, clarifying clients' individual interpretations of favoritism is essential and it helps to distinguish perceptions from actual behaviors.

Redirected anger is common in sibling aggression. Children who are angry with parents for unfair treatment are likely to aggress against a sibling who represents a safer target. Attacking "parent representatives" may be seen as an effective way to "get back" at parents, even when parents are unaware of the aggression. This is demonstrated in a case involving Frank and his sister Kathleen. Frank perceived that his father favored Kathleen. She would refer to herself as "Daddy's little girl" and it seemed she could do no wrong in his eyes. The father was quite hard on Frank and tolerated no mistakes, frequently punishing him. Frank was furious with his father for his seeming lack of approval and favoring of his sister. At every opportunity, when his father was not present, he would torment Kathleen. He never hit her, but he actively threatened her and as she put it, "played mind games." When asked in adulthood if he remembered why he treated his sister with such hostility, he replied that he was trying to get back at his dad.

It is important to add that cultural practices frequently support parental favoritism. Differential treatment linked to social expectations about family relationships may seem innocent and even loving, such as in the case of "Daddy's little girl," or necessary, as in "the family's last great hope," but usually do not come without consequence, particularly to the sibling relationship. Practitioners can expect to run into culturally supported justifications for differential treatment and favoritism. A practitioner strategy for addressing such arguments involves openly discussing culturally sanctioned expectations for family relationships for the purpose of critiquing the value of supporting ongoing differential treatment. For example, a practitioner raising favoritism with a father:

*Practitioner*: Many fathers take great pride in having a daughter be 'Daddy's little girl.' It sounds like you do, too.

*Father*: Yes. That's the way it's supposed to be . . . fathers and their girls . . . right?

*Practitioner*: Maybe. I know we get those kinds of messages from society. But I also wonder about how a "Daddy's little girl" relationship affects other relationships in families. In what ways has your special relationship with your daughter impacted your other relationships in the family?

*Father*: Well, I know that sometimes my wife and son get jealous.

*Practitioner*: How do you know that?

The practitioner continues to explore the implications of the father's favoring of the daughter.

## The Myth of Equality

It is important here to address a common myth and social taboo that practitioners are likely to encounter when addressing favoritism: "I love all my children the same." While parents may believe this sentiment, as a practical matter, parents do not and cannot treat their children identically, as discussed in Chapter 2. Even when they make efforts at sameness, children are unlikely to perceive it this way. Siblings are usually of different ages; have different needs and temperaments, unique talents and desires, varying cognitive abilities and understandings, and distinct appearances; have individual diets; and may not be of the same sex. Differential parental treatment is a necessity, and the same treatment is both an impracticality as well as unfair. For example, giving the same 8:00 p.m. bedtime to siblings aged 10 and 2 is equal treatment, but not fair. In another example, two siblings close in age sit at the kitchen table painting pictures. One child spends hours perfecting each line while the other spends a total of 5 minutes haphazardly scribbling. It would be equal treatment to hang both pictures on the refrigerator door. But is it fair? The child that spent hours drawing may feel that she spent more time on her picture, took it more seriously, and that she is the true artist, that sharing the refrigerator with her sibling's less serious endeavor undermines recognition of her talents. However, if the 5-minute drawing was excluded, its artist would likely also cry foul. Hanging either one or both pictures results in perceptions of injustice and possible favoritism. Parents cannot treat their children the same, and contrary to popular myth, research has demonstrated that many, if not most, parents do have a preferred child (Lauricella, 2010; Suitor et al., 2008).

Practitioners should raise the impracticality of same treatment and attempt to frame parenting as giving each child what they need, meaning that sometimes one child will get more and at other times the other child or children will get more—dependent upon their needs. It is likely, although unstudied, that well-functioning families shift attentions according to emerging needs, and parents fluctuate in regard to how they feel about each of their children. Flexibility and the ability to adapt to changing needs have been cited as a key aspect of healthy families (e.g., Minuchin, 1974).

As a practical matter, children are unlikely to appreciate parents' efforts to treat them the same anyhow—just try cutting a piece of cake or pouring a glass of soda equally! Using a Darwinian lens to explain this phenomenon, Sulloway (1996) argues that because individuals have a self-interest in perpetuating their genetic line, and share only 50% of their novel genes with biological siblings (with the exception for identical twins), the acceptable arrangement for sharing resources is not equal but instead "two for me, one for you." The "one for you" represents 50% of the "two for me." Genetic self-interest generates efforts to win more resources than one's siblings, and as such, "equal" represents losing or possible disfavor. An objective of practice should not be correct differential treatment by creating equality, but rather supporting a fair treatment and openly addressing perceptions of disfavor. Perceptions are easily dismissed and ignoring claims of injustice is problematic as it is tied to sibling resentment and possible aggression.

## Ignoring Claims of Injustice

Complaints of favoritism are so common in family life that parents typically dismiss them as meaningless whining and as normal child behavior. However, ignoring allegations of injustice has been linked to increased sibling resentment and aggression (Wiehe, 1997). Children's perceptions of injustice and patterns of parental dismissal often emerge during assessment of transactional sequences (e.g., enactments, tracking), as well as in the TCSA problem identification step where each family member is asked for their perception of the problem. Practitioners are encouraged to actively assess for favoritism beliefs, particularly when differential treatment is noted, and for dismissal of claims of injustice.

Children frequently use two strategies to try to right the wrongs of unfair treatment. The first is to make their perception of injustice known to their parents by complaining about it. The second is to complain about their sibling, in ways that aim to simultaneously diminish the favored position (e.g., tattling). Paradoxically, children's efforts to raise awareness of unbalanced treatment can serve to perpetuate their disfavored status. Parents commonly experience claims of injustice as whining, overreacting, and annoying, which increases negative feelings toward the complainer. In a complementary sense, the child's attempts to report injustice may serve to enhance the position of the favored child by their parents (e.g., who are seen as happy, easygoing), while diminishing their own (e.g., viewed as difficult, whiney, babyish).

During assessment, practitioners should note dismissal of claims of injustice, and when they occur, ask if what they have observed is common. For example, during the first family meeting, Tanisha (age 15) accused her mother of favoring her younger sister Yolanda (age 11):

*Tanisha*: It's so unfair! She gets away with everything, and I get blamed for everything. I hate her!

*Mother*: Tanisha, that's not nice! And, it's not true, Tanisha. You make a big deal out of everything.

*Tanisha*: (*throwing her hands up with frustration*) I can't win.

*Practitioner*: Tanisha, it sounds like you have tried before to express your view that you are not treated fairly?

*Tanisha*: All the time!

*Mother*: You should know that Tanisha is a big complainer. She complains about everything ...

*Practitioner*: (*interrupting*) And when you do express your feelings that things are unfair, what happens?

*Tanisha*: This! My mother always denies it and tells me I am too emotional ... or something like that.

*Practitioner*: So, your feelings of unfairness are not acknowledged? You don't feel your perceptions are taken seriously?

*Tanisha*: Never.

*Mother*: Because they are untrue.

*Tanisha*: (*to Yolanda*) Ugh, I hate you.

Here the practitioner has observed how the family handles claims of injustice and then questioned the family directly about it for two reasons: (1) to more clearly understand the family process and (2) to share the observation with the family, opening the door for further discussion and intervention work.

## Task Strategies for Ignored Claims of Injustice

Separating perception and behavior is particularly helpful because, as discussed earlier, it is essentially impossible for parents to treat their children the same. Siblings are typically of different ages and a 5-year-old requires different parenting than a 2-year-old. Children also have different strengths and needs. Because parents cannot essentially give their children the same treatment, the focus becomes one of perceptions of fairness.

There are two reasons to take injustice claims seriously. First, children's perceptions of favoritism are sometimes accurate, and pursuing them in greater depth can demonstrate ways in which treatment is unbalanced that may be initially invisible to parents and practitioners. Second, whether or not the claim that treatment is unfair is objectively true, it is true for the child. A basic practitioner engagement skill for building trust in clinical relationships involves acknowledging client perceptions, "starting where the client is" (Goldstein, 1983; Rooney, 2009). Enabling clients to tell their story and express their version of reality is important for client-centered practice, therapeutic relationships, and clients' motivation to participate in the change process. Dismissals of injustice claims can be viewed as competing perceptions of reality. Practitioners should demonstrate interest and validate opposing views.

During treatment it is often beneficial to help clients learn to distinguish between acknowledging perceptions versus agreeing with them. Often, a simple acknowledgment of a long-dismissed perception can serve to reduce client stress and lessen family conflict. In cases where parents have had a difficult time accepting their child's viewpoint, I have sometimes posed a somewhat parallel scenario to them, questioning how they might feel if they expressed a frustration with their significant other and were immediately told that the perception was false or "crazy" (which often opens up a can of worms!). This can help parents relate to the experience of being dismissed, and move to a place where they can acknowledge their child's perception without necessarily agreeing with it.

From a practice perspective, the focus should be kept on parent behaviors in relation to children's needs. Children in the same family require different parental resources and treatment, and the question becomes whether or not the differential treatment is justified and fair. Sometimes differential treatment may be difficult for children to identify but they still believe favoritism exists.

Their feelings may stem from an intuitive sense that their parents feel less warmly toward them although they are unable to identify specific examples of how this is manifested. Again, children's intuitions may be correct. During the course of treatment it may become evident that individual meetings with parents are necessary to unmask and address feelings related to preferring or disliking one child more than the others. This should be done when it becomes difficult for a parent to take on tasks to address patterns of biased interaction (e.g., always protecting the preferred younger child from the more disliked older). Tasks can then be devised to address emotional obstacles to positive parental engagement with children. Finally, favoritism claims may be made as manipulative gestures, without a genuine belief they are true. Distinguishing between real and fake injustice accusations is difficult; however, if pursued as real, explorations often reveal the genuine intent of parent and sibling behavior.

## Assessment and Task Strategies for PDT and Favoritism

Four patterns of PDT/favoritism triangles are common in families. These include parent coalitions with younger siblings, parent coalitions with older siblings, split-parent–child coalitions, and scapegoating. Each area has unique task considerations.

### *Parent coalitions with younger siblings*

As previously noted, parents frequently defend younger children who are in conflict with older siblings, giving rationales such as "You should know better, you're older." Parents who give support to younger children enable them to instigate conflicts with their older siblings because they know their parents will take their side. Typically, smaller and weaker children do not take on their bigger and stronger others unless they are confident that a person with greater size or authority will come to their rescue. The true danger, of course, occurs when allies are not around to serve as protectors. Older siblings may take such opportunities to retaliate.

Claims that older children are the aggressors in sibling conflict should not be taken at face value but rather evaluated in the context of parent side-taking. Practitioners should highlight parent–child coalitions that make outsiders of older children and openly discuss how such patterns can create resentment, hostility, and aggression. Efforts to restructure triangulations can often quickly bring aggression to an end by disrupting the patterns that support it.

It is important to note that parents generally believe that they are doing the right thing by protecting their younger child and are unaware of the impact it has on the older or the sibling relationship. Practitioners should take care to frame their side-taking behavior as being well intended, but problematic.

### *Parent coalitions with older siblings*

Older children in conflict with their younger siblings have the advantage of size, strength, and usually higher cognitive sophistication. They are likely to use these benefits when frustrated, resentful, or wanting to meet their personal objectives. Without parental intervention to teach and uphold prosocial sibling behavior, older children are likely to feel free to be aggressive. Moreover, parents who ally with olders against youngers give tacit permission to be aggressive without consequence. For example, Sam has complained on multiple occasions that his older sister Stacy hits him. His father's common response is, "You probably deserved it," while his mother nods in agreement. Stacy knows she can hit Sam freely and that Sam has no recourse or ability to protect himself.

A variation of parent–older child coalitions involves younger children perpetrating aggression with older siblings because they know the older child is highly rule abiding. Children are often anxious about disappointing their parents and violating their rules, so they refrain from retaliating. In cases in which the older children are favored, concern about maintaining their advantaged position may prevent them from engaging in violence. Younger children may learn through trial and error that they can attack an older and not worry about the older striking back.

### *Quadrangles: Split-parent–child coalitions*

As discussed in Chapters 2 and 3, a family dynamic in which sibling aggression is likely to be common is the quadrangle. The quadrangle involves a conflictual spousal system with two parent–child coalitions, each parent aligning with a different child. Each child is favored by their allied parent and disfavored by the other. The spousal conflict is reenacted by the siblings, with each child taking up their allied parent's position. They are fighting for the team, so to speak, even if they are not aware that their discord is tied to their parents' conflict. Often, each child is given tacit permission by their allied parent to aggress toward the rival child. Children may be particularly bold when their allied parent is home but the rival parent is away.

A feature of the family quadrangle is complementary labeling of children using "good" and "bad" labeling. As discussed in Chapter 2, good/bad designations are problematic for sibling relationships. In quadrangle families, each parent is likely to view their allied children as good and the rival child as bad, just as they see their spouse as "the bad one" in the marital relationship. Conflicting spouses frequently position their nonallied children as enemies in statements such as, "You are just like your father (*or mother*)," which are rarely meant to be flattering. Rather, it is meant to be hurtful while suggesting, "You and I are dissimilar and not on the same team." Moreover, it suggests to allied children that their siblings are playing for the enemy team.

Although the idea of sibling competition over parental affection would surprise few, a rarely talked about feature of family life is *parent rivalry* over their children. Parents frequently vie for a more favorable position with their children, and sometimes even ask their children to identify who they favor (even if in a joking manner)—for example, "Who treats you better? Mommy or Daddy?" In well-functioning families, these questions may be benign and have little to do with true feelings or reflective of coalitions. However, in high-conflict families, parent competition over children may result in quadrangle patterns, favoritism, and sibling conflict. Practitioners should assess for both sibling *and* parent rivalry.

The quadrangle is a pattern common to families that divorce. It occurs prior to family separation but loyalties commonly persist after the divorce. In custody arrangements where children are placed primarily in one parent's care, one of the children no longer has their ally around. They are now under the supervision of their "enemy" parent. Allied children are moved into positions of greater power. With the rival parent gone, allied children are at greater liberty to aggress toward siblings with the confidence that they have parents that will support them. Nonallied, or disfavored, children become outsiders in their primary places of residence. Assessment of quadrangles should be part of sibling aggression treatment with divorced families. Intervention work should aim to help the family transition to their new living arrangements, which may include modifying rigid and outdated coalitions. Parents and their nonallied siblings can be helped to learn about their positions in a conflict that is over, let go of old loyalties, and develop new relationships.

### *Scapegoating and disfavoritism*

The fourth variation of favoritism involves families selecting one child to blame for family problems, or "scapegoating." The scapegoated child is frequently accused of wrongdoing without merit. In families that scapegoat, there may not be any favored children, but one that is clearly disfavored. Disfavoritism involves a process where "parents single out one or more of their children for differential negative treatment" (Brody et al., 1998, p. 269), and has been linked to problematic outcomes such as family conflict and increased shame in the disfavored child (Brody et al., 1998). Patterns of disfavoritism and scapegoating give tacit permission to siblings to mistreat the disfavored child. Practitioners should assess parental support of sibling aggression toward children, particularly for those who are being consistently blamed without merit.

## DIRECT COMPARISON

As discussed in Chapter 2, siblings are compared more closely than any other relationship. From my practice and classroom teaching experiences, it seems that experiencing close comparison promotes greater competition that can escalate to aggressive tactics. This connection has been noted elsewhere (e.g., Sulloway, 1996), but has yet to receive empirical scrutiny.

Parental comparison in particular seems to motivate competition and possible aggression. When parents engage in active comparison they convey to their children that they are being evaluated, and one will emerge in a more favorable position than the other. Children are often highly attuned to which activities excite their parents and which do not. Holding a favored position in an area that excites parents is likely to result in rewards of resources (e.g., money, emotional investment, time). Siblings want to win more favorable comparison (if it is in their reach), and will compete to do so.

Conversely, less sibling comparison means less conflict. In practice, parents and siblings can be taught to engage in less comparison and instead promote individual accomplishments, contributions and talents, and sibling support and teamwork. Practitioners working with sibling aggression should observe for direct sibling comparison because of its potential to result in increased competition and aggression.

It is important to briefly mention that direct comparison can be positive when it fosters closeness, healthy competition, and highlights positive trait similarities. Parents who praise their children for all being compassionate and loving siblings help build warmth while minimizing competition to be the "most compassionate." An additional example would be saying to siblings, "I really enjoy how when you compete you also cheer each other on, and are friendly and supportive." Of course, such comparisons must be well timed and reflect actual behavior. Healthy competition is important for child development as it promotes greater effort and skills, and teaches about how to win and lose graciously.

As discussed in Chapter 3, complementary labeling and niche picking are two processes that are influenced by direct comparisons. Complementarity involves evaluations of personality characteristics in terms of opposites, and niche picking refers to the process of choosing interests and activities that often define individuals in regard to their areas of expertise. Each is taken up here as an area for assessment and for informing intervention strategies.

## Complementary Labeling

Practitioners should make note of active labeling of children in families and explore descriptions that seem potentially divisive. For example, good/bad complementary labeling seems to be of particular concern for sibling relationships (Schachter, 1985). Labels carry different values across families. In one family a particular label may be viewed favorably while another perceives it negatively. For example, for parents who place high value on intellect and describe one of their children as "the smart one," the other occupies a negative and diminished position, "the unintelligent one." By comparison, in a family that negatively perceives intellectualism, the label of "smart one" places the child in a disfavored position. Because the value of labels varies across families, learning what are divisive comes from assessment of complementarity.

The use of negative labels is highly problematic. They are defining, inhibiting, and self-fulfilling. A child who is labeled as "bad" is likely to internalize the designation and act badly. As discussed in Chapter 3, a child labeled this way is unlikely to change it by behaving well. Practitioners must immediately put a halt to parental use of negative labels. During a first treatment meeting with a family, the parents introduced their 2-year-old boy as their "little terror," and their 3-year-old boy as "Steven." The complementary nature of labels positioned Steven as the good one and the 2-year-old as bad. The parents then asked, "What do we do about our little terror?" The practitioner responded by immediately calling the label to their attention and talking about how helping their child will entail abandoning this designation and altering their perception of his actions. The practitioner suggested selecting a substitute and benign label such as "little boy" in place of little terror, or simply referring to the child by name. A "little terror" is a powerful person that often triggers an automatic reaction to restrain and punish, whereas a "little boy" is less threatening, less powerful, and suggests interventions aimed at supporting and teaching him prosocial behaviors. The parents immediately acknowledged that their label was problematic. During the task selection process they proposed using "little one" or the boy's name during both times of affection and frustration.

Labels frequently reflect sociocultural expectations that typically serve to constrain understandings of individuals. Gender, for example, plays an important role in the types of labels assigned. For example, in Western societies, females are more likely to be labeled with expressive traits (e.g., overemotional, nurturing, compassionate, loving, sensitive, fearful), whereas men are described using instrumental traits (e.g., assertive, brave, strong) (Bem, 1974), often opposite designations. Practitioners can deconstruct gender-based labels by openly discussing how they influence relationships, such as promoting unbalanced views of children, labeling, favoritism, and aggression. Similarly, culturally based labeling can be disentangled by openly discussing cultural "rules" that promote labeling and overt sibling aggression (e.g., labeling a girl as "tough" because she can physically dominate her brother). As an interesting aside, Edwards and Weller (2011) suggest that sibling aggression may reflect attempts to define and refine gender identity, in relation to the other—that is, who is more masculine and who is more feminine. Exploring these themes may reveal that a source of conflict is over who will define gender identity and labeling in sibling relationships.

Many labels are not problematic and are instead positive, promoting a positive sense of identity and individual pride. That said, helping parents evaluate their children according to discrete behaviors rather than global labels should minimize aggression related to unfavorable comparisons to siblings. Moreover, practitioners can assist with recognizing unique talents and individual accomplishments without diminishing other children's sense of self. Finally, minimizing problematic and active direct comparison is an important part of fostering sibling support using team-building strategies, which are taken up later in this section.

### *Task strategies for complementary labeling*

Assessment of active comparison and problematic complementary labeling suggests interventions to stop these behaviors. Strategies include facilitative confrontation, reframing descriptors, challenging distorted thinking, and focusing on discrete behaviors rather than global designations. Practitioners must also be careful to avoid problematic labeling through the use of formal diagnoses.

### *Facilitative confrontation*

Negative labels are reinforcing and frequently serve as self-fulfilling prophecies, where children succumb to the environmental interpretations of their intent, own the descriptors, and enact them as part of their identity. Practitioners can use facilitative confrontation that involves drawing on a positive therapeutic relationship to challenge client behaviors and ideas (Shulman, 2008). Practitioners should first share their observations with families and highlight the ways comparison and labeling are contributing to sibling aggression. It often helps to have parents actively think about how their children might be influenced by their descriptors. Framing challenges in the form of questions is a useful tool for facilitating reflection as they decrease defensiveness (Caspi & Reid, 2002). Asking parents how they think their use of labels influences their children's behavior and relationship may be initially more productive than telling them that their behavior is problematic.

Parents and siblings can agree to stop using labels but may find it exceptionally challenging to avoid making comparisons. It is an improvement for parents to refrain from labeling in front of their children, even if they continue to do it in private. However, the names parents choose provide the lens for how behaviors are interpreted. Ultimately, having parents avoid labeling or reframe their children's labels will likely be more productive in lessening sibling competition and aggression. It is helpful for children to hear the behavior being interpreted in positive ways, even if it involves continued labeling. Negative labels can be reframed into positive ones.

### *Reframing*

As presented in Chapter 3, all behaviors can be labeled in multiple ways. For example, a child who refrains from immediately answering a stranger's question could be labeled as shy. This same behavior can also be thought of as contemplative, calculating, restrained, or private. How behavior is interpreted guides decisions about how to interact with the labeled individual. One responds differently to "shy" than to "calculating." A brother labeled as "calculating" who does not respond to his sister's personal questions may be seen as aggressive compared to a brother who engages in the same behavior but is called "private." Similarly, a "hyper" child could be thought of as "high energy." Each label conveys different parenting approaches—high energy is more positive and less likely to suggest favoritism than the traditionally negative hyper.

Reframing is a common intervention strategy that aims to change the meaning of behaviors and can be effective in changing attitudes from negative to positive (Robbins, Alexander, Newell, & Turner, 1996; Robbins, Alexander, & Turner, 2000). It is particularly useful in helping families view behaviors differently and in ways that are less likely to negatively impact the sibling relationship. Practitioners using this strategy may select a child behavior and ask the family to identify other ways the same action could be interpreted. The practitioner may need to "prime the pump" and offer examples to assist the family in this exercise.

As noted earlier in this book, a particularly problematic but common sibling labeling process involves the use of the labels good and bad (e.g., angel and devil) to describe sibling pairs. Practitioners must overtly address good/bad complementary labeling when identified. Families should be strongly encouraged to halt such descriptions as they cloud understandings of behavior and impinge efforts to halt aggression and promote positivity between siblings. Once a child is labeled as bad, this perception becomes the lens for interpreting the child's actions. It is difficult for family members to recognize good behavior and the child's investment in being well behaved diminishes.

### *Challenging distorted thinking*

The noted communication theorist Paul Watzlawick (1977) posited that once an individual has a theory about an observed event, evidence that contradicts theory is interpreted in ways that paradoxically support it. To use a Watzlawick example, if one believes that he has "bad luck" and encounter more red lights than he should when driving the car, his red light theory will be supported by his interpretations of when he does and does not encounter them. When he does come across a red light, he thinks to himself, "You see, I'm right that I have bad luck with red lights." However, when he encounters a green light he may say, "What a fluke!" or "I finally got lucky!" or he may not notice the light at all. Both statements confirm that his theory is correct despite being evidence to the contrary. Contradictory evidence is missed, dismissed, or ignored. The driver does not say to himself, "Ah, a green light, I must reevaluate my whole theory about red lights." It is an interesting aspect of the human experience that evidence that supports or refutes one's theory confirms one's belief in it.

The same process can be applied to good/bad labeling. Evidence that the bad one is attempting to do good confirms the child's badness to the labeler via statements like, "She must want something" or "Maybe they upped his medication." Again, such statements serve to reinforce the child's bad label rather than call the label into question. As an example, Maria (age 18) carried the label of "bad" whereas Julio (age 16) was "good." Julio went to a party, drank alcohol, and crashed the family car into a tree while driving home intoxicated. When their parents learned of the crash, they blamed Maria saying that if it were not for her bad example Julio would have not done such a thing. They added that a "good sister" would have protected her brother and not let him do "such terrible things." The event did not change the parents' view of their children but rather, served to reinforce their views. That is, Julio's bad behavior reinforced his position as the good one. Calling children "bad" is often a self-fulfilling prophecy.

Practitioners should promote stopping the continued use of bad/good labeling and help families reinterpret child behavior. Falsely attributing bad or hostile intent is a common feature of poor sibling relationships and of bad labeling. Learning to correctly check for and identify accurate intent is a prosocial skill (Kramer, 2011). Reinterpreting behavior can be assisted by reframes and questioning accusations of intent. A method of identifying intent is to focus on discrete behaviors rather than use labels to guide interpretations.

### *Focusing on discrete behaviors*

Practitioners can help families change their focus from global descriptions to discrete behaviors. Learning to respond to individual actions enables clients to break out of labeling patterns. To use the earlier example of Julio and Maria, helping the parents separate each child's individual behaviors in the car crash event from their lenses clouded by labels promotes more accurate understandings of each child's responsibility. To facilitate this separation of labeling and behaviors, the practitioner asked the parents how they would view their son's behavior if they were being told the story about another child who got drunk and crashed the car. They responded by saying they would think the child acted highly irresponsibly and should be punished. The practitioner noted the power of labeling and how that has changed their view of his behavior. The parents agreed. The practitioner then asked if their daughter's behavior that evening was also distorted by her label. The parents agreed that she had done nothing wrong that evening and that blaming her was probably not the proper response. The practitioner suggested tasks that involved separating views of behavior from labels. An example of a task the parents agreed to implement entailed them by making a note in a journal about each time Maria engaged in a positive behavior. A second task involved them praising the behavior. The target of this intervention was to help the parents cognitively reconstruct their view of their daughter in incremental fashion.

### *Diagnostic labeling*

Practitioners must take care to avoid the labeling trap when making formal diagnoses and using them as interpretive lenses once they have been made. Practitioner training often directs them to see aggressive behavior as indicators of mental health problems. They may be tempted to see child perpetrators of aggression as warranting diagnoses such as "conduct" and "oppositional defiant," or even "intermittent explosive" and "antisocial personality" disorders. Considering aggression in the context of family dynamics may suggest that violent children may have issues that are strictly internal. For example, the child who is disfavored will likely be resentful, feel like an outsider, and choose aggressively as a means of coping with a rigged system (i.e., in which he/she is always the loser and/or problem). Although violent behavior is unacceptable, it does not immediately warrant a formal diagnosis. Assigning a diagnosis to already-disfavored or scapegoated children essentially blame them for a systemic problem, and will further isolate them and cause increased resentment for all family members. It is important for practitioners to assess family and environmental dynamics that may support resentment, frustration, and violent acting out, prior to assuming the problem is located within the aggressive individual and diagnostically labeling them. Again, once labeled, all future behavior is interpreted through this distorting lens.

## Niches

Niche partitioning refers to siblings entering different areas of interest in order to best win parental resources while minimizing the competition between them (Sulloway, 1996). One child may discover that she has a talent for dance, whereas her younger sister excels at softball. These sisters do not need to compete directly for recognition or superiority within their niches. Each has her own "turf." By comparison, brothers who both play hockey compete directly to win a favored position within that niche. They are likely to compare performances and be compared by others. To be compared favorably may result in greater parental and internal (e.g., self-esteem) rewards. While the benefit of such competition is often improved skill level, the child who is compared less favorably risks lower investment and may select a different niche in which to define himself.

Children who occupy the same niches are more likely to compete and also to spend time together compared to children who have different interests. The more individuals share living experiences the more they typically experience conflicts. Individuals who spend little time together should have lower conflict but also lower connectedness. The combination of wanting to win more favorable parental investment and personal rewards, with increased shared time and space, increases the likelihood of conflict and aggressive tactics when niches are shared. Strategies to decrease sibling aggression often require attention to shared niches, diversification, comparison, and parental involvement.

## Task Strategies for Shared Niches

When assessment reveals shared niches with heavy comparison and competition, further inquiry into aggressive tactics, intentional harm, and domination is recommended. Two approaches related to shared niches are offered here: planned diversification and reinforcement for teamwork.

### *Planned diversification*

Planned diversification involves helping parents and children deliberately carve out separate sibling niches so that each will have their own areas of expertise, confidence, identity, and self-esteem. This strategy minimizes comparisons and direct competition for resources. Practitioners should share the concept of niches with families, discuss its positives and negatives for sibling relationships, and ask whether or not remaining in a particular niche is worth it from personal and relational perspectives. If remaining in the same area is preferred, ways to diversify within the niche should be considered. For example, two brothers who excel at and want to continue with baseball may select different positions to develop as their own—for example, one a first baseman and the other a short stop. Diversification work also includes helping families broaden niche fields, attend to niche values, and develop strategies to be separate within shared niches.

### *Broadening niche fields*

Working with parents to broaden the niche field may be necessary in helping children diversify in their interests. Niche fields refer to the number of possible activity options provided by children's environments. Some parents demand that all their children engage in one activity whereas others support their children in almost anything they choose. Parents who limit the number of niche options force shared activities that exacerbate competition and its often corresponding aggression. In order to help children find separate niches, practitioners may need to encourage parents to be open to new interests, which include those that do not excite them. For example, an intact family consisting of four brothers was referred to counseling for sibling violence. The father made it clear that he expected all his sons to play football. He had played in college and wanted the same for his children. Early discussion of the violence indicated that it was linked to the pressure they each felt to succeed. The boys reported that their father would show them more or less affection based upon whether they performed well or poorly during games. In a session that did not include the father, two of the sons admitted to not enjoying football and wanting to quit. A diversification strategy involved addressing the father's emotional investment in the football niche for his sons and helping him weigh the benefits of allowing his children to pursue other interests. Although reluctant at first, the father slowly became open to his sons engaging in other activities.

### *Attending to niche value*

Practitioners must also attend to and help families recognize that not all niches are equal in their value to parents. This is illustrated in the case example of the father who is excited by and is highly invested in football. Although he may support other endeavors, football is a high-value niche and this is clear to his sons. Children pay attention to what excites their parents and which activities seem to garner the greatest rewards and which receive the least. Diversification approaches must include open discussion about niche value and parental support. One of the sons who reported wanting to stop playing football shared that he was interested in taking guitar lessons. For his father, this represented a betrayal to family values and tradition. It was clear that he regarded music as a low-value niche. However, rewards for niche involvement come from a variety of places. For example, his mother played a musical instrument and became excited about the prospect of having her child share an interest. Although the switch to a new niche initially created distance between the father and son, it also lessened the resentment, frustration, and aggression that occurred in their relationship and with his siblings. Over time, this boy became an excellent guitarist and joined a rock band that yielded high rewards from other sources, such as fans, his music teacher, and other musicians.

### Separate within shared niches

In cases where siblings both excel at the same endeavor and the activity provides a major source of pride, enjoyment, and self-esteem, practitioners should avoid diversification strategies and instead focus on intervention to sustain participation in shared niches while minimizing direct competition. One strategy is to separate the siblings by having them engage in their niche activity in different locations. For example, two sisters who excel at dance could begin working with different coaches at different sites, and compete in separate competitions. The result of diversification is less shared time and less opportunity for conflict. That stated, it is important to note that a risk of this approach is disengaged and less close sibling relationships. Because sibling support is highly beneficial to individual experience, interventions aimed at creating separate spaces should include efforts to connect siblings in areas outside their shared niche.

### Reinforcement for teamwork

A second approach is to enable siblings to continue participating in the same niche but change the perspective of *siblings as rivals* to *siblings as teammates*. This requires assisting both parents and siblings in making a major cognitive shift from individual achievement and recognition at the expense of others to mutual accomplishment and affirmation. Competition between siblings is not eliminated or avoided but rather redirected. The common reactive enmeshment between competitive rivals is refocused to positive involvement. Destructive competition is replaced by constructive contests with the aim of providing encouragement and support and improving each other's skill sets. Siblings are helped to think about behaving in ways that are best for the team (e.g., "us against everyone else") rather than for themselves. Of course, resistance to joining with the enemy should be expected. Practitioners may need to discuss the mutual benefits of teaming and constructive competition.

In order for teaming to be effective, it is often necessary to teach siblings and their parents about acknowledging positivity, engaging in prosocial and supportive interaction, and using positive reinforcement. Encouraging and rewarding good sportship (the gender-neutral term for the traditional "sportsmanship") is a strategy for accomplishing a sibling team stance. It is important to reemphasize the role of parents in building a sibling as teammates orientation. Parents must participate by supporting positive interaction and avoiding evaluative comparisons. Rather than focusing on labels, attention should instead be given to discrete displays of skill and individual achievement, paired with praise for sibling support, affiliation, and mutual affirmation. Moreover, parents should be guided in creating and maintaining family rules that prohibit belittling, teasing, expressing glee at other's misfortune, and open claims of superiority that come at the expense of others.

### *Case study: Reinforcement for teamwork*

The Martins, a Black family, consisted of a mother and a father, and two daughters, aged 10 and 12. The girls enjoyed and excelled at basketball. At the end of games, the family would compare who did better (e.g., scored more points, had a better average percent at the free-throw line), which usually resulted in protests, yelling, crying, and intense expressions of resentment. The negative reactions to these postgame comparisons were increasing as was the sibling conflict in relation to nonbasketball interactions. The family was aggravated and stressed by the constant fighting and after the 12-year-old spread a nasty rumor about her sister at school, the parents "couldn't take it anymore" and sought family therapy.

Because both siblings wanted to continue playing basketball, diversification of interests was not the appropriate course of action. Instead the treatment focused on building teamwork and sibling support. Tasks were formulated to build a relationship of good sportship. For example, when one did something particularly well, such as made a difficult shot, the other's task was to congratulate her with a "high five," and the recipient's job was to acknowledge the praise by smiling or saying, "Thank you." The parents' tasks involved ignoring bickering and instead acknowledging and rewarding acts of support. For example, when one daughter said "Nice job" to the other, the parents' task was to say something like, "I loved that you just supported your sister! I am proud of you!" This was further emphasized with statements to both such as, "You both make a great sister team!" In addition to these tasks, both the daughters and families were taught to avoid making negative comparisons and took on tasks that instead recognized individual accomplishments.

During treatment, the father raised an interesting discussion about the famous sibling women's tennis pair, the Williams sisters. He noted how supportive they seemed to be of each other even though they were often each other's greatest adversary in tournaments. At that point the 12-year-old proposed that maybe it was because the tennis stars were Black. The practitioner, who was White, asked the 12-year-old to explain her assumption, to which she replied, "I thought I heard them say that because they were Black women in a mostly White sport that they needed to stick together." The practitioner wondered aloud if the Williams sisters felt like it was them against everyone else. "Yes," replied the 12-year-old, "I think they do." The practitioner said, "So, they operate like a team, even though they are rivals?" The family agreed with this assertion and the conversation became about how the "Martin sisters" (which the practitioner intentionally began calling them) could be a team, while still engaged in competition, such as when on opposing teams or playing one-against-one in their driveway.

At the end of treatment, the siblings were regularly congratulating each other for each other's performances and offering statements of encouragement when either had a bad game. The bickering almost entirely ceased and the two seemed to be genuine friends. They referred to each other as a team. It should be noted that during the course of treatment, the sisters balked at supporting each other and had flair-ups. However, the lack of parental attention to negative encounters, thus no longer reinforcing them, and the new focus on gaining parental favor via prosocial sibling behavior, plus altering the nature of the sibling competition from being the better player to being the best sister, all served to overcome initial resistance. In short, there was no longer an incentive for being antagonistic, as the rewards shifted and came from only engaging in positive sibling interactions.

### *Teamwork and cultural values*

Western cultures emphasize *individualism* that gives precedence to independence and personal responsibility over the needs of collectives. This perspective supports competition and prioritizes individual needs over sibling and family loyalties. Mainstream cultural narratives that simultaneously devalue sibling responsibility and normalize sibling aggression complicate attempts to develop sibling connectedness. At the same time, Western societies are increasingly diverse and consist of cultural and ethnic groups that emphasize family loyalty. For example, among others (e.g., Indian, Italian), many Latin American cultures emphasize *familism* (Updegraff, McHale, Killoren, & Rodrguez, 2011), which places family well-being higher than individual choice. That said, it is important to note that it is problematic to generalize about Latin American cultures because they represent multiple diverse groups. High levels of familism have been linked to greater sibling closeness and support in Mexican-origin families (Updegraff et al., 2005a). Familism may have other important functions in relation to siblings. For example, African American adolescents reported that sibling warmth in conjunction with high levels of familism was linked to less risk-taking behaviors (Soli, McHale, & Feinberg, 2009).

Efforts to employ "siblings as teammates" strategies should consider the role of cultural values such as familism. For some, interventions to build family loyalty will be harmonious with cultural values. Intervention efforts should draw upon these cultural strengths. Sibling tensions may be related to conflict over cultural practices, particularly for immigrant families who may struggle to emphasize familism in a setting that promotes individualism. For example, sibling conflict and resentment may arise when one promotes personal needs while the other believes that sibling loyalty should take precedence. Finally, less is known about the role ideas like familism has in regard to sibling relationships in White, European-origin groups. Attempting to build a "sibling as teammates" orientation conflicts with Western notions of independence and competition. To address such obstacles, practitioners can openly discuss cultural and family values to learn more about how to work with families to build sibling support while protecting belief systems. As suggested earlier, individual competition can be preserved in relation to peers, with support from siblings.

## Parental Support for Aggressive Behavior

Parents can support and promote aggressive behavior in their children in a variety of ways. These include providing *overt* support for employing aggressive tactics (e.g., "Hit him back!") and by assigning positive outcomes to violence (e.g., "It makes you tougher"), as well as *tacit* approval via the lack of action when siblings engage in aggression, modeling violence (e.g., spouses belittling each other, child abuse), and excitement about violence on television or in video games. During assessment, practitioners should note statements and elements that give overt support or tacit approval for sibling aggression. Such support for aggression should be highlighted and halted.

### *Overt support*

Sibling aggression is occasionally supported by parents under the guise of wanting their children to become resilient or "tough." They believe that experiencing hostility with a sibling better prepares them for peer attack and living in dangerous neighborhoods. As discussed in Chapter 1, there is no evidence that experiencing sibling aggression makes children tougher. On the contrary, victims of aggression are likely less resilient as they experience greater psychological distress and are more likely to be revictimized by a range of sources than those who are not victimized (Cuevas et al., 2010). This view of "learned toughness" is often a gendered issue. For example, a boy who has been hit by his sister may be told, "Be a man, stick up for yourself!" Or the sister may be given permission to be violent using another gender-based rationale—for example, "I don't care if your sister hit you first, you don't hit girls." In either case, the sister has been given tacit permission to hit her brother, and in the former, the brother is told that the hurtful violence is good for him—a problematic message.

Parental emphasis on manliness or machismo may inadvertently suggest that aggression is not only acceptable but a positive sign of male development. Earlier in this chapter a case example of a father who demanded his four sons all play football was presented. During treatment, the father was asked to consider other activities for his sons in order to diversify their interests and lessen direct competition. The father's initial response was to approve of other activities only if they were "manly sports like football." He gave lacrosse, hockey, and boxing as examples—that is, sports that require intense physical tactics such as hitting or "checking." This father conveyed to his children that he prized aggression. He was inadvertently sending two conflicting messages: (1) be manly and tough by being aggressive and (2) stop hitting your siblings. Moreover, the father also initially shared that "talking about problems" showed weakness. This left the children in a bind. How were they to deal with disagreements and conflict without being aggressive and without talking about them?

Assessment of overt support sibling aggression entails asking for each family member's perception of violence in terms of its severity, rationale, and consequences. This is usually done during TCSA's problem identification step. Families that see violence as beneficial or benign are less likely to be motivated to address sibling aggression.

### *Tacit support*

Assessment should also include observation and inquiry into tacit support for sibling aggression. For example, parents who avoid entering sibling conflict when serious aggression occurs give unspoken approval for its continued use. Allowing siblings to resolve their own conflicts is a common advice given to parents because it promotes the development of an autonomous relationship in which children can experience closeness and learn to resolve their own difficulties. Children can learn conflict resolution skills first hand by engaging directly with each of their siblings. It is common for parental involvement to entail taking the role of referee, which changes the nature of the conflict to vying for parental support rather than resolution of the initial disagreement. Parental intervention can perpetuate sibling conflict. Refraining from entering sibling conflict is a good advice in positive relationships where aggression is mild. However, parents must halt violent exchanges in order to ensure their children's safety. Once violence is halted, sibling autonomy should be promoted.

Parents must convey that egregious activity will not be tolerated by articulating clear rules for behavior and reinforced with negative consequences. Perhaps more importantly, positive consequences should be given for prosocial handling of aggression such as restraint and deescalation of behaviors (e.g., walking away or saying, "Let's talk about this"). Many parents assume that children will interact well without having been taught skills for good behavior. Assessment should include evaluation of rule clarity regarding violence, and knowledge of prosocial skills.

Parents often make the assumption that their children know how to resolve their own conflicts. Unless strategies for resolving disagreements are expressly taught and reinforced, it is likely that children will resort to aggressive tactics. It is not uncommon for parents to express to practitioners that their children "should know better" than to hit each other or engage in name calling. Indeed, children may not know better. Sibling aggression treatment often includes explicit coaching of how to engage in and support prosocial skills.

A variation of tacit support for aggression involves coalitions and can be seen in the Dexter and Bart case example from earlier. Bart's mother gives unspoken approval for his use of violence against Dexter by taking his side. Moreover, she is more upset by Dexter's seeming unwillingness to allow Bart to join him with activities than the hitting. She unwittingly conveys the message that violence is acceptable. Like many parents, she sees sibling aggression as normal, which gives tacit support for violence.

Parent modeling of aggression is another variation of giving tacit approval for its use by siblings. Parents who act aggressively toward their children or with each other teach children that such behavior is an acceptable way to express needs. Sibling violence has been linked to other types of violence (Turner et al., 2010) and assessment must include inquiry into parent–child and partner aggression. Parent–child aggression may not meet the level that requires child welfare reporting but conveys tacit support of such tactics as well as being deleterious. Halting aggression perpetrated by parents is important for family health and for addressing sibling fighting.

Another area that gives tacit support for violence involves its glorification in other relationships, including fictional ones. Such behavior may teach siblings that aggressive actions are prized. For example, parents who delight in or support the celebration of destruction in movies (e.g., when the hero blows up the enemy's home), television (e.g., entertainment wrestling), and video games (e.g., shooting and killing rivals) may be conveying support for "toughness" and aggressive "win-at-all-costs" tactics. Although controversial, there is some evidence that violence in the media and in video games can promote aggression in children (Krahé & Möller, 2010; Krcmar, Farrar, & McGloin, 2011). Practitioners should take note of reports of glorified aggression and stories of sibling reenactments of media violence. Questions about how violence is viewed in larger contexts such as in the media, neighborhoods, with peers, and by other family members provide insight into whether or not aggression is tacitly supported. Practitioners may want to help parents monitor their own enthusiasm for violence and limit their children's observations of glorified hostility via stricter supervision and automated parental controls.

## Task Strategies for Parental Support for Aggressive Behavior

Assessment that reveals parental support for sibling aggression suggests task strategies that aim to change family culture to see aggression as problematic and to take action against it. This often involves confronting families about their positive view of aggression both in regard to sibling interaction and enthusiasm for violence in the media. Parental modeling of aggression is addressed. Implementing no violence contracts, teaching siblings restraint and prosocial methods for managing conflict, and helping family members identify when they are losing emotional control are all helpful strategies. Finally, tasks that promote a perception of connectedness and siblings as "teammates" rather than rivals are encouraged.

## Ineffective Supervision

A fourth family dynamic that supports sibling aggression is ineffective supervision of children by guardians. Four variations of this dynamic include (1) guardians overwhelmed by pragmatic demands (e.g., employment, domestic chores), (2) guardian dysfunction in which they are emotionally unable to handle the demands of childcare (e.g., substance abuse, mental illness), (3) willful neglect, and (4) guardians who grant children great autonomy (e.g., alone time after school and before parents return home). Because the first three variations commonly involve sibling caretaking, discussion of unstructured sibling caretaking arrangements is included and precedes the fourth. This fourth variation, high autonomy, often fosters boredom and independent decision making, which exacerbate sibling aggression.

### *Parents overwhelmed by pragmatic demands*

Parents may appear disinterested but may also be overwhelmed by the day-to-day pressures of life and have little energy or time for their children. For example, a mother of three children all 5 years of age and under expressed that she frequently relied on the television to entertain her 5- and 3-year-olds in order to attend to her infant as well as other domestic chores. During treatment she shared, "I don't know how I would get all the things I need to get done if I had to watch them all the time. I'm barely functioning now!" In another example of parents relying on child independence in order to cope with life activities, a single father worked during the day and enrolled in evening courses in order to advance his employment opportunities. At home his time was split among preparing meals, washing clothes, and studying. In order to complete these activities he relied on his children to, as he put it, "entertain themselves." He felt he had no time to supervise and although he wanted to be involved, the pressures of living made that impossible at the time. As a consequence of feeling overwhelmed, guardians frequently allow their children a great deal of independence that may range from leaving them unattended in a playroom in front of a television to allowing them to roam the neighborhood unsupervised.

Another explanation for parents being overwhelmed is the lack of education many possess in regard to parenting, particularly about how to manage siblings. The amounts of knowledge parents possess matters in regard to child outcomes (Bornstein, Cote, Haynes, Hahn, & Park, 2010). For example, parenting knowledge has been linked to more accurate interpretations of children's behaviors (Bugental & Happaney, 2002), and less of behavior problems (Huang, Caughy, Genevro, & Miller, 2005). Many parents lack information on how to effectively discipline children and resort to yelling and threats of punishment as methods of control. For example, three brothers in the Lee family physically fought with each other multiple times each day. Their mother's only strategy was to yell loudly, demanding that they stop fighting. She was the only adult in the house and felt powerless to manage her children and keep them safe. She reported that she and her sister rarely fought, and when they did they immediately stopped when their father yelled at them. She saw yelling as the only parenting tool for sibling fighting and lacked information about other strategies.

Punishment is one of the most frequently used parenting tools, but is a problematic one, as discussed in Chapter 4. For example, using an international sample, Gershoff et al. (2010) reported that the mother's use of corporal punishment, expressing disappointment, and yelling were linked to more child aggression symptoms. Shaming and even the use of time-out were significantly related to greater child anxiety symptoms. Punishment does not teach alterative prosocial behaviors. For example, a father who sees his two children fighting and immediately puts them in time-out, or tells them they have lost their television-watching privileges, has not provided them with better strategies for handling disagreements. Indeed, what punishment seems to teach is how to avoid being caught (i.e., becoming more sneaky). Intervention tasks for lack of discipline skills involve education and trying out new skills during treatment sessions.

A variation related to both parenting education and low parental involvement concerns the common belief that sibling aggression is normal behavior. Parents hearing their children involved in a physical altercation may choose to ignore it and avoid intervening. During conversations I have had with parents, I have observed them talking over their fighting siblings and acting as though they were unaware that the children were even present. Similarly, I have observed parents close the door to a room where their children were screaming harsh insults at each other. When I have confronted parents who seem to ignore their children's hostilities, the most frequent response is that their children are "just doing what siblings do." The lack of involvement is related to a lack of information about the seriousness of sibling violence.

Discipline is a team effort and is hampered by "split-parenting," when caretakers disagree about the methods and issues for intervention. If one parent believes that sibling hostility is dangerous and should be stopped, but the other sees it as normal and of no real concern, addressing sibling aggression is complicated by marital disagreement. The one who sees sibling fighting as a nonissue will likely undermine the spouse's efforts to discipline aggressive acts. In a case involving the Wu family, Mrs. Wu wanted the children's fighting to end as it was "causing stress to the household all day long." When Mr. Wu arrived home from work, she would tell him of the children's ongoing fighting. His response was to tell her that it was normal for children to fight and she was "making a big deal out of nothing." Occasionally, Mrs. Wu would punish her children by taking away their toys, but when the children asked their father for the toys, he returned them feeling they had been too harshly disciplined. Mrs. Wu's effort to halt sibling hostility was undermined by her husband's views and actions. The children recognized their mother's powerlessness and actively disregarded her disciplinary efforts. Assessment of caretaker unity and split-parenting suggests intervention tasks that address marital disagreement and the undermining of disciplinary power by spouses. Although education about the seriousness of sibling aggression can help move parents to a more unified place, split-parenting behavior typically crosses child behavior challenges and often reflects marital problems. In my experience, sibling aggression treatment commonly includes marital counseling.

*Guardian dysfunction*

Ineffective supervision may be related to guardians who are too debilitated to provide proper care, usually related to substance abuse and/or serious mental illness. In both cases, parents may be emotionally and cognitively unable to handle the demands of caretaking. Both substance and mental health issues may be longstanding or transient challenges. In situations of long-term debilitation, child welfare assessment must be done and reports made when children are actively neglected. However, substance abuse and mental illness are both frequently characterized by periods of fairly healthy functioning and decompensation. During problematic periods, supports must be enlisted to assist with or take over caretaking duties until the guardian is well enough to resume such responsibilities.

Children of debilitated parents often take on adult roles in families, providing emotional and physical care for siblings as well as the poorly functioning parent. Providing assistance to caretaking siblings in the form of physical support (e.g., enlisting grandparents) is helpful. In cases where the assistance of family members is unavailable, and the debilitated parent is able to manage basic care for the family (e.g., food, shelter, heat, transport to school) but little more, providing education about sibling caretaking and discipline strategies as well as emotional support is often necessary.

*Willful neglect*

In another variation of lack of supervision, some parents willfully engage in low involvement with their children, believing that self-governance and lack of intrusion is best. As discussed earlier, many professionals promote sibling autonomy and caution against parental interference in sibling conflict. The reasons for poor oversight vary and may also be related to employment requirements and lack of parenting knowledge.

### *Unstructured sibling caretaking*

The above variations of ineffective supervision frequently enlist children to become caretakers for siblings. Indeed, it is quite common for parents to place their children in the care of their older siblings. Sibling caretaking varies considerably across cultures (Cicirelli, 1994) and has important developmental functions, including socialization (Reynolds, Dorner, & Orellana, 2011). It also includes care for a sibling's child. Poorer families rely more on extensive sibling caretaking than middle- or upper-class families who may turn to older siblings for temporary arrangements, such as babysitting. Girls and ethnic adolescents are called on to do more sibling caretaking (Walker, 1999), as are oldest children of both genders in immigrant, non-Western, and agricultural families (Weisner, 1987; Zukow-Goldring, 2002), and children with siblings with disabilities (McHale & Crouter, 1996). Although many have argued the benefits of sibling caretaking, some have noted potential dangers such as increased internalizing of problems (Walker, 1999), unintentional injury (Morrongiello, Schmidt, & Schell, 2010), and sibling aggression (Baum, 1998; Green, 1994). Caretaking for one's sibling's offspring has been linked to more school absences, increased school disciplinary problems, and care conflict to increased stress, depression, anxiety, and lower grades (East & Weisner, 2009).

Sibling caretaking is often assigned with inadequate structure or preparation. Parents may initiate sibling supervision with little more than statements such as "You are in charge now," usually directed at the oldest child. Although many parents find it difficult to manage their offspring, children placed in command of their siblings are challenged by a greater number of complicating features. First, children often have limited knowledge of disciplinary and control strategies and are ill-prepared to handle challenges to their authority. Second, the legitimacy of their authority is contingent upon their parents' support. They are parent representatives. If parents do not consistently back their caretaking siblings when caretaking problems arise, their power is seriously compromised. Third, in Western society, rules for sibling hierarchy are less defined by social norms and power arrangements seem to be fluid. For example, sibling relationships are frequently considered to be egalitarian, like peers. However, age and size differences suggest complementary positions during childhood, with older children having greater power and younger having less, whereas sibling hierarchy appears to shift to more egalitarian arrangements in adolescence (Tucker, Updegraff, & Baril, 2010).

Because sibling power arrangements are fluid and typically not discussed in families, placing one in charge creates notions of relationships that run counter to experiences and beliefs about the nature of hierarchy in families. This can be observed when a child is placed in charge and the siblings react with shock and upset. When the parent is out of the house, the younger children frequently challenge the new arrangement saying, "You can't tell me what to do, you're not my mother." Supervising sibling are expected to keep their siblings behaved (e.g., "out of trouble") and safe and feel the pressure to keep them under control. Supervising siblings may not know how to do this, particularly when their authority is challenged. Consequently, they may turn to their larger size and strength to establish their "true" position of power in order to get their brothers and sisters to cooperate, utilizing techniques such as threats of physical pain, damage to toys, and locking them in closets—all behaviors regarded as sibling abuse.

As an example, a mother contacted a family service agency because she was worried about her eldest son David's violent behavior. The mother frequently asked David to care for (i.e., "babysit") his much younger siblings, which resulted in his punching them. During treatment meetings, David expressed that his siblings refused to listen to his instructions, even when he was trying to protect their safety. He told of one occasion when his 4-year-old sister Susanna kept trying to stick a fork in an electrical outlet. David said that he had to repeatedly tell her to stop but that she ignored him and continued to try. He said the only thing that worked was slapping her hard and telling her he would do it again if she did not stop.

Intervention work should focus on educating caretaking siblings about discipline strategies, clarifying rules about hierarchy, and confirming parental support for supervising siblings. In general, practitioners should support sibling caretaking arrangements and work with families to identify strategies for making it work. Many families depend upon sibling caretaking for economic and cultural reasons. Practitioners may support older siblings' positions of authority by utilizing them as experts, particularly in immigrant families in which they frequently act as cultural brokers and often are knowledgeable about culture-specific considerations for handling sibling relational and power arrangements (Reynolds et al., 2011).

### *Granting high sibling autonomy*

Children left to care for themselves for extended periods of time with little oversight or knowledge of their activities are more likely to engage in sibling aggression (Caffaro & Conn-Caffaro, 1998; Linares, 2006). Larger children may be motivated to invoke their size and position of power to manage sibling disagreements, with little consequence. Poor oversight includes uninvolved parents who make little effort to learn about what happens between their children or ignore evidence that harm is being perpetrated.

Boredom is a consequence of lack of supervision. Without the provision of structured activities, children become bored and look for ways to stimulate excitement, and provoking a sibling using aggressive tactics is a frequent choice. Two siblings in the backseat of a car during a long trip may find it more stimulating to poke each other than to endlessly stare out the window. Similarly, it is more exciting to experience the power of provoking a sibling than watch the same rerun of a television show each afternoon.

Interventions for high sibling autonomy and poor oversight include making arrangements to increase supervision and parental involvement. Practitioners should pay attention to parents' abilities to supervise in regard to job and other practical constraints, as well as guardians' emotional abilities to cope with daily stressors. Because boredom is a feature of lack of supervision, intervention strategies should include giving purpose and structuring independent sibling time. For example, providing children with activities (e.g., completing a puzzle, building with blocks) can eliminate the redundancy related to lack of structure. Another approach to planning independent time is to establish and reinforce clear rules for behavior. As examples, rules about asking permission to leave the house before doing so, watching television (e.g., alternating who gets to choose the show to watch), and sharing toys, and rules that prohibit aggression are all helpful in giving structure to alone time. Other structuring tasks include regular "checking in" by both children and parents to increase supervision while preserving sibling autonomy. Finally, education regarding the importance of parental supervision, inquiry into evidence of aggression, the dangers of sibling violence, and the advantages of structuring independent sibling time may be necessary.

## Task Strategies for Ineffective Supervision

Interventions to address sibling aggression related to ineffective supervision include task strategies that increase guardian involvement, which may involve rearranging work schedules, drawing upon support systems, prioritizing demands, and addressing emotional obstacles to caregiving. In cases that involve sibling caretaking, task strategies include developing formal arrangements and rules for sibling caretaking. This may involve providing education and activities that promote skill development about how to discipline and provide oversight that does not rely on physical domination. For cases in which sibling autonomy is high, and sibling caretaking is not appropriate (e.g., children are the same age or close in age), task strategies include actions that provide structure and rules for unsupervised time, such as clear understandings of how to spend alone time together. As with all the FFD, tasks that enhance prosocial skill development are recommended.

## Focus on Negativity

Families with sibling conflict often focus on the negative interactions and intent and fail to acknowledge positive encounters. This focus fails to recognize that relationships are multifaceted. I frequently encounter this focus on negativity when I meet parents for the first time and they say something like, "All my children do is fight with each other!" This focus promotes rigid understandings of relationships, contributes to ongoing sibling negativity, and can dominate family life. It represents the fifth family dynamic that supports sibling aggression.

The focus on negativity is particularly common in families with frequent sibling bickering, which typically involves tattling to parents. It may be less present in more severe forms of sibling aggression such as abuse, as parents are usually not around when it occurs. That noted, practitioners should assess for negativity in all forms of aggression. Helping families alter their negative focus to one that promotes positivity and prosocial sibling behavior is a central aim of the two-pronged treatment approach put forth in this book.

Sibling negativity serves to unintentionally reinforce problematic interaction in two ways. First, negative parental attention typically comes with commotion (e.g., yelling, threats), and is often exciting, and often inadvertently rewards continued bad behavior. Negative parental attention is also more desirable than none. Children may use negative strategies to win parental investment, particularly in families where it is scarce. More commonly, parents frequently only parent when their children are engaged in unwanted behavior. When their children are well behaved, they engage in little parenting, failing to acknowledge the good moments. For example, a father reported that he asked his two middle-school-aged children to quietly play in another room so that he could work. The siblings peacefully played a board game together for 20 minutes, at which point they began yelling at each other about whether or not a rule applied to a particular move. The father entered the room and said, "All you two ever do is fight!" He scolded and punished them for disobeying his request that they be quiet by taking away their portable music players (devices they prized). The father only paid attention to their negative behavior and disregarded his children's cooperative and productive behavior, which occurred for a much greater length of time. It was a missed opportunity to reinforce prosocial behavior. The attention given to the fighting reinforces the problematic behavior by giving it attention (i.e., parental investment is rewarding), and by framing the relationship as one that is inherently flawed, a perspective the children are likely to adopt (e.g., "We always fight," "We are foes").

Second, as can be observed in this case, a negativity focus is usually accompanied by an extreme and rigid language that both overstates and oversimplifies behavior, such as *always* and *never* (e.g., "You two always fight," "You never share," "You bicker all the time"). This language blinds parents and children to positive sibling moments. It only sees siblings as enemies and fails to recognize them as humans who engage in conflict but who also have good moments. It distorts perspectives of attributed intent by providing a negative lens through which behavior is observed. A brother who is seen as an enemy will be viewed with suspicion, perhaps misunderstood as sarcastic when he gives his sister a compliment. The brother's intent is more likely to be considered genuine when a more holistic view is ascribed to the relationship, one in which the brother and sister both get along and disagree.

## Task Strategies for Focus on Negativity

Interventions to address a focus on negativity involve formulating tasks that redirect attention to positive encounters, relax rigidly defining language to promote more holistic views of sibling relationships, and positively reinforce prosocial behaviors. Acknowledging and reinforcing prosocial interactions promotes increased positivity because it feels good. By comparison, negativity feels bad and discourages motivation to invest in the sibling relationship in productive ways. Siblings cast as enemies will be less likely to seek each other out for fun or support. If the father in the case presented above had instead focused on and reinforced the positive behavior (e.g., "I am so pleased with you boys and how well you play together, even when you disagree sometimes. You really are great siblings!"), the siblings would feel better about spending future time together and the relationship in general.

Ideally, parents will acknowledge and reinforce positive behaviors at the time they occur. However, parents also need strategies for handling misbehavior when it occurs and many parents struggle to identify positive behaviors to reinforce when their children are in the midst of bad ones. In some cases, positive interactions may be few and far between, leaving parents with few opportunities to attend to. Practitioners can educate parents about prosocial behaviors and how to set up positive moments during conflicts. These can first be set up as in-session tasks, rehearsed, and then formulated as tasks to be implemented between sessions. Many behavior management approaches are available for parents to implement and many offer comparable strategies. Similarly, I offer a five-step Positive Behavior Approach (PBA) for parents to implement to move from rewarding negative to reinforcing positive behaviors. The actions put forth are not new but are organized in a straightforward and easy-to-use way. While this approach is most effective with younger children, it can be used with adolescents with some modifications regarding rewards and behaviors. The five steps are outlined here, followed by a brief description of each. Each step includes an example that illustrates its implementation.

## The Positive Behavior Approach

1. Clearly articulate expectations for behavior.
2. Calmly put a stop to the bad behavior.
3. Remind children of expected behavior (or have them generate it).
4. Have children implement expected behavior.
5. Reinforce positive behavior.

### *Clearly articulate expectations for behavior*

Too often, parents mistakenly believe that their children know how to be well behaved regardless of the situation. Clearly explaining or reestablishing rules for expected behavior is beneficial as it provides children with guidelines about how to act that are situation specific. Because they are overtly stated as behaviors, they can be easily reinforced. Moreover, the rules can be referred to when children misbehave (e.g., "Remember what the rules are?"), giving children an opportunity to self-correct and choose behaviors that can be rewarded.

A brother (age 7) and sister (age 5) frequently fought over sharing toys. The moment one child showed interest in a toy, the other demanded to play with it. To address this situation the practitioner worked with the mother to set up a task in which she explained rules for sharing toys. Before they were allowed into the toy room, the mother sat down with the siblings and explained rules for sharing that included the following:

- Politely asking the sibling for the toy, which must be stated as, "May I please have the toy?"
- The sibling can respond with "Yes" or "I'll give it to you in a few minutes."
- If the sibling says, "Yes" then the child is to say "Thank you." (Mother is to immediately give big praise to both behaviors, particularly to the child who shared.)
- If the sibling says, "I'll give it to you in a few minutes," then the child will find another toy to play with and will ask mommy to set the timer. (Mother will praise the behavior of finding another toy.)
- Each child was allowed 5 minutes with a toy and then is expected to give it to the other when the timer rang.

Because of the children's young ages, a simple but specific verbal statement for asking to play with the toy was given. This was to avoid confusion over more aggressive variations such as "Please let me have the toy" or "Give me the toy, please." It is important for the mother to be present to observe, guide, and immediately reinforce behaviors during initial implementations. Once the behavior appears to be mastered then it can be applied when the mother is not present but with modifications (e.g., a child setting the timer).

### *Calmly put a stop to the bad behavior*

When children do not follow the rules and resort to aggressive tactics, the parent should firmly but calmly demand that the misbehavior stop. Parents are not to yell, lecture, punish, or call much attention to the bad behavior, all of which can be reinforcing. A simple statement can be used such as "No! That is not the behavior I expect from you". Parents must use a tone and facial expression that conveys that they are serious. When children persist with misbehavior or protest inappropriately, parents can then offer a choice between the expected behavior or continuing the misbehavior and receiving a negative consequence. To continue the example of the siblings learning to share toys, the mother can say, "No! That is not the behavior I expect from you. You can either continue to grab and whine and not be allowed to play with the toy today at all, or you can ask politely and have it in 5 minutes." If the child chooses the negative behavior the parent must follow through on the consequence.

### *Remind children of expected behavior (or have them generate it)*

As illustrated in the case example, defiant children should be reminded of the expectations for behavior discussed in step #1. The parent can either tell the child directly (e.g., "Ask politely.") or prompt the child to recall it (e.g., "What was the rule for asking for a toy?"). All situations cannot be anticipated and often behavioral rules were not established prior to the occurrence of unwanted behavior. In such situations, parents can collaborate with children to identify rules. For example, an 8-year-old boy accidently tripped over his sister's foot while walking through a mall, and angrily retaliated by punching her in the arm. Using the steps of the PBA, the father immediately told his son that his punching was unacceptable and then asked him to identify a better behavior to be implemented when such situations occur. The boy struggled but eventually offered that he could have asked if the trip was purposeful or an accident and then said, "It's OK, accidents happen." The father praised his son for identifying a positive action and announced that this will be the new rule when the siblings accidentally make unwanted contact with each other.

### *Have children implement expected behavior*

Once children have been reminded of the expected behavior, it is necessary to have them implement it. Parents must take care to avoid believing that because children are able to verbalize expected conduct, they understand how to put it into practice. Observing actual implementation provides opportunities to further discuss or modify expectations as needed. More importantly, having children implement expectations enables parents to positively reinforce (e.g., praise) good behavior.

To continue with the sharing example, the daughter was reminded of the "sharing rule" of politely asking and then instructed to carry it out. The girl then politely asked her brother for the toy, and her mother immediately and exuberantly praised her daughter. The daughter smiled, full of pride for successfully enacting a desired behavior. Whether or not the brother agreed to share at the moment was irrelevant. The immediate objective was to help the daughter learn a new behavior without inadvertently rewarding a negative one.

Parents will occasionally meet and should expect child resistance to trying out new behaviors. For example, if the daughter had refused to employ the new behavior and instead demanded the toy, continued grabbing for it, or had a "temper tantrum," the mother would simply need to repeat steps #2 through #4, calmly demanding the negative behavior stop, reminding of expected conduct, and instructing her to implement it. As described earlier, a choice that includes a negative consequence may be needed to coax the child to implement the new behavior. Sometimes children become so worked up that they take a firm stand against following their parents' directives, such as when they are hungry, overtired, or not feeling well. At these times parents should halt attempts to have the child carry out new behaviors and remove them from the situation. Parents should not yell, threaten, or engage the child in discussion about the incident, but simply tell them that they can try out new behaviors such as sharing at another time when they are more ready. The steps may need to be employed a number of times before the new behavior is integrated into the child's skill set. Children may sporadically repeat the bad behavior after a long period of employing the positive one. Parents should not be tempted to express frustration in comments such as, "Haven't we been through this before?" but rather repeat the steps of the positive behavior model.

Resistance to trying out new behaviors typically subsides once children have experienced rewards for doing so on a number of prior occasions. In fact, once established as a consistent method of discipline, parents frequently only need to say "Try it again" when a negative behavior occurs in lieu of going through all the steps. For example, a few weeks after trying out the new behavior, the daughter again attempted to grab a toy from her brother's hands. Because the approach had been carried out previously, the mother only needed to say, "Try it again." The daughter stopped grabbing and asked her brother politely for the toy. The mother praised her implementation.

### *Reinforce positive behavior*

The final step of the five-step positive approach involves positively reinforcing the planned good behavior directly after the children implement them. Positive reinforcement can take multiple forms, including verbal praise, stickers on a behavioral modification chart, and increases in privileges (e.g., adding 30 minutes to television watching time). A big deal should be made out of good behavior the first few times it is done. For example, verbal praise should be enthusiastic and accompanied with high fives (with younger children), and adding stickers to charts or increasing privileges should include energetic verbal praise. Children's first attempts at new behaviors may be clumsy, but should be rewarded nonetheless. Using Skinner's behavioral principle of "shaping," approximations of wanted behavior are initially positively reinforced and only then those attempts that are more accurate than prior ones are rewarded (Thomas, 2004). The child incrementally learns how to refine the expected behavior. Positive reinforcement should be done immediately after the child has implemented the desired behavior. Parents should also be specific in their feedback (e.g., "I like the way you said 'thank you' when he gave you his toy!").

Positive reinforcement should be implemented for at least the first 5–10 times the newly planned expected behavior is successfully implemented. After that, intermittent reinforcement is recommended. Research has demonstrated the efficacy of initial continuous reinforcement followed by tapering rewards (e.g.,

Tucker, Sigafoos, & Bushell, 1998). Once the behavior becomes part of the child's skill set, parents need no longer reinforce it and can instead focus on developing additional prosocial skills.

In sum, a focus on negativity assessment directs practitioners to help parents and children refocus attention from destructive encounters to positive ones. This transition frequently requires education about parenting strategies that promote positivity and prosocial behavior. Practitioners and parents can utilize Kramer's prosocial behavior list presented toward the start of this chapter to target tasks to move siblings toward more positive relationships. Refocusing to positive interactions requires helping parents minimize attention given to negative behaviors, creating good behavior rules prior to sibling interaction, and giving children opportunities to retry efforts to implement expected behavior.

## CONCLUSION

This chapter provided sibling aggression intervention strategies framed by five common family dynamics that exacerbate it. Although each family dynamic may serve to individually influence sibling relationships, aggression between brothers and sisters is often supported by multiple processes. All or any combination of the presented FFD may be present in a sibling aggression case. As such, selection of task strategies may reflect multiple dynamics that have been identified during assessment. The FFD are offered as guiding frameworks and not as rigid prescriptions. They also do not cover the full range of considerations that emerge in sibling aggression cases. Enhancing sibling positivity was presented as a central treatment objective of the two-pronged approach put forth in this book. The PBA was introduced as a model for promoting sibling support while stopping negativity and aggression. Case studies for each of the FFD will be presented in the next chapter. Each will also include task menus and illustrations of the task planning and implementation process, the central problem-solving sequence of task-centered practice.

# 7

# Task Menus: The Five Family Dynamics

In recent years there has been a greater emphasis on action-oriented methods in the social service professions (Reid, 1997). These approaches make use of tasks, usually carried out by clients. There has been increasing recognition of the power of clients taking direct action to address their problems through clearly articulated tasks (Burns & Nolen-Hoeksma, 1992), and the use of between-session activities (e.g., "homework") is becoming more widespread across a wide range of psychotherapeutic treatment modalities (Ronan & Kazantzis, 2006). Task planning and implementation are the central problem-solving mechanisms in task-centered practice; however, tasks can be used to augment practically all helping approaches (Reid, 2000). Although clients and practitioners typically develop tasks together, having a list of suggested actions to address specific problems can be a helpful resource. Reid (2000) offered a compilation of task suggestions for a wide array of psychosocial problems called "task planners." Formulated largely from the literature and practitioner expertise, each task planner provides a description of an individual problem, referencing the literature used to formulate an understanding of the problem and task suggestions, and then lists client and practitioner tasks in what are called "task menus."

This chapter offers task menus for the Five Family Dynamics (FFD) presented in the previous chapter. They are intended to be used with the Task-Centered Sibling Aggression (TCSA) treatment approach, and provide an added resource. Because the dynamics involve varied considerations, multiple task menus appear under some of the FFDs. For example, sibling aggression tied to direct comparison may be a function of complementary labeling, shared niches, or both. Separate task menus are provided for each.

## USING THE TASK MENUS

In task-centered practice, clients are actively involved in defining solutions to their own problems and tasks are not assigned or given as "homework." Task menus should be utilized as guides and not rigid prescriptions to be imposed upon clients. They should be offered as a list of possibilities for clients to consider and evaluate in relation to their situations. The role of the practitioner is to facilitate client problem-solving efforts and to assist in the identification of actions that clients may have not thought of or initially understood. Practitioners provide education, sharing information from the literature and professional experiences.

The art of practice is to balance practitioner input with client self-determination. Task menus can aid this process by allowing clients to consider a range of actions that do not come directly from the practitioner. That is, clients may be more open to looking through a task menu than accepting direct practitioner input, particularly in cases where clients are distrustful of authority (e.g., involuntary clients).

Ultimately, clients are responsible for implementing tasks and provision of task planners organizes the problem-solving process, emphasizing that change is to be brought about through client action (Reid, 2000). Again, task menus are meant to supplement client and practitioner problem-solving ideas. Task menus can be viewed as a "jumping off" point and discussion of actions may generate new ideas. They are not intended as complete intervention programs. Discoveries of new actions that work can be added to the task menu—which can then be utilized with subsequent cases. Task menu suggestions should be modified to individual client circumstances. For an in-depth review of task planners, see Reid (2000) and Naleppa and Reid (2003).

This chapter focuses the task menu component of task planners because in-depth problem descriptions culled from the scholarly literature and practice experience were already provided in the previous chapter. These included detailed descriptions of assessment and task strategy considerations. The following task menus repeat many of the actions discussed in the previous chapter but in list form, providing quick and simple access to suggested treatment actions. That said, I highly recommend using the task menus *after* Chapter 6 is read, which provides an in-depth explanation of the family dynamics that exacerbate and support sibling aggression, and the strategies put forth to address them. Without this background, the task menus may not make sense, may suggest more client than practitioner responsibility, and risk being implemented too mechanically and without a full understanding of the dynamic processes that these task strategies are meant to address. In addition, Chapter 6 also integrates sporadic cross-cultural considerations that are only sparingly included in the following task menus. Finally, for the most part, the task menus are intended for cases of destructive conflict and violence, and not serious abuse. Treatment of unidirectional abuse (i.e., physical, sexual, psychological) requires careful choices regarding working with the family together or separately. For example, in cases of ongoing and severe abuse, conjoint sibling sessions are usually avoided to protect the victim from further maltreatment (Caffaro, 2011). That said, the dynamics that support conflict and violence also support abuse. Practitioners should consider and make appropriate use of the strategies put forth in the following task menus when treating sibling abuse.

## THE TASK MENU IN DETAIL

The task menu is comprised of three components: tasks, elaboration, and practitioner role. A fourth component, the provision of an example, is occasionally included to add clarity by illustrating the use of particularly complex tasks.

Similarly, special "notes" are provided to further explicate ideas. Tasks constitute the main component. Elaboration and practitioner role appear as occasional subheadings that provide additional information to help guide implementation of a specific task.

## Tasks

Considerable attention has been given to tasks in Chapter 4. Tasks represent the actions to be taken to ameliorate psychosocial problems as defined by clients in collaboration with practitioners. The tasks listed under this task menu heading are intended for clients. In the context of the FFD task planners, clients are family members. Information about tasks intended for particular family members is noted in brackets following the task—for example, [parent task] or [child task]. Tasks tagged with [sibling task] are meant to be carried out by siblings with each other, as interactional activities. Finally, the parent refers to a range of adult caretakers of children (e.g., guardians, grandparents).

Most tasks presented here are intended to be carried out between sessions, as home tasks. However, the term "session task" is used for activities that practitioners and families may find helpful to implement or initiate during the treatment meeting. Some tasks can be done either in session or as home tasks (i.e., carried out between sessions) and are marked as [family task; session task]. That said, it is recommended that where possible, almost all tasks be tried out during session using rehearsal, role play, or enactments to ensure proper understandings of implementation.

## Elaboration

Tasks are stated at varying levels of abstraction and complexity. Elaborations are provided to offer greater specificity and details about how to implement tasks, particularly those that are broadly stated. For example, the task, "Parent will create rules for shared sibling time" is followed with an elaboration that provides examples of rules—that is, "For example, siblings will alternate selecting the television show to be watched. A chart to document who selected last will be maintained by the parent."

## Practitioner Role

This subheading refers to practitioner tasks and provides information regarding how to assist client implementation of in-session activities and task implementation. Most client tasks are straightforward and do not require the practitioner's assistance. For others, the practitioner's role is clear and does not require a special note using this subheading. This subheading is only included when tasks include practitioner participation or assistance. For example, an important practitioner role is educating clients about dynamics that have been observed and likely linked to the target problem. A practitioner who observes triangulation involving an aggressive child may need to explain this family systems concept in order for families to recognize the utility of a task that asks them to modify side-taking patterns.

It is important to note that clients bring to treatment their own perspectives of problems and possible solutions. All the FFDs represent indirect ways in which sibling aggression is supported by family interaction, and will challenge clients with new ways of viewing the problem. For example, parents may initially see sibling aggression as being located within a problem child and want treatment to focus on helping the child become better behaved. They may not recognize how their favoring of one child over others is contributing to the problem child's aggression. Practitioners typically must provide information about family processes and links to problems. Clients expect their practitioners to be experts and appreciate when knowledge is shared. Practitioner provision of education identified the approach by clients who have utilized task-centered sibling aggression treatment as a particularly beneficial aspect of the approach (Caspi, 2008).

## TASK MENUS FOR THE FFDs

It is important to note that these task menus emphasize *client* tasks, and should be shared with clients to aid task selection. Practitioner actions are considered in depth throughout this book and should be done in conjunction with client task planning. For example, practitioners may utilize tracking strategies to identify transactional sequences for the purpose of restructuring alliances within families. Discussions of alliances and patterns that support sibling aggression include client participation in the formulation of tasks to address problematic structures. Practitioners can refer to actions provided under *practitioner role* in the task menus. Practitioner role provides practitioner actions (usually during sessions) to support client tasks. These are to be used in addition to family and sibling intervention techniques offered in previous chapters. Finally, some tasks are repeated under multiple task menus because of overlap in the dynamics and of the utility of particular actions to address sibling concerns.

An outline of the task menus put forth to address the FFD that supports sibling aggression is offered in Figure 7.1.

### The Task Menus

#### *FFD 1: Parental differential treatment (PDT) and favoritism*

The family dynamic of PDT and favoritism suggests a range of tasks. In these cases, altering parent–child relationships and coalitions should lessen or stop sibling aggression. Although the sibling relationship is addressed indirectly (i.e., through parent–child relationships), the connection between sibling aggression and parental favoritism/differential treatment should be made explicit.

FIGURE 7.1 Task menus for sibling aggression.

**FFD 1 - Parental Differential Treatment and Favoritism**

*Task Menu: PDT and Favoritism*

**FFD 2 - Direct Comparison: Complementary Labeling and Niches**

*Task Menu: Complementary Labeling*

*Task Menu: Shared Niches*

**FFD 3 - Parental Support for Aggressive Behavior**

*Task Menu: Parental Support for Aggressive Behavior*

**FFD 4 - Ineffective Supervision**

*Task Menu: Ineffective Supervision- Increased Parental Involvement*

*Task Menu: Ineffective Supervision- Structuring Autonomous Sibling Time*

*Task Menu: Sibling Caretaking*

**FFD 5 - Focus on Negativity**

*Task Menu: Focus on Negativity*

Observations of differential treatment and claims of injustice typically emerge during enactments and during tracking of family interactional sequences, as well as during the problem identification step of TCSA. PDT and favoritism are similar but distinct concepts with overlapping family dynamics and intervention considerations. Frequently, PDT and favoritism are simultaneously present in families with sibling aggression. Both require explicitly raising of the observed dynamic (i.e., PDT and/or favoritism) using facilitative confrontation. For example, when the practitioner observes a parent dismiss a child's claim of injustice during a treatment session, the practitioner should call attention to the interaction. Task menus for PDT and favoritism and its variations are offered here.

### *Task menu: PDT and favoritism*

1. **Express perception of unfairness in a productive way [child task]**
   *Elaboration*: For example, in a calm voice and when composed. Ask parents to identify a good time to schedule a talk about something important and express it at that meeting. Take ownership for the perspective (e.g., "I feel") rather than taking an accusatory position (e.g., "You are unfair"). [Family task] Identify and agree upon a signal to note perceived favoritism when it is occurring.

2. **Acknowledge child's claim of injustice [parent task]**

   *Elaboration*: Repeat the child's claim back in a serious manner. Ask the child to tell you more about his or her perception. Work with the child to schedule a meeting to seriously explore issue. Use validation and empathy.

   *Practitioner role*: Help parents learn to appreciate their children's differing perspectives, even when they do not agree with them. Education about the skills of validating perceptions and putting themselves "in child's shoes" to build empathy to increase affective connections.

3. **Record parental treatment to distinguish PDT and favoritism [family task]**

   *Elaboration*: A chart can be created and placed in public location (e.g., refrigerator) to record aspects of parenting of behavior that can include, as examples, time spent with each child, amount of financial resources provided, affection pronouncements, privileges, and side-taking, depending upon the child's claims of unfair treatment.

   *Practitioner role*: Chart can be created with practitioner's assistance as a session task.

4. **Clarify what children mean by "favoritism" or "unfair" (e.g., uneven attention, warmth, privileges) [done in session]**

   *Elaboration*: Children are frequently unable to verbalize what it is that parents do that make them feel that favoritism is occurring. Asking about side-taking between members and noting it during exploration of interactional sequences may reveal patterns that suggest outsider status to children—which may be interpreted as favoritism.

   *Practitioner role*: Help family make distinction between differential treatment and perceived favoritism. Raise the impracticality of same treatment and attempt to frame parenting as giving each child what they need, which means that sometimes one child will get more than others.

5. **Reflect on own behaviors and feelings [parent task]**

   *Elaboration*: Actively engage in honest appraisals of how you feel about your children and how you treat them differently. Directly after a child makes a claim of injustice, write down in a journal what you did that triggered that accusation.

   *Practitioner role*: Practitioners may suggest scheduling separate meetings with parents to aid in self-appraisal activities. This may include helping parents understand how their relationships with their spouses, birth order, gender and other considerations influence their notions about their children. In addition, parents issues with PDT or favoritism with their own siblings, particularly when growing up, may be explored as a way to address the influence of multigenerational concerns.

6. **Find and engage in positive activities and interaction with child making the claim of injustice [parent task]**

   *Elaboration*: Spend time alone together in an activity the child enjoys. Compliment the child on moments when the child engages in good behavior.

   *Practitioner role*: Encourage parents to recognize and acknowledge positive behavior during sessions. For example, if playing a game together, make note of when parents are more critical of or positive with one child than another.

7. **Alter side-taking response [parent task]**

   *Elaboration*: Rather than automatically siding with the usual child, do something different—for example, side with outsider child, stay out of sibling disagreement, tell children they have valid points and to sort out disagreement together.

   *Practitioner role*: Help parents identify alternate responses to side-taking by highlighting repeating sequences of interaction noted during enactments. Confronting side-taking when it is observed helps parents think about what they could do differently at the time.

8. **Review sequences of interactions related to sibling conflict and identify different behaviors to employ to alter sequence [family task; session task]**

   *Elaboration*: If it is identified that a parent takes one child's side over another during a sibling conflict, the parent may choose to side with the disfavored child as a task (*Note*: a restructuring task) or select to remain neutral and allow the siblings to problem solve on their own.

   *Practitioner role*: Revisit identified transactional sequences that emerged during problem identification stage. Assist in providing ideas for altering sequences.

9. **Support sibling in claims of mistreatment [favored child task] [Related parent task: Prohibit expressions of glee or boasting and promote sibling support]**

   *Elaboration*: Favored children sometimes demonstrate glee during disfavored children's protests, even boasting of their preferred position. Create rule for behavior (see the PBA in Chapter 6). For example, the favored child could say, "I am sorry if this seems unfair. I'll help you talk to Mom and Dad."

10. **Select behavior(s) from Kramer's (2011) list of essential competencies for promoting prosocial sibling behavior (in Chapter 6) [sibling tasks]**

    *Elaboration*: Items from this list can be utilized as expected rules using the PBA outlined in Chapter 6.

    *Practitioner role*: Share the list with the family and use to guide mutual formulation of tasks.

### *FFD 2: Direct comparison—Complementary labeling and niches*

As already discussed in some length, sibling aggression is exacerbated by direct comparison by parents, by the siblings themselves, and by others (e.g., teachers, coaches, grandparents). Direct comparison was organized into two distinct types of dynamics. The first is complementary labeling that involves applying labels to children that usually reflect opposite traits. The second is niche partitioning, for which a separate task menu is offered.

***Task menu: Complementary labeling*** Complementary labels emerge from direct comparison and are problematic for sibling relationships. Labels are confining, defining, and foster competition. They both shape one's internal sense of self and provide the lens for how behavior is interpreted by others. Labels influence how family members are positioned in terms of relationship quality, power, and potential favoritism. Labels often carry different values for parents, with some more favored than others. Of particular concern for the sibling relationship is the complementary labeling of good and bad (Schacter, 1985).

Practitioner interventions usually entail facilitative confrontation to help families stop sibling comparisons, and cognitive reconstruction that involves altering the way children are perceived and distorted by labels. Focusing on discrete acts rather than global labels, reframing designations, and evaluating the intent of behavior are practitioner actions that can change interpretations of sibling behavior. Finally, practitioners must be careful not to model problematic labeling when formulating formal diagnoses, which carry the same problems of labeling in general.

1. **Stop using labels [family task]**

   *Elaboration*: The family agrees to refrain from describing each other using labels. When siblings are young, this is a parental task. This task involves increased self-awareness. A chart can be kept in which the use of labels is marked in order to raise self-awareness about using labels. An interactive task can be devised so that family members call attention to each other's use of labels. Tasks that involve refraining from a behavior are most effective when a substitute positive action is available. The third task in this menu, *focus on discrete behavior*, represents that substitution for labeling.

   *Practitioner role*: Uses facilitative confrontation to bring comparative labeling to the family's attention. Uses education to explain how labeling is problematic.

2. **Don't compare siblings**

   *Elaboration*: The family agrees to refrain from making sibling comparisons and using siblings to shape how personality is defined for each child. When siblings are young, this is a parental task. This task also involves increased self-awareness. A chart can be kept in which comparative statements are marked in order to raise self-awareness. An interactive task can be devised so that family members call attention to each other's use of comparison. Tasks that involve refraining from a behavior are most effective when a substitute positive action is available. The third task in this menu, *focus on discrete behavior*, represents that substitution for labeling.

*Practitioner role*: Use facilitative confrontation to bring comparative labeling to the family's attention. Explain how labeling is problematic and identify alternative substitute behaviors.

3. **Focus on discrete behavior [family task]**

   *Elaboration*: Individuals make note of behaviors directly after they occur in lieu of labels. For example, if a child is being silly the parent can say, "You are *acting* so silly" rather than using the label, "You *are* silly." Realistic differences can be noted. For example, if one child is usually more silly than a sibling, the child may be described as "often silly." The comparison "more silly" should be avoided as it is sibling comparison that may imply social status differences within the family.

   *Practitioner role*: Educate about skills of focusing on discrete behavior and avoiding comparison.

4. **Keep journal of actual behavior [parent task]**

   *Elaboration*: Labels distort perceptions of behavior. To promote accuracy and to separate labels from behavior, parents record the actual behavior that occurred. This is particularly useful with good–bad complementary labeling. All behaviors, both good and bad, should be objectively recorded without interpretations or assumptions of intent. For example, "Was rebellious" represents an interpretation and intent assumption, whereas "Threw homework book on the ground" describes the action without suggesting intent. Similarly, recording a child saying "Please pass the salt" to a sibling objectively describes the behavior, whereas "Was polite" is an interpretation (e.g., may have a different meaning in the sibling relationship). Older children can keep journals as well.

   *Practitioner role*: Assist in formulating structure for journals.

5. **Reframe labels to reflect positive traits [family task]**

   *Elaboration*: To assist with cognitively reconstructing perceptions of sibling behavior, select different designations that positively recast the original label. Consider and list alternative descriptions. New positive labeling should minimize polar opposite descriptions of siblings.

   *Practitioner role*: Educate about reframing, explaining its use as a step to halt negative labeling and ultimately stop using global labels altogether. Assist family in considering alternative descriptions. Model the use of reframing, drawing attention to reframes by making them explicit.

6. **Evaluate intent to formulate neutral or positive attributions [family or sibling task]**

   *Elaboration*: False and negative intent is commonly ascribed to behaviors exhibited in conflictual relationships. For example, the act of complimenting in a negative relationship may be interpreted as hostile or manipulative, even when the one complimenting was trying to be genuine. Aggressive children tend to ascribe hostile motivations to others, particularly when they feel threatened (Orobio de Castro, Slot, Bosch, Koops, & Veerman, 2003). Attributional retraining in which members are taught to infer nonhostile intent to ambiguous provocations may be effective (Hudley & Graham, 1993). Automatic interpretations of motive are internally challenged. Family members check for the true intent of behaviors (i.e., what a person meant to do). Match attributions of intent to verbal and nonverbal cues such as facial expressions, and assume accidental behavior when there is not enough information to determine intentionality (e.g., toy broken by sibling could be hostile or accidental).

   *Practitioner role*: During session, actively challenge attributions of negative motives. Educate about and model "checking in" to evaluate intentions of behavior (e.g., "Is that what you meant to do?").

   *Example*: Brothers Joel and Tyrone had a playful snowball fight that turned into an angry encounter with the intent to harm each other. The next day, Joel picked up snow and started packing a snowball. Although Joel seemed to be looking for a nonhuman target (e.g., scouting street signs and trees), Tyrone immediately assumed that Joel was being aggressive toward him. When the practitioner asked, "Did you intend on throwing the ball at Tyrone?" Joel expressed that he did not want to get into another fight with his brother and was honestly planning on throwing it at a tree. Joel's behavior was prosocial and intended to support the sibling relationship rather than harm it. However, his intent was falsely attributed. After some discussion in a treatment session, Tyrone and Joel decided to check with each other about intent. Each said they were committed to being honest. Although the boys agreed with the practitioner's assertion that it was easier said than done (to be honest in the heat of conflict), they all felt it was better to try out the task.

7. **Select behavior(s) from Kramer's (2011) list of essential competencies for promoting prosocial sibling behavior (in Chapter 6) [sibling tasks]**

   *Elaboration*: Items from this list can be utilized to assist sibling's selection of prosocial interactional behaviors that bypass understandings distorted by labels.

   *Practitioner role*: Share the list with the family and use it to guide mutual formulation of tasks.

***Task menu: Shared niches*** Siblings compete less directly for parental resources when they diverge in their interests, activities, and areas of expertise—that is, when they occupy different niches. Competition for resources often includes aggressive tactics and can escalate to violence. When siblings share niches they must compete directly to outdo each other to gain more favorable positions, to achieve greater rewards (e.g., parental investment or favor).

Practitioner assessment of shared niches by siblings suggests attending to how competition within niches is related to aggression, and how it is managed by parents. When possible, diversification of interests is a useful strategy for minimizing competition, direct comparison, and aggressive tactics. Diversification may require selecting different niches, modifying activities within shared niches, or engaging in niches in separate locations. Expanding niche fields and addressing niches values as they relate to PDT, favoritism, and parent–child coalitions also represent sibling aggression treatment strategies. Practitioner exploration of niches with families includes asking and evaluating the positives and negatives of shared niches, about the possibility of one or more of the children selecting different niches, and about diverging within the same niche. Practitioners may raise cultural, ethnic, and gender issues that influence niche selection.

1. **Identify positive and negative aspects of remaining in shared niche from both personal and relational perspectives [family session task]**

   *Elaboration*: Each family member provides perspectives on benefits and drawbacks of siblings sharing a niche. Responses can be noted on a whiteboard or chart.

   *Practitioner role*: Practitioner facilitates exploration of payoff for remaining in niche, its negative consequences, and whether one or more siblings trying out new areas for possible niche development may reduce competition and aggression.

*The following tasks are for when it is decided that siblings should no longer share a niche:*

2. **Select new area of interest that is different from sibling's area of expertise**

   *Elaboration*: Child shares ideas about alternative activities they would like to try.

   *Practitioner role*: Evaluating feasibility of activities for ongoing niche development (e.g., available resources, geography, parental support).

3. **Evaluate personal investment in children's niches and openness to investing in siblings engaging in different activities [parent task]**

   *Elaboration*: The purpose of this task is to consider expansion of niche fields. This task involves self-reflection that may be aided through journal keeping or utilizing a rating scale to make investment distinctions (e.g., 0 = low excitement; 10 = high excitement). For example, a range of potential niche interests may be raised and each evaluated in regard to parental investment. Areas that receive low ratings by parents but high enthusiasm by children can be discussed in regard to advantages and drawbacks to supporting niches.

*Practitioner role*: Explain concept of niche fields and benefits of supporting a wider range of niche choices. Assists parents in weighing the benefits of allowing children to pursue other interests. This discussion is often done in meetings with the parents that do not include the children.

*The following tasks are for when it is decided that siblings should continue in the shared niche:*

4. **Select new activities/role within the shared niche**

   *Elaboration*: Each child discusses how they can be unique within the same niche. For example, two children who both play basketball may decide that one child will focus on defense while the other will develop herself as a shooter. Three brothers who all do well at soccer decide that they will select different positions rather than all try to be a midfielder. One selected the position of forward, the second remained at midfield, and the third became a defender. This task frequently requires the support of coaches, instructors, and others involved in the child's niche activity.

5. **Identify ways for children to engage in same area of expertise while minimizing shared time [family task; can be done as a session task to identify external tasks]**

   *Elaboration*: Family identifies ways to keep siblings within a shared niche but in separate spaces. This includes finding differing locations, instructors, coaches, and days/times for children to engage in niche activities. For example, parents of two children who are both doing martial arts place the siblings in separate karate schools. The purpose is to lessen direct comparison and direct competition.

   *Note*: Less shared time provides less opportunity for conflict but risks sibling disengagement. Tasks to assist the development of sibling support and prosocial skills should be paired with this task (e.g., tasks 8–10).

6. **Focus on individual behaviors rather than global definitions of talent and identity [family task]**

   *Elaboration*: Strong niche identification processes may be lessened by focusing on behavior rather than labels associated with niches (e.g., "the basketball player" and "the pianist"). A focus on behaviors enables multiple children to occupy the same niche without one being designated as the best or the winner. Examples of statements that emphasize behavior are, [For the basketball players] "You rebounded particularly well today! And you (another sibling), that was a great pass to win the game!" Similarly, if a child creates a painting, the parent should praise the child for being a talented painter rather than describing the child as "my artist."

7. **Identify alternative sources for rewards for niche involvement [child tasks]**

   *Elaboration*: An alternative to diversifying child interests within shared niches is to diversify the reward sources. Rewards (e.g., praise, notoriety, recognition) can come from multiple places (e.g., coaches, grandparents, older siblings), in addition to parents. Direct competition for parent resources and favor may be lessened by identifying alternative reward sources.

   *Practitioner role*: Separate meetings with children (without parents) may be necessary to raise the issue of low parental investment and excitement about niche choices. Moreover, discussion can focus on how siblings fight *solely* for parental rewards (e.g., "to be the best") and how alternative sources may help bolster niche success while minimizing direct competition. This discussion should lead to tasks that include overt contact with alternative sources about provision of support.

   *Note*: A significant reward source relates to feeling good about oneself (e.g., higher self-esteem, self-confidence) for outperforming a sibling. Tasks that help siblings seek alternate sources for comparison and pride (e.g., peers) can help to minimize competition with each other. These tasks can be paired with "siblings as teammate" activities, which are described next.

*The following tasks are related to building a "siblings as teammate" orientation, a change from "siblings as rivals." Although developing a teammate orientation is a recommended strategy for addressing most sibling aggression cases, it is particularly useful when working with siblings in shared niches. Teammate tasks are taken on by parents and children and aim to build sibling commitment and loyalty. Tasks involve assisting a cognitive shift from focusing on their own performance and needs to acting in ways that are best for the siblings as a system (i.e., "the team"). This may entail creating an "us against everyone else" perspective. Practitioners should anticipate resistance to joining with the rival. The mutual benefits of teaming and constructive competition should be discussed.*

8. **Create a loyalty contract [family task]**

   *Elaboration*: Family agrees to meet and draw up an agreement of responsibilities to protect and support siblings to promote a teammate orientation. The emphasis is responsibility to the team rather than to oneself. This can be related to professional athletes who must demonstrate team loyalty (e.g., one rarely hears a professional athlete say that they outperformed a teammate). The agreement will include consequences for negative behavior such as belittling, teasing, expressing glee at a sibling's misfortune, and open claims of superiority. Rewards are given for demonstrations of sibling loyalty.

*Note*: Parents must support sibling teaming and avoid behaviors that aid to sibling competition (e.g., cheering on one child to do better than the other, using statements such as, "Let the best man win."). Cheering on all siblings and praising teamwork is necessary. This task can be done in concert with the next as good sportship is an aspect of team loyalty.

*Practitioner role*: Attend to and raise family cultural values related to balancing familism and individualism. Help family draw upon cultural strengths for building loyalty or help deconstruct belief systems that impede connectedness.

9. **Engage in good sportship [child task]**

   *Elaboration*: Rules for competitive behavior are framed as good sportship. Rules include engaging in behaviors such as giving praise, "high fives," and support ("Don't worry, you'll get it next time!"). Such behaviors can be formulated as discrete tasks (e.g., "Will tell my sibling 'good job' each time he scores a point against me").

   *Note*: The sports metaphors of sportship and siblings as teammates are not intended to suggest that these tasks are reserved for athletic niches. Sibling aggression related to shared artistic, education, and other niches can benefit from prosocial behavior such as good sportship and sibling loyalty. Practitioners can draw upon Kramer's (2011) list of prosocial competencies to generate specific task ideas for building sibling support.

10. **Positively praise positive sibling interaction [parent task]**

   *Elaboration*: Parents look for and positively comment on positive behavior such as complimenting, "high fives," or giving pep talks to a sibling. Behavior modification boards can be utilized with younger children where recognition (e.g., stickers, check marks) is given for supporting a sibling.

   *Practitioner role*: Assist in focus on positive behavior and in the use of positive reinforcement techniques for both planned and spontaneous wanted behavior. For example, during a treatment meeting, a boy described a recent piano recital in which he made a mistake that cost him the competition. In response, his sister said, "That was a very hard piece. I make mistakes in it all the time. I thought you did really well considering you had to play it in front of a large audience." This spontaneous expression of loyalty and support was initially left unacknowledged by the parents until the practitioner called attention to it. A task was selected to listen for such statements, praise them, and then record them in a journal.

### *FFD 3: Parental support for aggressive behavior*

Aggressive behavior can be overtly or tacitly supported by parents in a number of ways. Overt support includes directly encouraging and assigning positive outcomes to violence (e.g., "It builds character"), and by supporting dominance themes (e.g., machismo, patriarchy). *Tacit* approval of aggression is conveyed through parental inaction in the face of sibling violence, modeling violence, and by becoming excited about portrayals of harmful aggression in the media. Both overt support and tacit approval convey a family culture that endorses violence. Practitioner interventions must confront approval for violence and assist the family in building a culture of peace and support. Assessment should include inquiry into client perceptions of violence and whether or not and when it is perceived as beneficial, benign, or problematic.

***Task menu: Parental support for aggressive behavior*** In this task menu, item 1 should be completed with the family during a treatment session and prior to selecting other tasks.

1. **Establish a "no violence" rule [session task with family]**

   *Elaboration*: This can be done as a formal contract that lists behaviors that should be prohibited. Behaviors should include no verbal assault (e.g., name calling, belittling, taking pleasure in others' failures), no physical assault (e.g., hitting, kicking, slapping, tackling), no relational aggression (e.g., spreading gossip, social exclusion), and obviously no sexual assault, including leering, teasing about body parts, and exposure to sexually explicit material. The contract should include consequences for violations and rewards for abiding by the agreement.

   *Note*: Parents must model the behaviors outlined in the contract, avoiding violence themselves. Parents can take on tasks to support each other and use prosocial conflict resolution behaviors. Aggressive behaviors between parents do not need to meet the level of abuse to consequentially model unwanted behavior. For example, name calling should be avoided and replaced with respectful problem-solving discourse.

   *Practitioner role*: Assist family in identifying violent behavior. Practitioners may need to provide education about the negative consequences of sibling violence to families that perceive it to be benign or even beneficial. Moreover, practitioners may need to highlight the ways in which sibling aggression has already been harmful to the families they are treating.

   *Note*: "Rough play" may be beneficial and a way that siblings can engage in physical affection in ways they perceive to be socially appropriate, and should not be prohibited in all cases. Rules for engaging in rough play can be included (e.g., immediately stopping when one wants to cause harm to another). Sibling relationships that are highly volatile and likely to immediately escalate from play to intent to harm should be prohibited from rough play entirely.

2. **Praise and positively reinforce conflict that abides by no violence contract [parent task]**

3. **Intervene to stop sibling conflicts when child disobeys no violence contract [parent task]**

   *Elaboration*: Parents stop sibling fighting by separating them. Parents provide structure for application of conflict resolution skills. Consequences for violations of no violence contract are applied [item 1].

   *Note*: Parents should not intervene in conflicts that do not involve negative aggression or those that breach the no violence rule.

   *Practitioner role*: Educate parents on strategies to immediately halt fighting (e.g., separating, reminding of prosocial alternatives and consequences).

4. **Restrain from participating in negative conflict [sibling task]**

   *Elaboration*: When angered or frustrated by a sibling, leave the immediate situation by going to another room. Avoid retaliating to provocations. Incorporate anger management strategies such as counting to 10 before responding, deep breathing, and dismissing verbal provocation as meaningless.

   *Practitioner role*: Educate about skills of restraint and anger management strategies.

5. **Engage in positive conflict resolution behavior [sibling tasks; first attempts should be done as session tasks]**

   *Elaboration*: Conflict resolution behaviors such as clarifying personal objectives, listening, being flexible, clarifying feelings, remaining focused on immediate disagreement (i.e., avoiding tangents involving other areas of resentment and conflict) can each be selected as individual tasks for implementation.

   *Note*: Parents reinforce implementation of these prosocial behaviors.

   *Practitioner role*: Provide education about conflict resolution steps and behaviors.

6. **Supervise children's exposure to violent media, with the goal of halting such exposure**

   *Elaboration*: Parents restrict access to violent media and promote nonviolent programs (e.g., movies, video games). Electronic parental controls can be utilized. Parents can participate in violent media engagement with tasks to explicitly discuss observed violence and its outcomes and links to reality.

   *Note*: When parents convey to their children at very young ages that viewing violence is problematic, children usually self-select to avoid violent media and consider it to be unappealing.

7. **Monitor own enthusiasm for violence in media [parent and sibling tasks]**

   *Elaboration*: To assist in the revisioning of violence from exciting, fun, and positive to a view that recognizes it as problematic, parents and children challenge themselves to reconsider the meaning of what they are watching. These can be guided by questions such as, "Why is this exciting?" "What messages might my behavior be sending my children?" "Does what we are watching convey the false reality that violence leads to positive outcomes?" A behavioral task for self-reflection is maintaining a journal.

   *Practitioner role*: Provide education about the consequences of building a pro-violence family culture through violent media engagement. Share and assist with adoption of cognitive self-awareness actions and activities.

8. **Actively engage in activities that support emotional self-discipline and self-control [sibling task]**

   *Elaboration*: Enrollment in martial arts programs, which typically emphasize self-discipline and violence avoidance. Keep on one's person a written promise of commitment to acting respectfully and nonviolently. Use cognitive tasks such as repeating phrase, "I will not retaliate" and "I will not hit others." Reward self (e.g., statements of praise) when overcome with impulse to engage in negative aggression.

   *Practitioner role*: Provide coaching and assistance for identifying self-control activities.

9. **Help your sibling recognize when he or she is losing control [sibling task]**

   *Elaboration*: A mutually executed task can be developed and agreed upon in session where a child can say to the other, "You are losing control." The child in control can also walk away from the other at times of emotional escalation. The siblings are asked to work together to prevent escalation.

   *Practitioner role*: Children may need education about how to detect facial and other behavioral cues about when and when not to interact with a sibling. In addition, the practitioner may help children become other-oriented rather than focused only on their own needs. For example, if a child tells his agitated (e.g., slamming closet doors, stomping feet) sibling to "Keep it down," conflict is likely to result. Children may need to be taught to avoid each other when agitated, or be other-oriented and show genuine concern for their well-being (e.g., "Are you OK? You seem really upset.").

10. **Select supportive and team-oriented behaviors**

    *Elaboration*: Select items 8–10 from the task menu "Shared Niches" to build a "siblings as teammates" orientation. Select tasks from Kramer's (2011) list of prosocial behaviors presented in the previous chapter.

### *FFD 4: Ineffective supervision*

As noted in the previous chapter, three distinct dynamics are associated with ineffective supervision of children: (1) parent overwhelmed by pragmatic demands (e.g., employment, domestic chores), (2) parent dysfunction that impedes ability to handle the demands of childcare (e.g., substance abuse, mental illness), and (3) willful neglect. All three dynamics commonly involve sibling caretaking. A fourth dynamic that does not involve sibling caretaking entails situations when children have great autonomy, such as afterschool time when parents are still at work and when parents allow siblings to spend lengths of time together without being present. This fourth dynamic often leads to boredom and self-governance, both of which exacerbate sibling aggression.

The first dynamic, parental stress, involves sibling caretaking that can be initiated deliberately or unplanned. Deliberate sibling caretaking entails formally placing one child in charge of the others, whereas unplanned arrangements emerge in the face of parental noninvolvement (i.e., physical or emotional). Unplanned sibling caretaking is also common in the second dynamic, parent dysfunction. Parent substance abuse and mental illness often result in the parentification of children, that is, where children take on adult responsibilities before they are emotionally prepared, including caretaking of parents and younger siblings. Parentification is generally considered to be debilitating. Unplanned sibling caretaking is frequently a feature of the third dynamic, willful neglect.

All four ineffective supervision dynamics require parents to take on tasks reflecting greater involvement with their children. Practitioners must attend to the use of siblings as caretakers and evaluate whether or not they were planned or unplanned, should be sustained or replaced with adult supervision. Decisions to sustain sibling caretaking usually involve tasks related to clarifying roles and establishing formal rules. Two task menus related to ineffective supervision are offered here. The first focuses on increasing parental involvement. Practitioners may need to take time out to provide education about the important role of parental supervision, particularly in cases of sibling hostility. The second focuses on managing sibling autonomy, and the third involves tasks aimed to strengthen sibling caretaking arrangements. Sibling caretaking is central to the functioning of many families and practitioners should avoid reflexive efforts to stop it. Assessment should include evaluation of whether or not it is supportive or debilitating to the functioning of the family and its individual members.

### *Task menu: Ineffective supervision—Increased parental involvement*

1. **Identify activities siblings can do during unsupervised time [family task]**
   *Elaboration*: Family collaboratively generates ideas to implement. These may include together activities such as completing a puzzle, playing a video game, chores, and building with blocks, as well as independent activities (e.g., homework, reading).

**2. Parents spend increased time with children [parent task]**

*Elaboration*: Identify specific times in which parents will be physically present with children. Mutually reviewing availability with a calendar may be necessary. Moving other obligations (e.g., work, yoga class) to make time for parent–child togetherness. Because there are different types of obstacles to increased parental involvement, task strategies for each are presented here:

*2a. When related to emotional issues*: (*Note*: Individual meetings with the practitioner and parent are recommended to facilitate task identification and selection to overcome emotional obstacles.) Identify feelings that underlie emotional disengagement (e.g., frustration, resentment, anxiety) and explore strategies to address them, such as cognitive behavioral methods (e.g., tracking and challenging internal dialogue, restructuring), keeping feeling journals, and identifying links to past experiences. Anxiety-reducing strategies such as deep breathing and identifying supports (e.g., friends) to assist during childcare occasions. Strategies may include incrementally increasing time spent with the children (e.g., first week 10 minutes, next week 20 minutes). Anxiety of being alone with children is often related to feeling at a loss for ways to control children. Provision of discipline tools for handling defiance, unruliness, and sibling conflict can be helpful strategies for reducing anxiety related to spending time with children. Finally, tasks to increase spousal support and alliances should be considered as split-parenting (i.e., parents who have different discipline approaches and do not coordinate parenting efforts) frequently serves to undermine the authority of the primary caretaking parent, who becomes emotionally overwhelmed at the prospect of managing his or her own children.

*2b. When related to pragmatic constraints*: List constraints and identify which responsibilities to delegate to others (including children), such as preparing dinner and walking the dog, and which can be addressed by hiring professionals when possible (e.g., house cleaning, home repairs). If related to job requirements, evaluate ways to modify or change work hours with employer. In rare situations, it may be necessary to assess with clients whether or not it is worthwhile keeping the job or looking for a new one that is better suited to increased supervision. Finally, enlisting others (e.g., grandparents, friends, babysitters) to provide supervision should be considered.

*2c. If willful*: It is important to note that willful neglect is often related to emotional obstacles. Willful avoidance ranges from maintaining close but not immediate proximity (e.g., remaining in the kitchen while the children are in the family room for prolonged periods of time) to abusive neglect. Resentment toward one's children can result in direct hostility that may manifest as avoidance and neglect, as well as physical and verbal aggression. A safety assessment must be completed when neglect is suspected, and neglect must be reported when identified.

Willful neglect may be identified during treatment or be the reason treatment is initiated, usually by court mandate. Involuntary clients raise different treatment challenges than those who willingly seek treatment (Rooney, 2009). Involuntary clients are commonly resistant to treatment, frequently believing that they were wrongly judged. Practitioners can join with clients' perspective by framing task selection as actions to get the authorities "off their back." This approach preserves self-determination in selection of treatment objectives while satisfying court requirements (Rooney, 2009). Concrete actions to address legal concerns represent initial tasks and as trust builds in the practitioner–client relationship, exploration of emotional obstacles can be addressed.

In cases where parents voluntarily seek and participate in treatment, willful avoidance should be explored in individual sessions and task strategies include many of the same put forth in the earlier discussion of emotional obstacles to providing competent supervision of siblings. These include: identify, acknowledge, and address feelings of resentment and hostility that underlie emotional disengagement; employing cognitive behavioral methods; keeping self-reflection journals; identifying links to past experiences; utilizing emotional control strategies such as deep breathing and restraint; and identifying supports (e.g., friends) to assist during childcare occasions. Strategies may include incrementally increasing time spent with the children (e.g., first week 10 minutes, next week 20 minutes).

*2d. Parent dysfunction*: Another obstacle to guardian involvement is debilitation due to other issues, such as substance abuse and mental illness. These issues often result in the parentification of children, in which they take on adult responsibilities before they are emotionally prepared, including the provision of both emotional and physical care for parents and siblings. Parentification is generally considered to be debilitating. Sibling aggression related to debilitated parents involves multimodal interventions that may include referrals for, or direct treatment of, substance abuse and mental health concerns. Other guardians must be enlisted, even if temporarily, for caretaking and to help parentified children regain their childhoods. Finally, child welfare assessment should be completed in order to ensure child safety. Cases of neglect or abuse must be reported.

### *Task menu: Ineffective supervision—Structuring autonomous sibling time*

1. **Establish clear rules for behavior for independent sibling time [family task; session task]**

   *Elaboration*: Make a list of expectations of behavior. This may be done as a session task or by the family at home. The list can be posted (e.g., on the refrigerator) to remind participants and reinforce formal understandings. Examples include developing rules about asking permission to leave the house before doing so, watching television (e.g., alternating who gets to choose the show to watch), sharing toys, and rules that prohibit aggression. These should be spelled out clearly and mutually agreed upon. Consequences for violation of rules should be included in rule discussion and on written documents that include rules.

2. **Reinforce clear rules for independent sibling time behavior [parent task]**

   *Elaboration*: Parents use positive reinforcement (i.e., rewards) when siblings follow expected behavior and uphold agreed-upon consequences.

   *Practitioner role*: Provide education regarding reinforcement strategies to promote wanted behavior. The PBA presented at the end of Chapter 6 can be shown and explained to parents for possible adoption.

3. **Parents will regularly "check in" with siblings [parent task]**

   *Elaboration*: A time interval is selected for parents to visit the siblings either in person or electronically (e.g., phone, video chat) and inquire about status and to provide opportunities to reinforce positive, and implement consequences for problematic, behaviors. Positive and negative behaviors may be those agreed upon using task item 2, reinforce clear rules for independent sibling time. Initially, time intervals should be short (e.g., 5 minutes) and incrementally extended with successful periods of positive behavior. The use of timers is often helpful for maintaining consistent contact. This task can be used in conjunction with or as an alternative to the following task in which children report to their parents.

4. **Children will regularly "check in" with parents [child task]**

   *Elaboration*: A time interval is selected for the children to report to a parent/guardian either in person or electronically (e.g., phone, video chat) to share their sibling status about positive or negative interaction. Positive and negative behaviors may be those agreed upon using task item 2, reinforce clear rules for independent sibling time. Initially, time intervals should be short (e.g., 5 minutes) and incrementally extended with successful periods of positive behavior. The use of timers is often helpful for maintaining consistent contact. This task can be used in conjunction with or as an alternative to the above task in which parents systematically check in with their children.

   *Practitioner role*: Create a backup plan with the family for occasions when siblings are engaged in active aggression, particularly when the parent/guardian is at a remote location. Meet with children individually to inquire about how the reporting is going and to assess whether or not coercive tactics are being used to force positive reports from siblings.

***Task menu: Sibling caretaking***

1. **Identify disciplinary and control strategies for the caretaking child to implement with siblings [family task; session task]**

   *Elaboration*: Done either as a session task or as a family task at home, caretakers are given strategies for managing their siblings, such as time-outs, distraction, positive and negative reinforcement, and behavioral modification charts.

*Practitioner role*: Provide education about discipline and control strategies.

2. **Clarify and abide by rules about hierarchy [family task; session task]**

   *Elaboration*: Families rarely openly discuss sibling hierarchies and children often assume that they have symmetrical relationships with brothers and sisters, particularly if close in age. A clear discussion of who has authority over whom and at what times and locations should be explicitly discussed. For example, the caretaking child may only hold formal authority over siblings when parents are not at home. Younger children may have greater authority in their own bedroom, even over older siblings. Variations may exist based upon age and gender, but all should be overtly determined.

3. **Parents support legitimacy of caretaking child's authority**

   *Elaboration*: Children under the care of their siblings will often complain to their parents about their caretaking sibling. Parents must support the caretaking child's authority by siding with them and not with the complaining siblings. A statement such as, "When your brother (or sister) is in charge, you must do what they say even when you disagree." In addition, parents may support the caretaking child's challenged authority by saying, "You are correct, your older sibling is not your mother (or father), but he/she is your caretaker and in charge when I am not here." Parents should avoid acting as judges about which child is right or wrong and instead support the caretaking child publicly (i.e., in front of siblings) while privately coaching about positive discipline strategies and correcting behaviors that are problematic.

4. **Abide by rules related to hierarchy [younger child(ren) task]**

   *Elaboration*: Children who are being cared for by siblings have a role in minimizing sibling aggression. Tasks should be formulated to reflect individual behaviors that aim to assist caretaking siblings. Tasks can include asking for permission and following instructions, as well as chores.

   *Practitioner role*: Secure explicit agreement about all children's responsibility for nonaggression, including challenging and provoking, in sibling caretaking arrangements.

### *FFD 5: Focus on negativity*

Sibling conflict is often accompanied and supported by the family's negative view of sibling behavior. Statements such as "You two always fight!" illustrate a perception that the sibling's relationship is only negative. Sibling relationships are complex and involve both positive and negative aspects. Even seemingly hate-filled relationships have their good moments. When families focus on negativity, positive interactions are overlooked. Opportunities to reward prosocial behavior are missed. Parents sometimes mistakenly assume that children should get along and may not believe that positive behavior needs to be parented (e.g., acknowledged, praised). Rather, parenting is only seen as required when fights erupt. Giving attention to only negative behaviors rewards and reinforces them, albeit inadvertently (as the parents wish is for bad behavior to end), giving support to ongoing sibling aggression. In the FFD, the practitioner works with the family to alter their focus on sibling negativity to one that emphasizes prosocial behavior.

***Task menu: Focus on negativity***

1. **Identify and chart positive sibling behavior [parent task]**

   *Elaboration*: "Catch" siblings spontaneously being good to each other. Record the behavior in a chart or journal.

2. **Inquire about positive sibling behavior [parent task]**

   *Elaboration*: Ask children about positive moments that may have taken place when the parent was not in proximity to observe. If children start complaining about each other, tell them only reports of positive behavior are permitted.

3. **Create a formal contract that outlines expected sibling behavior [family task; session task]**

   *Elaboration*: The creation of the contract should be a collaborative effort that includes children and involves identifying already-existing positive sibling behaviors. Presently occurring and expected behavior are both made overt. This can be done as a session task or completed by the family at home.

   *Practitioner role*: Assist the family in identifying what constitutes prosocial behavior. Help to structure the contract to state objectives in terms of taking rather than refraining from action (e.g., "Alternate turns selecting what television show to watch" rather than "Don't hog the remote").

4. **Acknowledge and positively reinforce positive sibling interaction [parent task]**

   *Elaboration*: This task can be linked to task item 3 involving the formation of a formal sibling behavior contract. Parents should acknowledge and praise behaviors in the contract. Additionally, spontaneous prosocial behavior involving behaviors not listed in the contract should also be acknowledged and rewarded.

   *Practitioner role*: In some cases, families may wish to employ a behavioral modification chart. The practitioner should provide education about how to create and use one effectively, which includes noting positive behavior immediately and overtly, and selecting appropriate rewards.

5. **Comment on individual behavior rather than using global descriptors that reflect extreme definitions (e.g., "always," "never") [family task]**

   *Elaboration*: During conflicts, family members will use language that focuses on the "here and now" and remark only on the behavior that just occurred. Replace, for example, "He's always poking me" with "He was poking me."

In another example, "You are always mean to me!" is replaced with "Calling me ugly hurts my feelings."

*Practitioner role*: Educate about the problems of using global descriptors and how its use restricts flexible and holistic understandings of behavior and relationships, as well as distorts interpretations of the intent behind actions.

6. **Learn conflict resolution skills [sibling task; family task]**

   *Elaboration*: Positive actions to take when engaged in negative interaction are selected for implementation. Individual skills can be selected as tasks. Conflict resolution skills are done under the supervision of parents and after successful applications, siblings carry them out autonomously. Parents positively reinforce attempts to engage in productive conflict resolution.

   *Practitioner role*: Provide education about conflict resolution actions for both parents and siblings. Encourage family to try out strategies as session tasks prior to home implementation.

7. **Explore true intent of behavior [family task]**

   *Elaboration*: A focus on negativity distorts the ability to accurately determine the motivation behind behavior. Actions are perceived to have hurtful intent when one is in a negative relationship. Tasks to assess true intent can include asking about the reasons for behavior during calm periods (e.g., not in the middle of conflict), matching verbal and nonverbal cues, and assuming accidental behavior when there are not enough data to confirm intentionality. Attributional retraining in which members are taught to infer nonhostile intent to ambiguous provocations may be effective (Hudley & Graham, 1993).

   *Practitioner role*: During session, actively challenge attributions of negative motives. Educate about and model "checking in" to evaluate intentions of behavior (e.g., "Is that what you meant to do?").

8. **Select behavior(s) from Kramer's (2011) list of essential competencies for promoting prosocial sibling behavior (in Chapter 6) [sibling tasks]**

   *Elaboration*: Choose individual action from the list to implement as between-session tasks. A planned behavior can be implemented multiple times. Siblings can record applications and outcomes. As basic competencies are mastered, others can be selected for implementation.

   *Practitioner role*: Share the list with the family and use to guide mutual formulation of tasks.

## CONCLUSION

This chapter offered practitioners and client potential actions to address dynamics identified during assessment of common family patterns that exacerbate sibling aggression. These task strategies are recommended actions that are intended to aid practice, and not to be used as rigid guidelines. Moreover, the task menus are offered as starting points for intervention development. It is hoped that practitioners and clients continue to actively identify and develop additional tasks to continually add to the above menus. The task menus will not address all dynamics and concerns related to sibling aggression and new task menus should be formulated for additional challenges. Additional issues and considerations for TCSA implementation are taken up in the last chapter. The next chapter provides a case study that demonstrates the use of TCSA and the task menus in action.

# 8

# Case Study: Task-Centered Sibling Aggression in Action

This chapter presents a case study that illustrates the Task-Centered Sibling Aggression (TCSA) treatment approach in action. It describes the work with a family in which two brothers are being aggressive toward each other. The practitioner worked with the family over six sessions in a not-for-profit community family service agency. They met once a week for 6 weeks. Each meeting lasted for about 1 hour. The first meeting and start of the second are provided in great detail to illustrate implementation of TCSA, its sequence, steps, and unique considerations. Meetings 3–6 are summarized for ease of reading and understanding.

## CASE STUDY: THE MARTINS

The Martins are a middle-class family of four that includes a mother, father, and two boys, Peter (age 7) and Brian (age 10). The mother called a local family service agency looking for counseling for Brian because of his increasingly problematic behavior at home and school, which included refusals to do homework, chores, talking back, and "being mean" to Peter. The practitioner is male in his mid-50s and is also middle class. Working from a family systems practice orientation, the practitioner asked that all families residing in the household attend the sessions. The practitioner contracted with the family to meet for six sessions, reflecting TCSA's basic principle of planned brevity.

## FIRST MEETING

Following the steps of TCSA, the practitioner begins with the social stage.

### Social Stage

He welcomes them into his office, greeting each by introducing himself. He instructs them to sit wherever they would like. He observes the two boys arguing over a chair. The mother tells them both to "cut it out" and then tells Brian to let Peter have the chair. She then turns to the practitioner and says with a slight chuckle, "This is why we're here!" She then introduces each boy and her husband by name.

Although tempting, rather than jumping straight to the boys' conflict, Mrs. Martin's exasperation, or Mr. Martin's disengagement, the practitioner instead provides a brief window of time to allow their nerves to settle and ease the transition into treatment. He asks about whether or not they had any difficulty finding the office and they briefly discuss difficulty finding a time when all members were available to attend the meeting. Mr. Martin seemed particularly resentful about having to adjust his schedule to come to treatment meetings. The social stage provided the opportunity to address his anger by validating it and agreeing to flexible scheduling arrangements. Mr. Martin relaxed and seemed to become more open to the practitioner and their working together. Had the social stage been skipped, his resentment may have become an obstacle to treatment and change.

Transitioning to treatment, the practitioner asks the family about how familiar they are with therapy and discovers that they had not been in treatment previously. The youngest boy Pete seemed particularly confused about what to expect. The practitioner explained that they would be talking about what happens in the family and that they would decide together on what needed to be done to make things better. He then formally introduced the family to task-centered procedures, informing them that they would collaboratively come up with tasks to implement to solve the problems they identify. The practitioner also explained that he would explain the process as they go and that they would know what he was doing and that there would be no secret agendas on his part. Once the family indicated that they understood and were ready to begin, the practitioner transitioned from the social stage to the next steps of TCSA, *Provide Overview of TCSA and Sibling Education* and *Target Problem Formulation* (TPF), which include problem exploration and identification. It is not uncommon for practitioners to simultaneously operate within multiple TCSA steps, alternating between them as the interview unfolds. In this case, taking the lead from the family, the practitioner begins with the TPF process (rather than the usual *Providing an Overview of TCSA and Sibling Education* stage), but alternates between them.

## Target Problem Formulation

The practitioner begins with problem exploration (the first step of TPF) with the family by sharing his observation of the two boys' conflict over the chair and acknowledges Mrs. Martin's irritation. He repeats back to the mother, "You said, 'This is why we came here.'" She nodded, sharing that Brian frequently picks fights with his younger brother.

*Practitioner*: So, you would like the two to fight less?

*Mrs. Martin*: Yes, but that's just the tip of the iceberg! I mean siblings will fight, that I understand. But I don't like it that Brian uses his larger size to push Pete around. But there are other problems with Brian. He talks back to me, he doesn't do his chores, he refuses to do his homework ... unless my husband is around, then he is an angel.

*Practitioner*: Really? He is so different when you are around? [*Directed at Mr. Martin.*]

*Mr. Martin*: He never gives me a problem. I am at work when much of this is going on. I am not sure why my wife has so much difficulty with him.

*Mrs. Martin*: He thinks it's my fault, that I am doing something wrong as a parent.

*Mr. Martin*: I didn't say that. I just don't know why he is good with me and not with you.

*The practitioner makes note of the marital tension but does not address it at this point.*

*Practitioner*: Mrs. Martin, what made you pick up the phone and call our agency at this time? Has Brian's behavior changed suddenly?

*Mrs. Martin*: No, I wouldn't say it was sudden. It's been happening for a while. He used to be such a good boy, but in the last year or two he has been getting worse and worse.

*Practitioner*: So why now?

*Mrs. Martin*: Well, right before I called here Brian had a big explosion. First he got into a big fight with Peter where he punched him in the face. I punished him for that but it made him go crazy and he threw his school bag with all of his school books in the outside trash can. Then, he cursed at me! I told him he lost the right to watch TV for a week and he cursed at me again! I didn't know what to do. I had enough. So, I called here.

*Practitioner*: Wow, sounds overwhelming!

*Mrs. Martin*: It was!

*Practitioner*: Did she tell you what had happened? [*to Mr. Martin*]

*Mr. Martin*: She did ... later that night. I think she called here first.

*Mrs. Martin*: I did. I called here first.

*Practitioner*: Oh?

*Mrs. Martin*: I have told him things like this before but he doesn't seem to think they are a big deal.

*Practitioner*: Brian, it sounds like you had a rough afternoon.

*Brian*: I guess.

*Practitioner*: What do you think set you off?

*Brian*: Pete. He's such a pain ... all the time!

*Practitioner*: Really? I know little brothers can sometimes be a real challenge. How is Pete a challenge to you? [*Note the practitioner's reframe of "pain" to "challenge." Challenges can be overcome with the right strategies.*]

*Brian*: He always gets what he wants and if he doesn't he cries like a baby ... [*Brian acts like a baby and looks directly at Pete.*] Wah, wah, wah!

*Pete*: Mom!

*Mrs. Martin*: Brian! [*Brian slumps back into chair and folds his arms.*]

*Practitioner*: Brian ... can you tell me more about what you mean by Pete getting what he wants?

*Brian*: If he wants to watch a TV show he just yells for mom. If he wants to use the computer, he just yells for mom ... even if I am using it for homework!

*Practitioner*: And then what happens? [*The practitioner begins tracking transactional sequences.*]

*Brian*: She always yells at me ... even if I haven't done anything. She just always believes him and never me.

*Mrs. Martin*: That's not true. I try to be fair. [*To Brian*] You're bigger and so I expect you to act like a big brother.

*Brian*: Come on, Mom! I never get what I want. Pete just has to whine a little and you give him what you want. You know he's your favorite. [*Pete smiles.*]

*Mrs. Martin*: It's not true. I love you both the same.

*Practitioner*: Pete, what do you think about this?

*Pete*: I don't know.

*Practitioner*: Do you think your Mom favors you?

*Pete*: Well, I am better ... I mean, I don't do things that get me into trouble like Brian.

*Brian*: I get into trouble because of you!

*Practitioner*: How about you, Mr. Martin, what do you think about Brian's perspective ... that he is treated unfairly?

*Mr. Martin*: Well, I think my wife is harder on him sometimes because he can be more challenging. If he acted better, maybe she wouldn't be so tough on him.

*Practitioner*: So you do think the two boys are treated differently? [*Mr. Martin nods in agreement.*]

*Mr. Martin*: Yes, I think so.

*Practitioner [to Mrs. Martin]*: And you, Mrs. Martin?

*Mrs. Martin*: Yes, but it's only because Brian misbehaves. If he didn't, I would treat them the same.

*Practitioner*: Interesting. OK, so it seems pretty clear that Brian's behavior is what we call a "target problem" ... that is, a problem we will focus on resolving together. In particular, his aggressive behavior toward Pete needs attention. It is of major concern to you and I am concerned that if we don't address it directly now that it may escalate into more dangerous violence.

*Mrs. Martin*: I agree!

*Practitioner*: At the same time, I understand that Brian believes he is being treated unfairly and seems frustrated by his situation. Is that right, Brian?

*Brian*: Yes.

*Practitioner*: OK, so we will have to focus a bit more on that, too, and maybe help change things so Brian doesn't feel that way. Starting with the sibling aggression concern, I have learned from working with families that they have found information about siblings and why they do or don't get along, or fight, and this is helpful to them. That is why the next step of TCSA called, "Providing an overview of sibling education" is included. I would like to take a moment to explain some things about siblings, if that's OK with you? [*The family shows their agreement and voices their interest in hearing more about siblings.*] Great! So, it sounds like we agree that a target problem is "sibling aggression"? [*The family indicates their agreement.*]

Now that the family and practitioner have determined that differential treatment and perhaps favoritism are present, and that a target problem is Brian's aggression toward his brother, the practitioner segues to the *Provide Overview of TCSA and Sibling Education* step. Later, he returns to problem exploration (within the TPF step) in order to find out more about the sibling aggression, including its frequency and severity. Problem exploration is also continued to identify additional challenges the family would like addressed.

## Provide Overview of TCSA and Sibling Education

The practitioner introduces the family to the task menus for the FFD (showing them Chapter 7). He calls their attention to the first dynamic, *Parental Differential Treatment and Favoritism*. The practitioner explains the importance of the child's perception of favoritism as a treatment concern, making a distinction between the parent's perception and the child's. He also shares how identical treatment by parents is a virtual impossibility and that despite parents' best efforts, children may still see them as being unfair. He calls attention on the handout to the "Ignoring Claims of Injustice" item and explains how attending Brian's perception is important.

*Practitioner*: So, as you can see, there is a link between different treatment of children and sibling aggression. The fact that Brian believes that things are unfair is important, whether or not things truly are unfair. Does that make sense?

*Mrs. Martin*: Yes, it does. But I don't want to give into his whining.

*Practitioner*: What do you mean?

*Mrs. Martin*: I don't want to let him get away with bad behavior because he thinks or says he is being treated unfairly.

*Practitioner*: Oh, I agree. Misbehavior should not be permissible. There are ways to address his challenging behavior and also help him feel things are more fair. [*To Brian*] What do you think, Brian? Would you be up for talking about ways to improve your behavior if things seemed more fair?

*Brian*: Yes. Sometimes I get so frustrated by how Pete gets away with things, and I don't, that it makes me do bad things?

*Practitioner*: Really? That's interesting. Can you tell me more about that?

*Brian*: I don't know. I just get angry ...

*Practitioner*: Do you have an example of when that happened recently? [*Practitioner is using the enactment strategy here. This is also a transition back to TCSA's target problem exploration step.*]

*Brian*: Well, last night I was playing with a model I made of a World War II airplane ... I spent hours building it. Pete came in and tried to grab it out of my hands. I wouldn't let him have it so of course, he cried for his Mommy. That made me so mad so I punched him. I know I am not supposed to hit him but I didn't know what else to do. It's my plane and I should be able to play with it myself.

*Practitioner*: Oh my, that's sounds very frustrating!

*Brian*: It was.

*Practitioner*: OK, let's find out more about what happened here. We need to find out more how the sibling fighting happens. I am going to ask you all a lot of questions so we can find out the sequence, the order, of events that happens when fights happen. Sounds OK? [*The family conveys that they agree.*]

The practitioner is using an enactment to track transactional sequences of family behavior. A pattern is uncovered that was summarized in the following way:

1. Pete challenges Brian.
2. Brian responds with physical aggression.
3. Pete calls for their mother.
4. Mrs. Martin comes to the siblings and asks what happened.
5. Pete reports that Brian hit him; Brian reports that Pete provoked him (e.g., tried to take model).
6. Mrs. Martin punishes Brian for hitting.
7. Pete's behavior is generally not acknowledged (Mrs. Martin's rationale is that Brian is older and should be nice to his "little brother.").
8. Brian gets angry at mother for punishing him, expresses that "It's not fair" and expresses his frustration by talking back, ignoring his chores, avoiding homework, etc.
9. Mrs. Martin becomes frustrated, not knowing what else to do, and calls Mr. Martin at work.
10. Mr. Martin becomes annoyed that he is being disrupted at his workplace and tells his wife he will deal with it when he gets home, but does nothing when he arrives home, using the rationale that the event happened a long time ago and that he is too tired to deal with it.
11. Mrs. Martin gets angry with Mr. Martin.

As the practitioner summarizes the above sequence, he writes it down. The practitioner asks for a second example of a sibling conflict and tracks the transactional sequence. The pattern is almost identical and he confirms with the family that this is the usual course of events.

*Practitioner*: Great! I think we have a feel for how things happen then. We are going to return to this sequence shortly. But first, it is important that I find out a little bit more about the sibling fights. For example, I would like to find out when and where these usually occur, and how often they happen.

*Mrs. Martin*: I think they almost always happen when they are in their play room. They are in there getting along fine and then I hear yelling. All I ask for is half an hour of peace! [*chuckling*]

*Practitioner*: Boys?

*Brian*: Yes, mostly in the play room, and sometimes in my bedroom and sometimes outside.

*Practitioner*: Peter?

*Peter*: The playroom mostly.

*Practitioner*: And when are these mostly taking place?

*Mrs. Martin*: Pretty much whenever they are in the play room ... after school, while waiting for dinner ...

*Practitioner*: Weekends?

*Mrs. Martin*: No, not as much on weekends. I think because my husband's around.

*Brian*: We still fight but Pete doesn't call Mom because he's afraid of Dad.

*Practitioner*: Oh, that's interesting. Is that right, Pete?

*Pete*: I guess so. He gets so mad if we bother him and he takes away our toys and tells us we are going to get a spanking.

*Mr. Martin*: Yes, I need my weekends to be peaceful. I don't need any of their nonsense.

*Practitioner*: So you don't put up with their fighting [*a statement to ally with Mr. Martin before asking him about his use of corporal punishment*]

*Mr. Martin*: No way.

*Practitioner*: So you take away toys and threaten to spank them. Have you spanked them?

*Mr. Martin*: Only a few times ... when they were little. I haven't had to in a while. [*Practitioner makes mental note of father's use of physical aggression to manage physical aggression, a behavior that falls under the FFD of "Parental Support for Aggressive Behavior." The practitioner will return to this dynamic in a subsequent session.*]

*Practitioner*: OK, so fights happen mostly after school and mostly in the play room. A strategy we can discuss later in this meeting is developing rules for afterschool time in the play room. Often, providing structure with clear expectations helps reduce problems.

*Mrs. Martin*: Oh, that sounds like a good idea!

*Practitioner*: OK, we'll get to that shortly. How often would you say these fights are occurring? Once a day? Many times a day?

After some discussion it is determined that the frequency of fights averages about 10 times each week (about twice a day, excluding weekends when Mr. Martin is home). The practitioner asks each family member to rank the severity of the fights on a scale ranging from 1 = minor to 10 = very severe. There was considerable disagreement between family members and it was decided that the severity scores of Pete (7), Brian (4), and Mrs. Martin (8) would be kept separately. Mr. Martin abstained from answering, saying that he was not around and could not provide accurate answers regarding the frequency or severity of sibling conflicts. The practitioner explained that in accordance with TCSA, the family would be asked to report on frequency and severity of the fights each week. He also explained the purpose of using the scores to monitor progress and treatment effectiveness.

## Task Selection

The practitioner made note of the limited time they had left in their first session and transitioned to the *Task Selection* step of TCSA. Because the focus of this first session was on sibling aggression and differential treatment and favoritism, the practitioner asked the family if this is the primary problem they would like to address at this time, and that further exploration into other problems would be taken up at the following meeting. The family agreed.

*Practitioner*: OK, so let's start with these two target problems: sibling fighting and perceived favoritism.

*Mrs. Martin*: If we could make even just a little progress with the fights and Brian's hitting, that would be a great step forward!

*Practitioner*: OK, so the next step of TCSA is to generate task ideas . . . things each of you can do between now and the next time we meet that will make things a little better. We will all throw out ideas and choose the ones that seem to be the best . . . the ones you feel most strongly about. Let's start by listing them. What have you tried? And, what have you found to be effective?

*Mrs. Martin*: Effective? Nothing really . . . that's why we're here [*she laughs*]! I have tried punishing Brian, but that doesn't seem to do anything.

*Practitioner*: Rather than starting with Brian's hitting, let's begin with his perceived favoritism. We can talk about alternatives to punishment shortly. Is that OK?

*Mrs. Martin*: Yes.

*Practitioner*: Any ideas of what you could do differently . . . to help Brian feel more included?

*Mrs. Martin*: I don't know ... I know he does feel like I am being unfair ... earlier you showed us that sheet about taking people seriously when they say things are unfair. That's something I can do.

*Practitioner*: That's a great task idea! What do you think, Brian?

*Brian*: It would be nice to be taken seriously.

*Practitioner*: Great. Mrs. Martin, what would that look like ... in action ... taking Brian seriously? What specifically would you do?

*Mrs. Martin*: When he complains about fairness I can ask him to explain how I was unfair and maybe how I could have done things more fairly.

*Practitioner*: Oh, I like that idea. I think that would go a long way with Brian. [*Brian is sitting on the edge of his seat, listening intently.*] Brian, if I read you correctly, you think this is a good idea?

*Brian*: Yes.

*Practitioner*: What could you do differently about how you approach your mother when you think she is unfair? [*After a moment of silence, the practitioner provides a prompt.*] I think sometimes the way you let your mother know you think she is unfair is to yell at her with a mean voice. Is that correct?

*Brian*: Yes, I do that. I guess I could say it more nicely.

*Practitioner*: What would you say?

*Brian*: In a calm voice I would say, "Mom, I think you are being unfair." I've tried that but she doesn't listen to that.

*Practitioner*: OK, well your mother is agreeing to try things differently. Perhaps you can work with her and try again. You act politely and calm and your mother will ask you to explain further. Does that sound like something you can do? It means no yelling, whining, throwing things, and so on ...

*Brian*: Yes, I can do that.

*Practitioner*: Great!

The practitioner then asks Mr. Martin and Pete to share their ideas about tasks each of them can do to assist with the perception of favoritism. Mr. Martin volunteers giving greater support to his wife when she expresses her parenting frustrations. In particular, he offers to call "family meetings" to discuss what had happened that led to Brian's claim of injustice and allow Brian and his wife to express their views in a calm and serious way. Both Mrs. Martin and Brian thought that family meetings were a good idea and Mr. Martin's calling meetings was selected as a task. Pete had difficulty identifying what things he could do to help Brian. To assist Pete and the family with additional task ideas, the practitioner shares the task menu "PDT and Favoritism." The family was pleasantly surprised to discover that some of their ideas were on the task menu.

Discussion of the task menu led to the selection of two additional tasks: one for the family and the other for Pete. Mrs. Martin continued to sporadically defend her behavior toward Brian by expressing that she did not think she was being unfair. She asked to select the task "Record parental treatment to distinguish PDT and favoritism" from the menu. Brian was excited by this task as well, believing it would demonstrate that his mother was playing favorites. The task they formulated entailed making a chart to hang on the refrigerator, recording all sibling disagreements, and including descriptions of how Mrs. Martin handled the boys' conflict. The practitioner worked with the family to achieve task specificity and identify who would create and manage the chart and record keeping.

Looking at the task menu, Pete agreed that he sometimes took pleasure when his mother scolded Brian and volunteered to try the task "Support sibling in claims of mistreatment." He shared that he thinks his mother does agree with him more than Brian about most things and that sometimes he feels badly for him. He agreed to tell his mother when he felt that Brian was being treated unfairly. The practitioner was skeptical that a 7-year-old was capable of taking his brother's side during a heated conflict between them, but supported Pete's desire to try to implement this task.

*Practitioner*: Wow, Pete, I am surprised that you would want to tell your mother that she is being unfair when it usually means she is on your side. Are you sure you want to do this?

*Pete*: Yes ... I mean, if Brian is being a jerk than I probably won't think Mom is being unfair, but if it seems like he is getting into trouble just because we were fooling around a little ... or something like that ... then I think I can tell my Mom that.

*Mrs. Martin*: He is such a mature child. He is so sweet! [*Pete smiles proudly and Brian rolls his eyes. Mrs. Martin sees Brian's eye rolling*.] Brian! I can't believe you would make that kind of face after your brother so nicely offered to stick up for you.

*Brian* [*dramatically*]: He's soooo sweet! Please.

*Practitioner*: Brian, it seems that you think something is not right here. Can you explain what it is?

*Brian*: Yes! It just seems like Pete found another way to be a "momma's boy" [*i.e., the favorite*] by telling my Mom that she's wrong. If I told her that she was wrong about something, I would get in so much trouble!

*Practitioner*: That's interesting. You think your mother is giving Pete special treatment right now? That she is favoring him? [*The practitioner intentionally models the "taking seriously claims of injustice" task that the mother agreed to take on*.]

*Brian*: Yes. Here I am trying to be good. I am here in this office talking about ways to make things better. Do I get a "He's so sweet"? No. You see how clear it is that he's her favorite?

*Practitioner*: I see what you mean. You are making efforts and get no praise, but your brother does.

*Brian*: Exactly.

*Practitioner*: Mrs. Martin, what do you think? Here is an opportunity to try out your task of "taking Brian's claims of unfairness seriously."

*Mrs. Martin*: Well, I can certainly see how Brian might think my complimenting Pete might be favoritism ... but I don't mean it that way ... I do think it was nice of Pete ...

*Practitioner*: I agree, it was nice of Pete. However, is Brian also correct that he is not receiving the same treatment for his efforts?

*Mrs. Martin*: I guess so ... although we are here because of him ...

*Practitioner*: Does that mean he should not get credit for trying?

*Mr. Martin*: He should be praised the same as Pete.

*Mrs. Martin* [*Angered by and directed to her husband*]: Well, I don't hear *you* praising him!

*Mr. Martin*: You're right; I should praise him and Pete both.

*Mrs. Martin [Sarcastically to her husband]*: Well, it's nice to have you involved. [*To practitioner*:] Yes, Brian is trying. I should compliment him too.

*Pete [Smiling]*: Yes, Mom ... you're being unfair to Brian. [*To practitioner*:] Just doing my task! [*He giggles, then Brian laughs, then both parents smile.*]

*Mrs. Martin*: Brian, I am really impressed by how you are here working to make things better. It means a lot to me and I know it must be hard for you. [*Brian nods.*]

*Practitioner*: That was really well done, Mrs. Martin! [*Practitioner uses this moment to address marital tension and create more positivity in the marital relationship. A positive marital relationship models prosocial behavior for children*:] Don't you think so, Mr. Martin?

*Mr. Martin*: Yes, I do. I know she loves Brian a lot and really feels that way.

*Mrs. Martin*: I do love him very much. [*Brian crosses the room and hugs his mother.*]

*Practitioner*: Brian, that was really nice of you.

*Mrs. Martin*: Yes, I have two sweet children!

*Practitioner*: Yes, you do. It means you and your husband are good parents and doing a really nice job with the boys.

*Mrs. Martin*: Then why are we here?

*Practitioner*: All families can use a little extra support from time to time. Raising siblings is more difficult than most think. But you are doing so many things right ... let's continue planning tasks to get the family to a better place. Sound OK?

The family agrees. The practitioner reviews the selected tasks with the family and begins to explore the details of task implementation plans, transitioning to the next step of TCSA, Identifying and Resolving Obstacles.

## Identifying and Resolving Obstacles

The central activity of this step is to anticipate task implementation implications and identify potential obstacles. When obstacles are identified, tasks are formulated to bypass them in order to promote successful implementation. "Backup" or contingency plans are made so that clients are prepared to manage obstacles if they arise. Clients are often quick to abandon task implementation and lose confidence in the power of particular actions when they run into challenges and are unprepared to handle them (i.e., do not have a contingency plan).

Many tasks seem straightforward at first but the practice of predicting what could happen to obstruct tasks often demonstrates the complexities of taking new action. For example, Mrs. Martin and Brian agree to tasks that are interdependent. Mrs. Martin agrees to take Brian's claims of unfairness seriously and Brian selected to use a calm voice when expressing injustice. The practitioner revisits these tasks and asks the family to imagine a sibling fight and asked the pair to identify what difficulties they may encounter trying to implement their tasks. At first, both Brian and his mother said that they could not foresee any challenges. The practitioner uses "What if?" questions (Caspi & Reid, 2002) in which various challenging scenarios are put forth. These questions force clients to assess obstacles that they had not initially considered. Often, the "What if?" questions serve to "prime the pump" for clients and help them generate their own ideas. The practitioner begins by raising the obstacle of emotional reactivity.

*Practitioner*: Brian, your task is to use a calm voice when telling your mother you think she is being unfair. *What if* you are so angry that you can't manage to use a calm voice?

*Brian*: I will try to remain calm, but ... I guess I would just not say anything until I calmed down.

*Practitioner*: What a great idea! How will you get yourself to calm down?

*Brian*: If I get so angry that I only want to yell, I think it is best if I go to my [*bed*]room and read a book or listen to music for a while.

*Practitioner*: Another great idea! OK, so if you find yourself angry ... rather than giving up on the task ... you will wait until you calm down before you try to talk to your mother. You will do this by going to your room and finding an activity to distract you?

*Brian*: Yes.

*Practitioner*: That sounds like a good backup plan. OK, now I am going to ask you another one that may be even more challenging. *What if* your mother doesn't do her task? I mean, what happens if you use your calm voice and respectfully tell her you think she is being unfair and she forgets her task and doesn't take you seriously? Maybe she just ignores you ...

*Brian*: Well, then I would just yell again.

*Practitioner*: Mmm ... we all want things to get better and that sounds like more of the same kind of thing that has all of you upset. Let's try to think of your task as not connected to hers. Is there a way for you to keep to your task even if your mother doesn't take you seriously? Can you think of a way to handle that obstacle?

*Brian*: I guess I could try the same thing I said earlier. I could just go to my room and wait a while, then try again. Maybe when she is less upset she will be more able to take me seriously.

*Practitioner*: That's very good but sounds very hard to do. Do you think you could actually do that?

*Brian*: Yes.

*Practitioner*: OK, then let's give it a shot. Mrs. Martin, what about your task? What do you think could happen to make it difficult for you to carry out your task of taking Brian seriously?

*Mrs. Martin*: I guess, like Brian, that I could be so frustrated that I am too upset to listen to Brian. I can see that happening. Sometimes I do get so aggravated.

*Practitioner*: Brian has a good plan for that; going to his room to calm down. What about you ... what will you do to ensure your task goes well?

*Mrs. Martin*: I think if I stop and take a deep breath, count to 10, then I can calm down enough to ask him to tell me more about his perspective.

*Practitioner*: It's tough to be accused of playing unfair when you are already aggravated. I like your idea, but are you sure that deep breathing and counting will be enough?

*Mrs. Martin* [*smiling*]: Good point! I think I need to do the same as Brian. I will find another activity and then when I have calmed down I will go back to him and ask him more about his feelings.

*Practitioner*: That sounds like a good idea. And, here's the same tough question I asked Brian ... what happens if Brian does not talk to you calmly as he has planned, but instead yells at you or whines or throws something? Will you give up your task?

*Mrs. Martin*: No. I will remind him to use his calm voice and will try to stay calm myself. But even if he yells at me or throws something, I will try to talk to him seriously when he is calmer.

*Practitioner*: Sounds like a good plan. It sounds like the both of you are committed to carrying out your tasks even if you run into obstacles. I have one more "What if?" for you, Mrs. Martin. *What if* you truly believe that Brian is wrong and deserves different or more harsh treatment than Pete? Will you still implement your task of taking Brian's perspective seriously?

*Mrs. Martin*: Yes. Actually, I don't think that will be a problem because up until now I have always thought I was being fair and doing the right thing ... so, even if I believe I am correct I will still take the time to try and understand Brian's perspective.

*Practitioner*: OK, good. It's important to remember ... Brian ... that your mother does not have to agree with you, change her punishment, take your side, and so on ... she just needs to listen to you and try to understand your view. That is her task. That will be a big step forward and a big change for your mother. Are you going to be OK with that for now ... not necessarily being agreed with but better understood?

*Brian*: Yes, I understand.

The practitioner continues the anticipating obstacles discussion with each of the selected tasks. Pete is asked about challenges to supporting his brother. Mr. Martin considers obstacles to supporting his wife and to calling family meetings, and the whole family work together to identify problems related to keeping record of Mrs. Martin's actions during sibling conflicts.

## Rehearsal

Once tasks have been formally selected and refined, and contingency plans for implementation challenges have been created, the practitioner transitions the family to the next TCSA step, Rehearsal. In this step the family has opportunities to try out their tasks in the treatment meeting prior to implementing them at home. Many tasks can be rehearsed without any setup or can be initiated using role play. Some tasks, however, require recreating a "real-life" situation to attempt them in a more genuine context. A strategy to recreating such situations is to use an enactment in which actual disputes are discussed or revisited.

Rehearsals provide opportunities to undertake tasks with the support and guidance of the practitioner before attempting them outside of the treatment session. They also often reveal unanticipated obstacles that can then be addressed as they were in the previous step. Tasks met with obstacles can be revised or abandoned, or contingency plans can be developed to maximize task success. It is better for tasks to fail during treatment meetings than in "real-life" encounters as the reasons for breakdown can be identified and addressed.

*Practitioner*: Brian and Pete, I am wondering if you can talk now about your last fight ... the one you were talking about earlier when you, Brian, hit Pete? Brian, can you tell me what happened that led to your punching him? [*Note that the practitioner is explicit about the behavior and avoids using language that minimizes the presence of violence—that is, "when you had a disagreement."*]

*Brian*: I used to be really into Legos ... I still like them but don't do it as much. I have whole collection of things I have built. Pete took a car I had made and started taking it apart . . . I told him to put it back and stop messing with it but he didn't . . . so I punched him.

*Practitioner*: Pete, is that how it happened?

*Pete*: Ya, pretty much. He never plays with his Legos anymore and I needed a few pieces for a building I was making.

*Practitioner*: OK, so Pete, you were building a Lego building . . . and Brian . . . what were you doing . . . before Pete took your car?

*Brian*: Playing a video game.

*Practitioner*: OK. And then, Pete, you went over to Brian's collection of Lego projects he had completed, took a car, and started taking pieces from it to use for your building . . . is that right?

*Pete*: Yes.

*Practitioner*: Then what happened? Brian asked you to not use his car?

*Pete*: Yes . . . not really asked as much as yelled at me. That made me mad so I kept taking pieces off, even ones I didn't need.

*Brian [to Pete]*: You're such a jerk!

*Mrs. Martin*: Brian!

*Practitioner*: Hold on for a few minutes, Mrs. Martin . . . let me understand from the boys what happened as you weren't there at the time. Brian, I can see that he has made you angry but I have a "no violence" rule and name calling is a type of violence. When Pete didn't stop taking apart your car, did you do anything else? Did you call your mother?

*Brian*: No. But, he called my mom before I hit him.

*Practitioner*: Really? Before? Is that right Pete?

*Pete*: Yes. I knew he was getting ready to hit me.

*Practitioner*: And, Brian, then you hit him?

*Brian*: Yes. He called mom and I knew what that meant . . . I was going to get into trouble either way . . . it's so annoying!

*Practioner*: That's the part you see as unfair?

*Brian*: Yes! He took my car . . . without asking me . . . and starting taking it apart and I get in trouble for it!

*Practitioner*: I can see how that sounds unfair. [*Practitioner intentionally models mother's task.*] So what happened then [*practitioner continuing to track transactional sequence*] . . . right after you hit Pete?

*Brian*: Well, my mother came downstairs and punished me for hitting Pete.

*Practitioner*: Did you try to explain to your mother what had happened?

*Brian*: Yes, I told her about Pete messing up my Lego car . . . but she didn't care . . . she just yelled at me for hitting. She said she didn't "care about the reasons" [*using a mocking tone to imitate his mother*].

*Mrs. Martin*: There is never a good reason to hit a person.

*Practitioner [bringing Mrs. Martin in]*: I agree, Mrs. Martin, hitting is not an acceptable option ... but what are Brian's options?

*Mrs. Martin*: Well, he could have told me what Pete was doing before he hit him.

*Practitioner*: Fair enough. Brian, why didn't you tell your mother before you hit Pete?

*Brian*: As I said, I knew she would be on his side ... she would say [*using same mocking tone*], "Brian, you're older. You don't play with the Legos anymore. Be a good big brother."

*Mrs. Martin*: Well all those things are true!

*Brian [in a whining tone]*: You see! It's not fair!

*Mrs. Martin*: It is fair, Brian. You are bigger and you should not hit.

*Practitioner*: I can see that we are back to the same pattern we talked about before. This is a good time to *rehearse* ... to try out the tasks we discussed earlier. Brian, you agreed to talk about your feelings that things were unfair in a calm and not whiney voice. Can you try that here? And Mom, your task was to try and understand Brian's perception. Pete, you are going to support your brother. Can we try these out here before you get home?

The family agrees to try out the tasks. Brian took a deep breath and then slowly, in a calm voice, explained to his mother how hard he had worked on the Legos and how he doesn't agree that Pete should be able to touch or play with his things without his permission. Mrs. Martin also implemented her task and replied to Brian that his belongings should be under his control and that Pete should ask permission before touching them. The practitioner prompted the mother to try to put herself "in Brian's shoes" to understand his frustration. This enabled her to use both validation and empathy in her responses. She told Brian that she could see how he felt her not making Pete stay away from his stuff was unfair and aggravating. The practitioner then encouraged Pete to also put himself in Brian's position and asked him what it would be like to have a younger brother who kept getting into his belongings without his permission. Pete responded that it would be annoying and after some prompting, was able to implement his task and tell Brian that it was unfair.

*Practitioner*: It sounds like developing some clear rules about personal belongings might help, too. Perhaps, Mr. Martin, this could be a reason to implement your task and call a family meeting to establish some rules?

*Mr. Martin*: That's a good idea.

*Mrs. Martin*: I agree, there should be rules about belongings ... but I also think there should be rules about being a big brother ... I want Brian to learn that a big brother has to set a good example ... he should share and try to help his younger brother.

*Practitioner*: I agree. I think rules for being brothers is a great idea ... rules for being a big brother and rules for being a little brother, too. I would like to see more sibling warmth and support and we will work toward this goal.

Stopping the punching must happen immediately. Let's quickly talk about alternatives to punching. Brian, what else can you do if Pete takes your things?

*Brian*: I don't know. I guess I will try to tell my mother in a calm voice ... sort of like my task.

*Practitioner*: Wow! How does that sound, Mrs. Martin?

*Mrs. Martin*: I think that's good. I am going to stop immediately getting on Brian for things ... I am going to try to find out more what Pete is doing and try to understand Brian's feelings more ... *if* they fight again ...

*Practitioner*: I am sure they will, but I am hoping with no more punching or name calling. OK, the last step of the TCSA model is contracting, where we will write down the tasks each of you agreed to implement between now and the next session. After we complete the contract I'll make copies so that everyone has their own. Along with the contract, I am going to give each of you a Task Review Form on which you will record your success at implementing the tasks. I'll explain that when we are finished contracting. We will finish up today by scheduling our next meeting.

## Contracting

The last TCSA step of treatment meetings entails developing formal, written, and mutually agreed-upon contracts regarding the work that is to be done between treatment meetings. Target problems and the tasks selected to address them are put in writing. Contracts also include checks that contingency plans to anticipated obstacles and task rehearsal were undertaken. The contracting step enables review of what was discussed and provides opportunities for clarification and formal commitment (see Appendix C for an example from this session, and Appendix B for a blank contract). It is helpful to provide each family member with a copy of the contract. The practitioner retains a copy as well.

Contracts are useful for helping prevent clients from forgetting or avoiding their tasks. Clients can look to the contract between treatment meetings to remind them of what they agreed to. The practitioner can convey that the contract is used to hold people accountable to their commitments.

The first time the contracting step is implemented, it includes an explanation of the task and problem review processes. The frequency and severity scores of target problems identified during the TPF step are reviewed. The practitioner explains that they will be asked to report on frequency and severity at each meeting in order to track progress. Clients are given a Task Review Form (see Appendix D) that asks them to rate their task performance directly after each implementation. Task implementation is rated on the following scale: 1 = not completed; 2 = partly completed; 3 = mostly completed; 4 = fully completed; N = no opportunity to complete. Successful tasks are often kept for subsequent implementations, while tasks that were not successfully completed are reviewed for obstacles and appropriateness. Focusing on the reasons clients used to score their implementations is usually more revealing than the numbers they chose.

Asking about what constituted a score provides opportunity for clarification about understandings and expectations.

The session ends with a discussion of the number of sessions the family and practitioner agree to, which is written on the contract. The next treatment meeting is scheduled.

## SECOND MEETING

The Martins returned the following week. The practitioner began this second session (and the beginning of the Middle Phase of TCSA) with the *social stage.*

### Social Stage

The practitioner initiated nontreatment-related discussion, asking the boys about the start of their baseball seasons to help the family transition from daily life to treatment mode. Brian and Pete shared their excitement about their upcoming first games, but after a very short time, Mrs. Martin interrupted to report that the children seemed to be fighting less.

*Practitioner*: Really? That's great news! OK, let's get started then, shall we? [*formally transitioning to treatment work*]

*Mrs. Martin*: Yes! This was the first week in a long time that I haven't had to deal with a huge fight. They still are having little ones, but no hitting . . . I am happy to report.

### Task Review

The first step of second meeting is the Task Review stage. The practitioner uses Mrs. Martin's readiness to start treatment by asking about how their tasks went the past week.

*Practitioner*: Let's take a look at your Task Review Forms and see how the tasks we selected are working out for you. Brian, why don't we start with you [*Mrs. Martin hands the practitioner Brian's completed form, and the practitioner locates the contract with written tasks*]. OK, here it is! Your first task was to calmly tell your mother about when and why she was treating you unfairly. I see you tried it three times this week. The first one you scored a "2 = partly completed" and the next two times you scored a "4 = fully completed." That's great!

*Brian*: Ya . . . the first time I told her but I didn't exactly remain calm . . . so I scored it a 2.

*Practitioner*: Well, first times are often tough to get right. But you did much better the next two times. Can you tell me about one of the 4s?

*Brian*: Yes. Pete was mimicking everything I said and even though I asked him to stop many times . . . and calmly . . . he wouldn't stop. So finally I just screamed at him to get away from me. My mom came running in yelling at me to be nice to Pete and punished me for yelling. At first I wanted to yell back, but I remembered my task. I took a deep breath and said, "Mom, I think you are treating me unfairly because you don't know what happened. You don't know that Pete has been copying me and wouldn't stop even after I asked him many times."

*Practitioner*: Wow! That sounds perfect. It must have been hard to restrain yourself from yelling.

*Brian*: Well, not really. Only for a minute.

*Practitioner*: Fantastic! And, Mrs. Martin, what did you do then ... in response to Brian's using his task?

*Mrs. Martin*: Well, to be honest, at first I was taken aback and thought, "Who is he to be telling me what I am doing! I am the parent here." But then I remembered that he was just doing what we talked about. So, I listened and tried to do my task of taking his claims seriously. Once I heard the story, I knew I shouldn't have jumped to conclusions.

*Practitioner*: Wow, that went incredibly well! Both of you did your agreed tasks really well on that occasion. What did you rate your task?

*Mrs. Martin [pulling out her sheet]*: I gave it a "3."

*Practitioner*: Why a "3"? I don't understand. [*Asking about reasons for scores is helpful in identifying encountered obstacles to fully successful implementations.*]

*Mrs. Martin*: Well ... after it happened I realized that I didn't finish the task. I forgot to ask Brian how I could have handled it more fairly. I mean, I never punished Pete for what he did. I guess that would have made it more fair.

*Brian*: I thought that was unfair, too, but didn't say anything about it ... since the first part went well.

*Practitioner*: Brian, that showed really good restraint and judgment. I am impressed. Mrs. Martin, you still completed the first part of the task very well. You remained calm and listened to Brian. I am sure he felt much more supported by you.

*Brian*: It did seem like she was more on my side.

*Practitioner*: The second part, asking Brian about how he would see things if they were more fair, that can be added in the future. I also wonder if you praised Brian for his carrying out his end so well and really making an effort to make things better at home?

*Mrs. Martin*: No ... but I guess I should have ... it is true. *[Turning to Brian:]* Brian, that was really good of you. You did so well this week with your tasks.

*Brian [smiles]*: Thanks, Mom.

The practitioner continues to quickly review task performance, highlighting what went well and identifying encountered obstacles. The family had done well with their tasks, with all giving ratings of "4 = fully completed" for their last two attempts at selected tasks. The only task exception was Mr. Martin's calling of family meetings, which he did not do and scored an "N." When asked what the obstacle was to completion, Mr. Martin explained that it had been a particularly busy week at work and he was not home much and when he was, he felt too tired to have a family meeting.

## Target Problem Review

The practitioner uses the family's task successes, and father's obstacle, to transition to the next step of the TCSA Middle Phase sequence, *Target Problem Review*. In this step, the practitioner assesses the current state of affairs regarding identified problems for immediate work, by asking about the problems' severity and frequency. In cases where families report the problem to be decreasing, the work is headed in the right direction and tasks are kept. When the problem is not improving or is getting worse, new directions are identified.

*Practitioner*: It seems like things went fairly well with the tasks . . . except perhaps for Mr. Martin, who had an overly busy week. Before we talk about how to plan future family meetings, let's see how things are going with the three target problems we identified last week. The first problem on the contract is "sibling fighting." How are we doing with that?

*Mrs. Martin*: As I mentioned earlier. Things are much better. They had a few heated disagreements, but no real bad ones. It was a nice change!

*Practitioner*: I bet! I gather from the Task Review Forms that there were three sibling fights this week . . . since the three of you (Mrs. Martin, Brian, Pete) recorded three task ratings for the sibling fighting tasks? [*The practitioner is empirically tracking frequency.*]

*Brian*: Yes, that's pretty much it. There were a couple other times but they weren't real fights . . . more like . . . just getting annoyed.

*Practitioner*: Well, brothers and sisters will get on each other's nerves from time to time. Only three fights? That's very good. It is a lot less than prior. You all agreed last week that the fighting was about 10 times a week. Would you agree with these numbers, Pete?

*Pete*: Yes.

*Practitioner*: Let's see how you would compare how bad or severe the fights have been. [*The practitioner is empirically tracking severity.*] Brian, how would you rate the overall problem of you fighting with Pete on a scale from 1 to 10 . . . "1" being very mild and "10" being extremely severe?

*Brian*: Well, last week I rated it a "7." I think we are at about a "4."

*Practitioner*: That's a big difference. What brought it down to a "4"? [*Note that the practitioner is looking for positive actions, linking tasks or identifying other positive steps to change, and does not just accept the number as is.*]

*Brian*: We are fighting a lot less and the fights aren't really that big.

*Practitioner*: So what do you think has brought about this change?

*Brian*: I am not sure. I think it's because I have been calmer and Mom is listening to me more ... not just taking Pete's side right away.

*Practitioner*: Have you also been making an effort to be nicer with Pete?

*Brian*: I think so ... but he's also being nicer to me. He's doing his task of asking permission before using my things.

*Practitioner*: Really? Pete, is that so?

*Pete*: I don't know.

*Practitioner*: How would you rate how severe or serious your fighting with Brian has been?

*Pete*: Well, we really didn't fight much this week. I guess not that serious.

*Practitioner*: Using the same scale of 1 to 10?

*Pete*: I would say a 2 or 3.

*Practitioner*: So you would also say things are better. What do you think has changed? Why are the fights not as serious?

*Pete*: Like you said, Brian has been nicer, and I think my Mom has been more calm, too.

*Practitioner*: It sounds like you have been really trying, too ... asking permission ... being nicer?

*Pete*: Yes. I don't like the fighting, or when Brian would hit me, and wish it would stop.

The practitioner continues this line of exploration for each of the problems, getting each member's input, and praising them for their positive and successful action. The family members all rate the three target problems with lower scores (i.e., marking improvement) than the previous week. The practitioner uses their positive movement and motivation to gently open conversation regarding the poor parental alliance noted in last week's session. It is an effort to introduce a potential additional target problem. The practitioner's reasoning for this is that, although at the moment spirits are high, sustaining long-term family change will be bolstered by helping the parents learn to coparent. A strategy for helping parents come together is to work out a coparenting plan of shared and consistent discipline.

*Practitioner*: I am so pleased that things are moving in the right direction. The children are really doing well and, Mrs. Martin, I am very impressed with how well you have done with fairly difficult tasks ... and largely on your own! Mr. Martin, does she share with you all the things she has done?

*Mr. Martin*: No, not really. I mean ... well, I ask how things are and she tells me they are better and that's about it. I know I haven't been getting the phone calls at work ... which is good.

*Mrs. Martin*: We don't really get to talk much.

*Practitioner*: So many couples are so busy these days. It makes it a real challenge to parent together. You know . . . at last week's meeting it came up that you have different ideas about how to parent . . . such as how to handle the boys' fights and whether or not to punish.

*Mr. Martin*: That's true. We don't agree on those things. But, since she is the one at home, I let her take charge.

*Mrs. Martin*: Well, sort of.

*Mr. Martin*: What do you mean? You make *all* the decisions about the children!

*Mrs. Martin*: I do not. And, you don't really support me. You give me the feeling that whatever decisions I make are not the right ones.

*Mr. Martin*: No, I don't. You call me at work and complain. They don't seem to fight when I am there, so I am thinking that it is not as big a deal as you are making it out to be.

*The couple's disagreement starts to escalate and the practitioner interrupts*:

*Practitioner*: Well, it does seem like you have some differences regarding at least this situation. It is very important for parents to work as a team. When they don't, it makes it very difficult to address problems with children when they emerge . . . and they will emerge as it is a child's job to test their parents' rules. In my experience, there is little more important than having parents learn to work together in making long-lasting improvements in families. I think it would be helpful to take up "parental disagreement about parenting" as a target problem.

*Mrs. Martin*: I agree. I think that's important.

*Mr. Martin*: Yes, and maybe we'll get to some of our other problems [*he chuckles*].

*Practitioner*: I see you are chuckling, but something tells me that you are somewhat serious.

*Mr. Martin*: Well, no marriage is perfect.

*Practitioner*: OK, so should we start with getting you two to work together on parenting?

The couple agrees that building a parenting alliance is an important objective and ask to include it as a target problem for immediate work. Discussions of coparenting often ignite and reveal other marital issues. The practitioner does not push to address marital problems at this point, but may if it becomes an obstacle to building a parenting alliance. The practitioner uses the adoption of a new target goal to transition to the next step of TCSA, *Target Problem Formulation or Reformulation.*

## Target Problem Formulation or Reformulation

The practitioner reviews the target problems selected the previous week and assesses with the family whether or not to continue with them, or to change, discontinue, or add any. The family decided to keep their existing target goals with the aim of discontinuing "distinguishing parental treatment from favoritism," and substituting it with the marital target goal of building the parenting alliance, starting at the next session.

### Task Selection

The family chose to keep their existing tasks and have "another go at them" as they seemed to be working. Their initial instinct was to discontinue them, but after consultation with the practitioner, they were convinced that 1 week of progress was only a beginning and that their challenges would require at least one more week, if not more.

### Identifying and Resolving Obstacles

Because no new tasks were selected, the discussion of obstacles focused on challenges the actually encountered rather than those they imagined could happen. Both Brian and Mrs. Martin agreed that their biggest obstacle to successful task completion was losing control of their emotions and becoming angry during moments of conflict. The practitioner reviewed the strategies they utilized to successfully manage their emotions the previous week (e.g., taking a deep breath, reminding themselves of their tasks) and both said they would try to implement the same strategies. There was some discussion about Mr. Martin's difficulties regarding calling family meetings. To address the obstacle of his busy schedule, a meeting was scheduled during the treatment meeting. Task specificity was achieved by identifying the exact time, location, and topic for the meeting. Mr. Martin agreed to try this task again.

### Rehearsal

Problem-solving Mr. Martin's difficulty in calling family meetings constituted the rehearsal step during this session. Because no new tasks were selected, and existing tasks were being implemented with success, rehearsal was not necessary.

### Contracting

The session was concluded by completing new contracts. Each was given a copy of the TCSA contract to complete and a Task Review Form. The same target goals and tasks were utilized, but new problem severity scores were included.

## SUMMARY OF SESSIONS 3–6 AND FOLLOW-UP

The Martins met with the practitioner for six sessions over the course of 7 weeks (they were away on vacation for 1 week). During the third session, which only the parents attended, the focus was on building a parenting alliance, using alternative methods to punishment and corporal punishment, which included an introduction to the PBA. At times the couple's exchange became heated, and other marital issues emerged, but the couple preferred to focus on parenting issues rather than their marriage. They were open to considering marital therapy, but wanted to wait until the initial 6-week contract of services was over.

The fourth and fifth sessions revealed that the siblings were fighting only once each week and rating them as mild in relation to severity. The practitioner noted that although they were not fighting, they did not seem to be enjoying each other's company either. Informing the family about the importance of supportive and warm sibling relationships, target problems and tasks were mutually selected to build positive sibling relationships. Both siblings seemed eager to have a better relationship, even expressing that they would like to be "like best friends." The parents were pleasantly surprised and selected tasks to support their children's relationship, including using positive reinforcement when nice moments were observed or reported.

The sixth session was the last in the initial provision of services agreement, and marked the Ending Phase of the TCSA model. The family reported that the intense sibling fighting had stopped and that the boys seemed be enjoying their time with each other more than before. Mr. Martin shared that he hears the boys laughing with each other quite often, which was a new occurrence. After engaging in the *Target Problem Review* step for the last time, the practitioner transitioned the session to the subsequent stage, *Identification of Successful Problem-Solving Strategies*. During this step, the family and practitioner retrospectively reviewed the strategies that had worked in resolving problems. The family appreciated and conveyed they would now employ the task-centered problem-solving process when they encountered difficulties. In particular, they identified the processes of prioritizing problems and selecting a limited number of tasks to try out to resolve them. Client integration of task-centered problem-solving procedures is one that empowers clients to solve their own challenges, and an objective of task-centered practice.

The practitioner brought their work together to an end by asking about their family situation in general, reflecting the next step of the TCSA Ending Phase. In general, the family reported that the children were doing well and that Brian's enthusiasm for school had changed. Mrs. Martin said that prior to beginning treatment, Brian resisted doing his homework and on occasion, even going to school. She said that since the sibling fighting had stopped, Brian's homework and school attendance had improved. Pete seemed happier as well. The one issue remaining for the family was the identified marital issues, which the practitioner raised as a way to transition to the last step, *Discussion of Future Work and Possible Recontracting*. During this last step, the practitioner explained that sibling conflict was an expected part of life and aggression was likely to reemerge from time to time. The practitioner added that if this occurs, they may want to revisit their tasks or problem solve with fresh tasks using the process they had used together. The practitioner warned of the dangers of violent and abusive behavior and asked the family to consider implementing a "no violence" rule. Finally, Mr. and Mrs. Martin shared that they would consider returning to work on marital issues but were not ready to begin that effort at the present time. The family thanked the practitioner, who congratulated them on jobs well done, their commitment to the family, and their commitment to making positive change.

### Follow-Up

Six months later the practitioner placed a follow-up phone call and spoke with Mrs. Martin. She reported that, in general, things continued to go well. There had been a few "flare ups" between the boys, but that they were able to resolve them quickly. She added that they were still considering marital counseling and hoped to begin that work sometime in the near future.

## CONCLUSION

This case study illustrated the first two sessions of TCSA treatment in great detail to provide an example of the model in action. The Martins are fairly typical of cases in which sibling aggression is the identified reason for treatment and where severe violence and abuse were not present. Although the case appeared straightforward, its seeming ease was facilitated by empirical and theoretical knowledge of family dynamics that support sibling aggression, the FFD task menus, and using a structured, well-explicated model, TCSA.

# 9

# Additional Applications

This chapter will offer additional considerations for the application of the TCSA treatment approach. Sibling aggression is complex and multifaceted, and while much can be addressed using the FFDs and their corresponding task menus, other dynamics contribute to sibling aggression and become issues for treatment. Brief discussions of dynamics not covered by the FFDs are offered here. A discussion of sibling themes in adulthood and practice implications follows. Then, sibling aggression prevention efforts are presented. This is followed by a discussion of TCSA applications across practice modalities and settings, and special considerations for working with perpetrators and structuring sessions. The chapter concludes with additional thoughts and future directions for sibling aggression treatment, research, and education.

## ADDITIONAL DYNAMICS THAT EXACERBATE SIBLING AGGRESSION

Like all forms of interpersonal violence, sibling aggression is multifaceted, involves multiple complex factors, and is often one of many problems families bring to treatment. The FFDs presented in the previous chapters can be used to address a wide array of sibling aggression cases, but they do not address all potential considerations. Additional practice issues are briefly presented here. Each can be addressed as individual problems or in concert with FFD task strategies. The following represent a small selection additional dynamics practitioners working with sibling aggression may encounter. Rather than try to address the full range, a few of the more common challenges are highlighted here. These include marital conflict, divorce, domestic violence, shared living, and disability.

### Marital Conflict

Sibling aggression and marital conflict have been linked in research (Stocker & Youngblade, 1999). There are a few ways in which marital discord exacerbates sibling hostilities. Four are offered here. First, many children respond to their parents' stress by becoming more disagreeable, negative, and aggressive. They are often anxious about when fights will erupt and whether or not their parents' relationship is stable. The household stress leaves them with little tolerance for additional tension in the form of minor sibling annoyances. Second, children are often angered with their parents for fighting but unable to address them directly. As such, sibling aggression may be redirected anger. Third, couples in conflict frequently recruit children to choose sides and enter into coalitions. The quadrangle (discussed in Chapter 3) represents a family in which each parent enters into a coalition with a separate child. Children on opposing sides of spousal conflict will see and treat each other as on the "enemy's" team. The sibling discord is a reenactment of the spousal conflict. Fourth, when spouses disagree on parenting strategies and discipline (i.e., "split-parenting"), authority is undermined, often creating a setting in which siblings can aggress without consequence.

Because marital problems exacerbate sibling aggression, providing couples therapy is often a part of sibling treatment. Marital harmony reduces stress in the home and models problem-solving and prosocial relational behavior. Marital discord often arises when practitioners inquire about how sibling conflict is handled. Parents often disagree about how to discipline misbehavior and aggression. Helping couples parent together is important for formulating parenting strategies for addressing sibling conflict. In some cases, it may be necessary to have parents-only treatment sessions in order to resolve disagreements and to address sibling issues consistently and as a united front in which one is not undermining the other's approach. Indeed, some have recommended meeting with parents prior to siblings as the first step in addressing sibling violence (Reid & Donovan, 1990).

In cases in which marital problems are deeply entrenched and unlikely to be resolved rapidly (e.g., divorce), practitioners may find it important to quickly move to sibling work. This is done to ensure client safety, and to begin building sibling positivity so that the children can utilize each other as supports to cope with the household tension. As noted earlier, sibling support can be helpful in "buffering" the negative effects of parental conflict (Caya & Liem, 1998; Jenkins, 1992).

Finally, it is not necessary to resolve all marital problems in order to help parents attend to their children's sibling aggression. Practitioners can help parents agree on parenting rules, despite other differences and resentments. This may involve providing education about how to effectively discipline children. Working with parents to keep their children out of their marital conflicts is a strategy that can be helpful for reducing household stress for children, and for not pressuring them to take opposite sides.

## Blended Family Adjustment

Little has been available to practitioners to guide sibling work in blended families, despite the prevalence of divorce and remarriage. While some have found that sibling aggression occurs more between step- than full-siblings (Turner et al., 2007), others have reported the opposite (Deater-Deckard et al., 2002).

Nevertheless, sibling aggression between step- and half-siblings is an issue that arises frequently in treatment (Caffaro & Conn-Caffaro, 2005).

Siblings in blended families must make many accommodations, including developing relationships with strangers (i.e., new siblings), adjusting to new homes, parenting, rituals, and the loss of their first families. Caffaro and Conn-Caffaro (2005) note conditions that may exacerbate sibling aggression in blended families, including that they typically form quickly with little input from children, and that siblings have no shared history and come from families with different values and ways of doing things. Sibling aggression may be a reaction to managing the stresses of adjustment.

The task strategies offered for the FFDs can be utilized with blended families, but consideration must be given to the unique dynamics of transition that can be addressed using the TCSA. Tasks can be formulated to assist accommodating to new lives. The transition to new relationships offers opportunities for prosocial skill development. Additionally, tasks can focus on restructuring coalitions that represent past family arrangements. For example, divorcing families often function according to quadrangle structures in which two parent–child alliances oppose each other. When the primary custody of the children is awarded to one parent, all the children now live together under the supervision of one parent. For some of the children, the parent in custody has been an ally. For the others, the parent has been a virtual enemy and the children exist as outsiders to the favored child's coalition with the custodial parent. As families transition from old arrangements to new, disentangling old alliances and formulated new relationships is important. For example, custodial parents must learn to see their outsider/enemy children as human beings (and their offspring) and not in terms of the myopic roles they have played in family dysfunction.

To repeat a statement from Chapter 2: "Outsiders act like outsiders" (e.g., resentful), and often use aggressive tactics to change one's status. Tasks should be formulated to create an inclusive environment in which all feel like "insiders." Also, tasks may focus on increasing private time between parents and their disfavored children, and avoid side-taking behavior. Finally, practitioners should help blended families clearly define parenting roles and who is in charge of whom. Step-children often avoid accountability by accusing step-parents of not being their "real parent." New couples must clearly define how parenting the other's children will be handled, with couples supporting each other rather than defining their "own" children. Ultimately, transitions take time and hopefully a sense of belonging to one unit without divisions of who belongs to whom will occur.

## Intimate Partner Violence and Child Abuse

The number of children exposed to intimate partner violence (IPV) each year is high (Graham-Bermann & Levendosky, 2011), and many studies have demonstrated that they are at a greater risk for psychosocial problems than children who are not exposed (Holt, Buckeley, & Whelan, 2008). Researchers have noted the connections between various forms of family violence, including IPV, parental abuse of children, and sibling aggression (Anderson, 2010; Appel & Holden, 1998). Practitioners working with families with IPV must extend their focus from only IPV and also assess for multiple forms of violence, including between siblings.

It is important to note that not all children are negatively affected by IPV (Piotrowski, 2011), which suggests that assessment should include identification of strengths. It may be that the nature of the sibling relationship partly explains why some children are at risk for problems while others do well in the face of observed IPV. There is evidence that sibling relationships have the potential to serve as "buffers" to the negative effects of domestic violence (Lucas, 2002). Hence, task strategies should include efforts to build sibling positivity and mutual support to assist with coping with violent parents.

Finally, children abused by parents also both perpetrate and are victimized by siblings. Assessment of sibling aggression is indicated in parent-to-child abuse cases. The FFDs have application to these cases as favoritism, differential treatment, labeling, negativity, ineffective supervision, and particularly support for violence are all common features of child abuse families. Similar to working with IPV, divorce, and other marital conflict, developing positive sibling relationships may help children cope with parent–child abuse.

## Shared Living

There are sibling aggression cases that are not embedded in the problematic family dynamics described in the FFDs, and are simply problems of coresidence. Conflict is expected of all individuals sharing physical space, whether intimate couples, office mates, college roommates, or siblings. Siblings share a great deal of time together. During childhood, they spend more time with each other than with any other relationship (McHale & Crouter, 1996). Shared living disagreements are bound to emerge, and in such cases, interventions focus on helping siblings coreside. Task strategies involve establishing rules for personal belongings, shared items (e.g., toys, television, computer), and together time, as well as teaching conflict resolution skills. Treatment meetings focus on the sibling subsystem and may require less parental involvement than cases in which the FFDs are present.

## Child-to-Parent Abuse

Child abuse of parents is perhaps the most underexamined form of family violence, but there is growing evidence that it is widespread (Routt & Anderson, 2011). It is different from defiance and has been defined as "any act perpetrated by a child or adolescent that causes a parent to feel threatened, intimidated and controlled" (Kennair & Mellor, 2007, 204). Research has attempted to identify characteristics associated with child-to-parent families and perpetrators, but findings have been inconsistent (for more information, see Ibabe & Jaureguizar, 2010; Kennair & Mellor, 2007). For example, some studies report that boys are more often perpetrators than girls, but others have found no difference (Ibabe & Jaureguizar, 2010). Perhaps more consistent are findings that suggest perpetrators tend to have been exposed to family violence themselves, and that mothers are victimized more than fathers (Routt & Anderson, 2010).

In my professional practice, I have observed that sibling violence is frequently accompanied by child-to-parent violence, although this coexistence has not to my knowledge been studied. There is some evidence that firstborns are more likely to be violent toward parents than laterborns (Ibabe & Jaureguizar, 2010), similar to sibling violence. It may be that families in which child-to-parent violence occurs involve a single perpetrator who dominates and terrorizes the household. In my experience, perpetrators often perceive themselves to be "outsiders" in families that consist of parent–child coalitions. The parents act to protect the younger children from the aggressive older siblings, which enrages them and they turn on the parents, which further perpetuates their outsider status.

Child-to-parent violence varies widely according to the child's age and types of aggression utilized (i.e., physical, sexual, psychological, financial). Intervention work must be adjusted accordingly. For example, a 10-year-old female who punches her mother requires different strategies than a 17-year-old male doing the same thing to his mother. Although both mothers may be frightened of their children, the girl's behavior may be triggered by anger while the boy's is motivated by domination. As such, practitioners may choose to hold conjoint meetings between the mother and the 10-year-old to identify patterns of escalation and develop an inclusive family culture, but may handle the adolescent case differently, which may require making reports to the authorities and individual sessions to develop safety plans for parents and siblings. Practitioners working with sibling aggression must also assess for child-to-parent violence, and conversely, identification of child-to-parent violence suggests exploration of sibling aggression.

## Disability and Mental Illness

Research into sibling victimization in families with a child with a disability or mental illness has been scant. It is likely that sibling aggression rates are higher in these types of families because of the challenge of managing behavioral disorders (Linares, 2006). The wide range of disabilities and mental health concerns makes it difficult to offer generalizations for treatment. Family and sibling dynamics will be very different depending upon the type and severity of the disorder. For example, there is some evidence that children with attention deficit hyperactivity disorder aggress more toward their siblings without a disability (Kendall, 1999). By comparison, children with diabetes or hemophilia are more likely to be victims. Parents of children with chronic diseases worry constantly about their welfare and maintain high vigilance and focus. It is not unusual for healthy siblings to receive little attention, feel like outsiders, become resentful, and act in aggressive ways.

Practitioners working with families with children with disabilities or mental illnesses should inquire about the quality of sibling relationships, and assess for support aggression. Goeke and Ritchey put forth an "inclusive orientation" framework that integrates knowledge from the extant disability literature, family systems theory, and the creation of inclusive classroom communities by socializing students to positive understandings of difference. In this approach, families are helped to change their view on disability to framing it "as a set of factors to which we (teachers, parents, siblings, etc.) can thoughtfully respond and as a potentially positive and enriching experience for all, rather than as a set of problems to be fixed within one family member" (Goeke & Ritchey, 2011, pp. 180–181). This three-step "strengths-based" approach involves (1) assessing the impact of the disability on the family and how it is understood (e.g., problem, unique positive contributions); (2) helping families reframe the family orientation of "deficient" to "different," which fosters empowerment and inclusiveness; and (3) helping parents to teach, model, nurture, and expect positive sibling interaction that is facilitated by providing structure in the form of routines, rules, and using positive reinforcement. A warm and positive sibling relationship is a protective factor against a range of problems (Kramer, 2011), including problematic externalizing behavior (e.g., aggression) for healthy siblings of children with disabilities (Fishman et al., 1996). Goeke and Ritchey's (2011) approach on building an "inclusive family culture" by using a strengths perspective and utilizing task strategies to structure and build sibling positivity offers a promising direction for work with families with children with disabilities and mental health challenges.

## SIBLING AGGRESSION THEMES IN TREATMENT WITH ADULTS

As noted earlier in the book, the majority of discussion regarding assessment and intervention for sibling aggression has focused on childhood, although many of the dynamics and considerations also apply to adult sibling problems. For example, parental favoritism, shared niches, and complementary labeling in adulthood have negative implications for the sibling relationship. Negative themes from childhood often extend into adulthood, even when the dynamic no longer exists (e.g., "Mother always did love you best").

Rules for relating with siblings in childhood also persist in adulthood. This can sometimes be observed at holiday gatherings in which married, economically independent, and well-adjusted grown-ups experience old feelings of rivalry and revert to adolescent behaviors with their adult siblings. There is empirical evidence that suggests that the quality of sibling relationships remains fairly stable over time (Dunn, Slomkowski, & Beardsall, 1994; Kramer & Gottman, 1992; Kramer & Kowal, 2005). Negative sibling relationships are unlikely to change without intervention (Kramer, 2011). Because sibling aggression is associated with a host of psychosocial problems, sibling themes are worth exploring in work with adults. For example, relational behavior and emotional reactions with intimate partners and coworkers may stem from sibling experiences. The strategies for managing problems with siblings in childhood are likely the same tactics used with other relationships of similar age. In addition, perceptions of one's personality and competencies are powerfully influenced by sibling relationships, as described in depth in Chapters 2 and 3. Indeed, sibling aggression themes have treatment implications. A few are highlighted here, including working with sibling aggression survivors, sibling hostilities in adulthood, and sibling elder abuse.

## Survivors (At Various Levels of Aggression)

Sibling aggression in childhood has long-term negative consequences for both victims and perpetrators. In my experience, I have had few adult clients seek treatment for problematic sibling experiences in childhood, with the exception of sexual abuse victimization. Rather, sibling issues often emerge during family history assessment at intake. Clients often disregard problematic and aggressive sibling relationships as inconsequential and disconnected from their presenting problems. However, sibling aggression may be part of the etiology of adult problems such as relational difficulties, depression, anxiety disorders, and substance abuse, among others.

Practitioners often must help most clients connect adult problems to childhood sibling aggression experiences. When these connections are made, sibling problems are taken up as secondary issues. For example, Mary and Matthew sought marital therapy after Mary threatened to leave the relationship. Matthew was confused by the threat because Mary had never voiced upset. When, during a couples therapy session, the practitioner asked Mary why she had not said anything to Matthew about her resentments, she said that he always "had to win" every disagreement. She added that it was better to give in than to fight. When asked where she learned that deference is preferable to conflict, Mary said, "It is just like when I was a kid with my brother. If I ever dared to disagree with him, he would hit me until I said he was right." Mary's sibling victimization experience "taught" her to suppress her own needs rather than engage in conflict and it emerged as a problem in her adult relationships. The therapist helped Mary connect her childhood experiences of fear to the way she handled disagreement in her marriage. Mary initially denied the connection but further exploration into her sibling experience revealed that she had been highly fearful of her brother and of being left alone with him, suggesting she was a sibling abuse victim.

### *Victims*

The term "survivor" is often used to describe adults who experienced sexual abuse during childhood. Survivors can also be applied to those who endured physical, psychological, and relational terrorizing. Wiehe (1997) puts forth a five-stage model for working with survivors. Although intended primarily for work with sibling sexual abuse cases, it has beneficial application for other forms of sibling maltreatment:

1. Acknowledging the reality of the abuse.
2. Overcoming secondary responses that include both the client's denial of its present-day impact and managing the denial of family members that what occurred was abuse. Group therapy with other abuse survivors is often helpful in navigating this step.
3. Forgiving oneself and relinquishing self-blame for the abuse.
4. Adopting positive coping behaviors that may involve distancing oneself from the abuser and supportive family members. It also means avoiding self-injurious behaviors such as substance use and lashing out as ways to cope with the emotional intensity of working through victimization.
5. Relinquishing survivor identity in which the abuse represents an important piece of the client's history and no longer a primary way of understanding oneself. Clients are helped to move to a more holistic view of themselves in which they are human and have strengths and weaknesses.

A particularly problematic long-term consequence of childhood sibling abuse is the internalization of negative attributes ascribed by the abuser. Siblings that were psychologically belittled and tormented with names such as "fat," "stupid," and "ugly" have commonly integrated these labels as part of their identity. Task strategies for working with survivors of psychological abuse include cognitive behavioral work to track the source of and halt negative internal dialogues, replacing them with reality-based positive self-talk.

It is important to note that victims of maltreatment are often revictimized. Sibling victims are more likely to experience victimization from multiple sources (i.e., "polyvictimization") (Turner et al., 2010). Practitioners must not be quick to assume that sibling maltreatment is the only source of trauma. Moreover, treatment must include attention to protecting victims from further maltreatment. For example, adult survivors of sibling maltreatment are at a higher risk of date violence (Noland et al., 2004), and likely aggression from spouses and adult peers (although either has yet to be directly studied).

### *Perpetrators*

Many, if not most, individuals who have been violent toward their siblings do not see their behavior as problematic. In fact, some may even fondly remember violent interactions (e.g., "I really let him have it! It felt really good."). Perpetrators frequently deny that their actions were harmful and in particular will reject claims that their behavior has had long-term negative consequences for siblings. Lack of empathy for victims is a common characteristic of those that perpetrate sibling abuse (Caffaro & Conn-Caffaro, 1998). Helping a perpetrator develop empathy for victims and take responsibility for actions is aided by starting with his or her perspective of the relationship. Frequently, perpetrators feel that *they* were the victims and disown accountability by stating that they had no other choice but to use violence in their situations.

For example, Troy excused his frequent physical assault of his sister by saying that his father always protected her and let her "get away" with calling him names. He added that he had to "put her in her place" when their father was not around and that it was the only way "to get back at" his "unfair" father. The practitioner used this rationale as an opening to explore his disfavored experience and accompanying pain and resentments. Troy began to recognize that his sister did little to instigate him and that his feelings toward her were clouded by his father's unbalanced treatment. As he began to take responsibility for the harm he caused his sister, he began to experience intense feelings of guilt and questions about who he was as a person. At one point, he asked the practitioner, "What kind of person beats up on a little girl? At the time, I thought I was tough, but now I think I was such a coward." He became increasingly angry with his father and began to grieve the missed opportunities to have a close relationship with his sister. The practitioner worked with Troy to reconnect with his sister by taking responsibility for his past behavior, supporting her in her own reactions, and beginning to build closeness. As a final step, task strategies included Troy undertaking family research to learn more about his father's life (he was deceased) with the aim of understanding him as a human being rather than an idealized individual who had legitimate reasons for disfavoring him. By talking with his mother, Troy learned that his father constantly worried about him being tough enough to endure the world "as an African American." She told him that his father loved him deeply but was particularly hard on him because he thought that was the best way to help him be successful. This was both a surprise and a relief to Troy. Although he did experience continued moments of intense grief about not having a closer relationship with his father, he now thought of him with affection rather than resentment.

The practitioner acknowledged Troy's own sense of victimization in order to help him move to a place where he could acknowledge and take responsibility for being a perpetrator. Practitioners should avoid a sole focus on perpetrators' hurtful behaviors as a strategy for helping victims, particularly when doing conjoint sibling work. Such actions will be viewed as taking sides with and favoring the victim, often a replication of the dynamics that exacerbated the original violence. Finally, it is important to note that identifying childhood sibling aggression and working with perpetrators to view it as serious and harmful and to take responsibility may be an important step in helping to prevent it in future generations. That is, a perpetrator who has come to terms with the seriousness of sibling aggression is less likely to dismiss or support violent behavior between his or her own children than an individual who has not done this work.

### *Sibling hostility in adulthood*

Although investigation into sibling aggression in middle adulthood has been essentially nonexistent, there is evidence that it remains prevalent in early adulthood. Studies using college samples report that sibling assault is alarmingly prevalent (Kettrey & Emery, 2006). It is likely that sibling aggression declines sharply in middle adulthood as individuals no longer share residences or are even required to keep in contact. That said, family members typically operate according to the interactional rules they learned in childhood and are likely to replicate aggressive behavior used in childhood in their adult sibling encounters. For example, during treatment for depression, Darla reported that she disliked family gatherings because all of her brothers would join together in making fun of her. She said that they saw it as amusing but she found it hurtful. When she protested, they called her a "baby" and told her she had no sense of humor. She said that she did not want to avoid family gatherings because she felt that her presence was important to her mother, but at the same time believed that confronting her brothers was useless.

In another case, David sought treatment because he had just turned 40 years old and was deeply worried that he had no prospects for marriage and would not have a family of his own. He described his relationship with brother Frank as "best friends" and said that they spent a great deal of time together. David also reported that Frank had a serious drinking problem and that he saw it as his responsibility to protect him (e.g., get him to work on time, stop him from driving while intoxicated). He also shared that Frank's drinking worsens whenever he does begin developing a relationship with a potential love interest. When the practitioner inquired into how he handled the conflicting relational demands, he said he becomes highly resentful of Frank and tells him he does not want to look after him anymore. He added that Frank will usually respond by telling him he does not want his care, which angers him further, and that it usually erupts into a fist fight. He reports that he once broke Frank's nose and had to rush him to the hospital. David shared that the fights make him feel incredibly guilty because he knows "that Frank doesn't know any better" and he retreats from his budding relationship with a woman in order to attend to him again.

Both cases illustrate sibling aggression in adulthood and highlight the importance of attending to sibling themes in adulthood. Conjoint sibling work should be considered. In the case of Darla, conjoint work with Darla and one sibling at a time would likely have a better outcome than meeting with the entire sibling set in which the brothers are likely to join together against her in the treatment room. Task strategies in adulthood target halting sibling aggression, developing sibling positivity, and creating a healthy balance between autonomy and connectedness.

### *Sibling elder abuse*

Elder abuse (a.k.a. maltreatment) is a serious problem affecting hundreds of thousands of individuals each year (Pillemer & Finkelhor, 1988). It may involve psychological, physical, sexual, and financial abuse. While adult children are the most frequent perpetrators of this type of maltreatment, siblings are among the least (National Center on Elder Abuse, 1996). However, violence against parents may be a sibling issue, borne out of perceptions of parental favoritism and resentment. Elder abuse related to sibling dynamics can be perpetrated by sibling caregivers or children caring for their parents. In fact, siblings may be the target of children who are violent toward their elderly parents. For example, Michael was designated by his mother as her primary caregiver and was in charge of her bank account. Michael's two sisters, who lived across the country, became increasingly concerned that their mother was being neglected. When they inquired about the elimination of a full-time caregiver, Michael told them that there was no money left in their mother's account. He then told the sisters that they should start paying for their mother's care. They suspected he was lying and using her money for his personal needs. The more they would ask about their mother's financial situation, the less he would share and began avoiding their phone calls and emails. The sister's believed that Michael's intention was really to torment them—that their mother was a "pawn" in their long-standing sibling conflict. This indirect form of sibling aggression is hostile to his sisters and mother, and constitutes both sibling and elder abuse.

Practitioners working with adult caregiving arrangements must attend to relationships beyond the immediate caregiver and person receiving care dyad to include family dynamics, and siblings in particular. Suspicion of elder abuse must be reported to state adult protective services. Parent maltreatment is often embedded in long-standing family dynamics, many of which began in childhood. These often are linked to relationships with siblings and perceptions of favoritism. Intervention work should focus on arranging family meetings when possible and addressing "old hurts," with the aim of having siblings work together for the best interest of the parent. Similarly, when siblings are the perpetrators, conjoint sibling sessions are recommended when the receiver of care is able to participate. Individual sessions with the caregiving sibling to address or uncover underlying hostility is indicated when the receiver of care is unable to participate. Again, relationships to parents are salient when working with sibling dyads.

Finally, sibling aggression in caregiving arrangements can range from mild to severe. Abuse must be reported, but less problematic forms should not be left unaddressed as aggression often escalates. Asking sibling caregivers about the quality of their relationship at the start of care provision offers opportunities to address resentments prior to intensification.

## Prevention

As noted in Chapter 1, little attention has been given to the prevention of sibling violence despite being both a widespread and a potentially dangerous social problem. Prevention efforts have been primarily directed solely at families.

However, stopping violence before it occurs requires a multisystems-level approach. These include important actions directed at children and families, educators and practitioners, researchers, and the culture at large. Each of these systems is taken up here.

### *Children and families*

In the few available offerings, sibling aggression prevention is not the central objective, which focuses instead on prosocial skill development to increase social–emotional competencies with siblings (Kennedy & Kramer, 2008; Kramer & Radey, 1997; Tiedemann & Johnston, 1992). Siblings who feel warmly toward each other are less likely to act in hostile and harmful ways, and intervention efforts to build positivity can serve as important prevention technologies. Individual prosocial skill development, parent training, and changing the social climate have been identified as effective prevention efforts for youth violence in general (U.S. Surgeon General, 2001).

### *Stopping aggression early in development*

It is expected that siblings will act aggressively toward each other at young ages. Toddlers, for example, have a limited repertoire of problem-solving strategies and will commonly resort to aggressive tactics to express their wishes (e.g., hitting out of frustration, forcefully grabbing a toy, shoving). Many parents and practitioners view these behaviors as temporary functions of age that the child will "grow out of" and dismiss or ignore the aggression. Alternatively, many parents scold the child. Both ignoring and scolding are behaviors that may serve to exacerbate hostility. Ignoring conveys tacit approval and scolding promotes "outsider" status in which the sibling is being protected (i.e., favored) by the parent. Preventing the escalation of harmful aggression requires attending to it from its first appearance but in a way that teaches the aggressor alternative prosocial behaviors and supports inclusive status.

As an example, Maria, age 3, slapped her 1-year-old brother when he reached for one of her toys. Their mother immediately yelled at Maria and said, "You let your little brother play with your toys!" Maria began to cry and tried to hit Roberto a second time. Her mother reacted by again yelling at Maria saying, "You are being a bad girl and going into time out!" Maria cried and from time out yelled, "Roberto, I hate you!" Although their mother's reaction provided a negative consequence for Maria's physical aggression, it may serve to create negativity in the sibling relationship. Maria, treated as an "outsider" (i.e., in a triangle with a mother–son coalition), expresses her resentment toward her brother—a problem that could escalate into increasing violence.

This is a moment early in their relationship where expressions of aggression can be used as "teachable moments" to provide children with prosocial behaviors for handling conflict with the aim of building greater warmth and inclusiveness. For example, using the steps of the PBA (described in Chapter 6), their mother could have intervened by firmly telling Maria that hitting was not permitted and then provided her with a productive alternative behavior such as gently holding her brother's hand to keep him from grabbing her toy and providing him with a replacement toy that he can play with (e.g., telling him, "You can't play with this toy, but you can have this one."), or actively sharing the toy (e.g., telling him, "You want this one? OK, you can have it, but just for a moment."), or calling for her mother's help if she becomes overly frustrated. Their mother then must actively and energetically praise the positive behavior (e.g., "You see how nice your sister is! She really loves you!"). Their mother can help protect Maria's interests while also helping to support the younger brother's curiosity and to build sibling affection.

Because the quality of sibling relationships seems fairly stable, resentments from early in life are likely to grow and possibly turn to escalating aggression if left unaddressed. By comparison, strategies to promote warmth and support early on are likely to set the course for long-term positivity and reduced problematic aggression.

When working with older children in practice, it is important to inquire about the sibling relationship early in treatment and, if characterized by some negativity, raise the dangers of aggression—even if the current relationship does not consist of harmful hostility. Preventing sibling aggression involves raising the potential for it to occur before it takes place, particularly when it is suspicious that relationships could be headed in that direction.

*Educators and practitioners.* Although there is evidence that siblings have an important role in human behavior and development, siblings have been largely neglected in formal education settings, university curricula, text books, and postgraduate training (Caspi, 2011a). Moreover, sibling aggression content has been essentially missing from these settings despite being prevalent in cultural and religious narratives, and is frequently portrayed in various media formats (e.g., movies, television shows). The lack of emphasis on siblings and the problems of aggression constrain prevention efforts. Additionally, and more problematically, it may give tacit support to its perpetuation.

Siblings receive even less inclusion in practice curricula (i.e., applied human service professions education). Sibling content occasionally makes appearances in family and individual therapy texts, but rarely is it the focus of attention. Currently, I know of no graduate education programs that offer sibling practice courses or even regularly include sibling practice content. Integration of sibling aggression content must come from faculty, who ironically, must receive their own training to be convinced and prepared to include such material in curricula.

I have observed a fairly recent increase in sibling offerings at continuing education workshops and scholarly conferences, but it still remains an underrepresented area. Presentations that focus on sibling aggression treatment are almost nonexistent. The lack of offerings is not necessarily a reflection of lack of practitioner interest, but is likely instead due to lack of awareness and prior education. My experience giving workshops is that practitioners are quite interested in the subject as evidenced by consistently high attendance and enthusiasm. More must be encountering sibling aggression in their practice.

Invisible aggression is difficult to prevent or treat. Awareness is an essential ingredient. Practitioners and educators must be trained to "think siblings" (Caspi, 2011a). Sibling aggression content is required in formal education settings as part of an overall strategy to begin prevention efforts.

*Researchers.* Although sibling aggression has received some attention by researchers, it has received little compared to other forms of interpersonal violence. As noted in Chapter 1, few treatment offerings have received empirical scrutiny. Researchers, like practitioners and educators, are not encouraged to consider siblings in their formal education. Investigations into the processes that support sibling hostility are important for developing sensible prevention strategies. Moreover, researchers should collaborate with practitioners to design empirically validated prevention programs. Prevention will benefit from the development of prevention technologies.

Research has had a long-standing struggle with dissemination of important findings. An increasing number of studies have demonstrated that problematic sibling aggression is widespread and has harmful consequences, yet the general public, policy makers, and many practitioners are unaware of this. Alternative methods of "spreading the word" (e.g., press releases to media, discussing findings in forums available to the general public) must be undertaken as part of a comprehensive prevention effort.

*Culture at large.* As discussed in Chapter 1, sibling aggression is perceived to be a normal, expected, and harmless behavior by the culture at large. Prevention efforts must also include actions to denormalize sibling violence. This requires confronting sources that continue to perpetuate cultural narratives that support violence between siblings by highlighting its negative consequences. As in the case of other forms of interpersonal violence (e.g., wife battering, peer bullying, child abuse), which were once overlooked and thought to be rarely occurring, private matters, or normative development, a cognitive shift with a new understanding of the dangers and prevalence of sibling aggression is necessary.

Sibling aggression is the only form of interpersonal violence that is viewed as acceptable behavior. In recent history, other forms of interpersonal violence (e.g., wife battering, peer bullying, child abuse) were once thought to be rarely occurring, private matters, or normative development. Efforts to change the cultural stance toward interpersonal violence have been important in preventing and reducing these other forms. Challenging constructions of sibling aggression normalcy may be aided by illustrating how violent behaviors such as punching, belittling, and shoving to the floor are not tolerated when perpetrators are a parent, teacher, coach, or babysitter. If these behaviors were perpetrated by a peer, it would be viewed unfavorably (e.g., "bullying"). I have found that highlighting the inherent contradiction of "normal violence" has been an effective strategy for beginning to alter understandings of this problematic social phenomenon.

Examples of activities to denormalize sibling aggression include public awareness and educational campaigns. These should target families, communities, schools, mental and physical health practitioners, researchers, policy makers, agency administrators, university faculty and students, and the media. In other words, to change the dominant cultural narratives that keep sibling aggression invisible, it is necessary to "spread the word" at every opportunity. Finally, because sibling aggression has been linked to other social problems (e.g., peer bullying, substance abuse), and seems to be a precursor to later violence such as date violence (Noland et al., 2004), prevention efforts should have positive implications far beyond reducing sibling violence.

## TREATMENT APPLICATIONS ACROSS PRACTICE MODALITIES AND SETTINGS

### Practice Modalities

A hallmark of task-centered practice is its integrative orientation (described in depth in Chapter 4), which promotes utilizing and drawing upon effective strategies from other intervention and theoretical frameworks. Accordingly, the TCSA treatment approach put forth in this book is meant to be used as an organizing structure for practice, to be implemented across practice modalities and settings. TCSA integrates structural family therapy and behavioral techniques, family systems, and ethological theories and will be most readily usable by practitioners using these sources. For those using different approaches, TCSA should provide information and strategies that are fairly easily incorporated into their practices. For example, the use of client tasks as a treatment strategy has increased across practice modalities and the suggested task strategies should be relatively easy to utilize. Finally, task-centered practice has seen many successful adaptations for a variety of treatment issues, which have targeted work with individuals, couples, families, and groups (Ramos & Tolson, 2008; Reid, 2000). Similarly, although TCSA is offered as a family treatment model, it is readily adaptable for individual and group work.

#### *Settings*

TCSA is readily adaptable for direct practice in the various settings sibling aggression emerges. The focus of this book was on work with families in clinical settings (e.g., community mental health, family therapy, private practice). However, sibling aggression is also an important feature of out-of-home care (e.g., foster) settings (Begun & Mersky, 2011), schools, camps, and any other places where siblings reside (e.g., group homes, orphanages, day care, nursing homes). Additionally, sibling aggression issues may emerge in work with individuals of any age. For example, it is common for resentments to emerge in hospital and hospice settings where siblings may be in their eighties or older. Individuals seek out and are referred to treatment for a wide variety of reasons that involve siblings both directly and indirectly. Inquiry into sibling relationships with individuals in almost any setting is likely to reveal important information and result in sibling aggression work for which TCSA is appropriate.

## Special Applications Considerations

### *Sibling sexual abuse*

A broad overview of sibling sexual abuse was provided in Chapter 1, where I noted that sexual abuse involves dynamics and intervention considerations that are distinct from other forms of sibling aggression. It is a unique variant of family violence that requires "specialized intervention" (Caffaro, 2011, p. 247). Although some overlap of family patterns with those presented in the FFDs may exist (e.g., ineffective supervision), they are not intended specifically for sibling sexual abuse. Some actions for abusive sibling relationships are similar, such as reporting to child or adult protective services and creating safety plans. Practitioners working with families with sibling sexual abuse are encouraged to make use of existing offerings that specifically target this unique area of practice (e.g., Caffaro & Conn-Caffaro, 1998; DiGiorgio-Miller, 1998; Haskins, 2003; Wiehe, 1997). TCSA can be utilized as an organizing framework with task strategies drawn from these offerings. For example, tasks can be formulated to improve supervision, clarify and strengthen interpersonal boundaries, and work with authorities.

### *Organizing sessions: Who attends and when?*

Selecting which family members attend sessions and at what time depends upon the nature and severity of aggression. Family meetings and conjoint sibling sessions make sense for less severe forms, whereas individual sessions are usually necessary for abuse cases. The approach put forth in this book is a family model and encourages beginning with meetings in which all family members are present. Abuse is a family problem in that it negatively affects all members and is often supported by family dynamics, and, as a collective, the family should work together. Indeed, most interventions emphasize family intervention. It is important to emphasize the importance of including fathers in treatment as they may play a particularly important role regarding the nature of sibling relationships (Brody et al., 1994; Caffaro, 2011; Noland et al., 2004; Stocker & McHale, 1992).

There are situations, however, in which perpetrators should not be included as their presence may silence victims, or they may utilize session work to further torment. Client safety should be the primary concern in making decisions about whether or not to include perpetrators in family meetings. Additional considerations include taking into account the "readiness" of victims and the guardian's capacity to supervise and protect their children (Caffaro, 2011).

Guardian-only meetings are recommended in order to support and clarify parenting and discipline strategies and to ensure that couples are working together. Disagreements about how to parent, opposing views of the seriousness of sibling aggression, and cross-generational coalitions are addressed in order to create a parental alliance—perhaps the most important element in developing positive sibling relationships and halting aggression. In fact, it is common for sibling aggression approaches to include guardian-only meetings as a central intervention step (e.g., Caffaro, 2011; Reid & Donovan, 1990). In fact, Reid and Donovan (1990) include guardian-only meetings as a first phase of treatment.

Practitioners using TCSA should consider a flexible approach that includes family, guardian-only, conjoint sibling, and individual sessions. Each configuration usually involves unique task-planning and implementation processes. For example, couples may develop tasks related to developing a parenting alliance, whereas sibling sessions may result in the formulation of actions related to sharing personal property. TCSA practitioners should also consider adding group work as either a central or adjunctive approach.

### *Groups*

Group work can be a helpful treatment modality to be used as an adjunct or as a stand-alone approach for sibling aggression, particularly for adolescents. Groups formulated for severe aggression typically separate victims or perpetrators. Victims receive validation and support from peers who have experienced similar maltreatment. A focus for perpetrator groups is accountability and development of new interpersonal skill sets. For less severe forms of aggression, groups work with both siblings, usually with a focus on developing prosocial and conflict resolution skills. TCSA is adapted for group settings in which the members work together to identify and formulate tasks, and to hold each other accountable for completing them.

### *Practitioner bias*

Practitioners' understanding of siblings influences intervention work. Because practitioners receive so little information about siblings in their training, they may hold biased views, informed by cultural narratives and personal experience (Caspi, 2011a). Such views may overlook siblings as both resources and sources of disruption. As a consequence, practitioners may fail to ask about sibling relationships entirely (Watson & McGoldrick, 2001).

A danger exists when a practitioner see sibling aggression as normative and benign. Not only do such views risk client safety, they also serve to perpetuate abuse by neglecting to address it. For example, a boy terrorized by a sibling may be referred to treatment for being disruptive at school. A biased clinician may avoid exploring the sibling relationship and even if the violence is disclosed, may fail to see it as problematic or linked to the school behavior.

Practitioner bias may also emerge in cases where one of the siblings has a disability or mental illness, and becomes the sole focus of attention and protection. Siblings often act aggressively when they feel like outsiders in their own families. Practitioners can collude with the family and reinforce this outsider positioning when they avoid consideration of the sibling relationship. Similarly, those working with children in out-of-home care settings may give greater priority to placement and parent–child relationships and miss the centrality of siblings, and neglect to identify sibling violence—particularly problematic when protecting children from violence is the reason for removal from families. Begun and Mersky (2011) have noted the complete lack of attention given to children living in families (i.e., biological and adopted) who care for children in the foster system. The experience of being a sibling to a foster child too often includes violence.

Practitioners may also be biased by gendered perceptions of sibling relationships. For example, aggression perpetrated by females is not considered in the same ways as when males are the aggressors. Moreover, interpersonal violence is almost always about power and control. Feminist therapy has long encouraged practitioners to integrate the unpacking of gendered social constructions in understanding relationships, particularly in terms of power arrangements (e.g., Walters, Carter, Papp, & Silverstein, 1988). Learning how a sibling's aggression is linked to gender suggests different interventions than if such issues are left unexamined.

Practitioner sibling biases are best addressed through education and self-reflection, often fostered in clinical supervision. The clinician who is aware of the deleterious effects of sibling violence is unlikely to engage in neglectful or misdirected practice. Practitioners must systematically incorporate sibling relationship assessment in their work. One strategy that promotes greater objectivity is the use of standardized instruments for assessment, as noted in earlier chapters.

## CONCLUSION

This book provided an overview of sibling aggression, introduced an emerging consolidated sibling theory, presented the TCSA treatment approach, and provided assessment and intervention strategies organized by five common family dynamics that exacerbate problematic sibling aggression. The treatment approach put forth seeks to meet two major objectives: (1) halting sibling aggression and (2) promoting sibling positivity and support. Task menus to meet these goals were offered to facilitate TCSA implementation.

I conclude the book with some final thoughts and suggested future directions for research and practice. Although the book attempted to be thorough, it is impossible to address all sibling aggression-related concerns and its many varied manifestations. Practitioners should use the presented information as guidelines for understanding sibling behavior and for carrying out treatment. Much is still unknown about sibling relationships in general and sibling aggression in particular. For the most part, research has focused on victims. Research is needed to further our understanding of perpetrators, their development, cognitions, and behavior, and the role of the family and larger institutions in their lives. In peer aggression, victims are also often bullies (i.e., "bully-victims"), a dynamic that has not been examined in the sibling domain. In particular, treatment methods for working with perpetrators of severe aggression must be developed and tested.

The next step in the development of TCSA is a more systematic testing of its efficacy. Preliminary evidence suggests that it is promising as an effective approach (Caspi, 2008). Because it is a highly structured model that emphasizes clear behavioral tasks and ongoing empirical problem evaluation, evaluating effectiveness should be relatively straightforward. Practitioners are encouraged to track progress and record situations in which the model worked and those in which it did not meet the needs of the situation. They should also actively add task ideas to current task menus and generate new task menus, and publish their work to aid other practitioners. Sibling aggression is a serious social problem and team efforts are required to address it.

# APPENDIX A

# Factors Connected With Sibling Aggression

The following are linked with sibling aggression. Most are findings from empirical investigations. The research from which these are drawn represent a wide range of rigor. Some findings are well established and others have only preliminary support. A few additional factors are included that come from prevalent theoretical frameworks and appear with enough regularity in the sibling discourse that they are generally accepted as important in sibling life and for practice. Citations are included for more in-depth understandings of concepts and study methods. A more in-depth presentation of the factors appears in Chapter 1 and these are referred to throughout the book.

Considering the range of empirical support, these factors should be utilized to *generally* inform assessment practices. Practitioners are encouraged to refer to this list to aid assessment in two ways:

1. *In cases in which sibling aggression is the reason for treatment.* The list can be used to aid in identification of
   a. Potential causes or factors that exacerbate sibling aggression. For example, marital conflict, a supporting factor, may be assessed and may require attention in order to treat the sibling aggression.
   b. Other potential problems that may be consequences of sibling aggression. For example, seeing peer aggression on the list can help practitioners inquire about peer bullying.
2. *In cases in which sibling aggression is not the reason for treatment.* The list can be used to aid in the identification of sibling aggression by considering the list as "risk factors." The more factors from this list that are present in the lives of clients the more likely sibling aggression is present. (*Note:* this list has not been tested for its predictive power.) Even if only one or a few factors emerge in practice, practitioners should inquire about sibling aggression.

The list is organized according to likely consequences and likely exacerbating factors that include family, parenting, individual, and additional concerns. It is important to keep in mind that many of these issues likely operate in reciprocal fashion with sibling hostility—each reinforcing the other.

## LIKELY CONSEQUENCES AND RECIPROCAL PROCESS

### Childhood

- School misconduct (Garcia et al., 2000)
- Academic difficulties (Kingston & Prior, 1995)
- Peer bullying (Duncan, 1999; Ensor et al., 2010)
- Poor peer relations (Dunn & McGuire, 1992; Ensor et al., 2010; Stormshak et al., 1996)
- Physical aggression with peers (Berndt & Bulleit, 1985; MacKinnon-Lewis et al., 1997)
- Behavior and emotional problems (Deater-Deckard et al., 2002)
- Psychiatric diagnosis (Cuevas et al., 2009)
- Psychological distress, including major depressive disorder (Kessler & Magee, 1994), anxiety, depression (Duncan, 1999), unhappiness, helplessness (Rosenthal & Doherty, 1984)
- Destructive thoughts about family members (Rosenthal & Doherty, 1984)
- Medical illness (Rosenthal & Doherty, 1984)
- Victimization by other sources (Kessler & Magee, 1994) and multiple sources (Turner et al., 2010)

### Adolescence and Early Adulthood

- Arrests (Bank et al., 1996)
- Interpersonal aggression (Williams et al., 2007)
- Psychological distress (Cuevas et al., 2010), including depression, insecurity, and feelings of incompetence (Hoffman & Edwards, 2004), anxiety and possible enduring anger, resentment, and challenges with expressing emotion (Graham-Berman & Cutler, 1994)
- Date violence (Noland et al., 2004)
- Greater consideration for using violent behaviors with others (Gully et al., 1981)
- Substance abuse (Button & Gealt, 2010)
- Delinquency (Button & Gealt, 2010)
- Aggression (Button & Gealt, 2010)
- Sibling negativity and lack of intimacy (Updegraff et al., 2005)

### Long-Term Consequences

- Lowered self-concept (Garey, 1999)
- Depression, insecurity, feelings of incompetence (Hoffman & Edwards, 2004)
- Relationship problems in adulthood (Wiehe, 1997)
- Posttraumatic stress disorder (Wiehe, 1997)
- Lower self-esteem and social competence (Morrill-Richards, 2010)

## LIKELY EXACERBATING FACTORS

### Family Dynamics

- Negative and conflictual parent–child relationships (Hoffman et al., 2005)
- Parent hostility toward a child (Williams et al., 2007)
- Spousal abuse (Haj-Yahia & Dawud-Noursi, 1998; Hotaling et al., 1990)
- Marital and intimate partner conflict (Hoffman et al., 2005; Stocker & Youngblade, 1999)
- Partner disagreement about parenting and split-parent identification (Schachter, 1985)
- Mother's marital dissatisfaction (Stocker et al., 1997)
- Maternal negative emotional expressiveness (Stocker et al., 1997)
- Maternal self-criticism (Garcia et al., 2000; MacKinnon-Lewis et al., 1997; Volling & Belsky, 1992)
- Financial stress (Hardy, 2001; Williams et al., 2007)
- Low family cohesion, disorganization, household chaos (Brody et al., 1994; Eriksen & Jensen, 2006; Kretschmer & Pike, 2009)
- Husband's losses of temper (Eriksen & Jensen, 2006)
- Low maternal education (Ensor et al., 2010)
- Family triangulation (Haskins, 2203; Kerig, 1995; Kiselica & Morrill-Richards, 2007) and its related parent–child coalitions (Vuchinich et al., 1994)

### Parenting Behavior

- Parental differential treatment (Dunn, 1991), particularly by fathers (Brody & Stoneman, 1994), and particularly by fathers favoring laterborn sisters (Updegraff et al., 2005)
- Active and direct judgmental comparison (Feinberg & Hetherington, 2001)
- Parents labeling their children "bad–good" and "easy–difficult" (Schachter, 1985, Schachter & Stone, 1985)
- Low parental involvement, particularly by fathers (Updegraff et al., 2005)
- Ineffective parenting (Bank et al., 2004)
- Inconsistent discipline (Bank et al., 1996)
- Coercive parenting (Means-Burleson, 2002)
- Maternal coercive, rejecting, and overcontrolling parenting behaviors (Eriksen & Jensen, 2006; Yu, 2008)
- Parental abuse of children (Button & Gealt, 2010; Wiehe, 1997)
- Parents use of violence to resolve parent–child conflict (Graham-Berman et al., 1994)
- Parental neglect
- Approval of aggression (Rosenthal & Doherty, 1984)
- Possibly corporal punishment (Eriksen & Jensen, 2006)
- Lack of supervision (Whipple & Finton, 1995)
- Nonintervention in sibling conflict (Bennett, 1990)

- Ignoring child-voiced claims of maltreatment (Wiehe, 1997)
- Neglecting to reinforce of prosocial behaviors (Bryant & Crockenberg, 1980)
- Restricting children's efforts to diversify interests and specialization (Sulloway, 1996)

## INDIVIDUAL

### Perpetrators

- Lack empathy for victims (Silverman, 1999)
- Possess aggressive temperament (Munn & Dunn, 1988)
- Wish to satisfy unmet personal needs for physical contact in emotion-deprived environments (Bank & Kahn, 1997; Haskins, 2003)
- Are also victims of abuse, including by siblings (Caffaro & Conn-Caffaro, 2005)
- Sibling caretaking of younger brothers and sisters (Baum, 1998; Green, 1984)
- Boredom (Prochaska & Prochaska, 1985)

## ADDITIONAL FACTORS

- Firstborns (Martin & Ross, 1995)
- Imitating models—for example, younger siblings imitating older (Patterson, 1986)
- "Cascading violence" in which the firstborn attacks the secondborn, which goes after the thirdborn and so on (Wiehe, 1997)
- "Jump pairs" (first and third) (Schachter et al., 1978) may join together against their middleborn siblings
- Close age-spacing (Aguilar et al., 2001; Noland et al., 2004)
- Presence of a male (Ensor et al., 2010; Hoffman et al., 2005; Lockwood, 2002; Randall, 1992), particularly with preschool-age children
- Older brother–younger sister pairs most common for sibling violence (Aguilar et al., 2001; Buhrmester, 1992; Button & Gealt, 2010; Caffaro & Conn-Caffaro, 2005; Graham-Berman et al., 1994)
- Culture practices (e.g., primogeniture, patriarchy) (Hoffman & Edwards, 2004; Sulloway, 1996)
- Disability (Hanson et al., 1992; Linares, 2006)
- Ethnic/cultural background (Rapoza et al., 2010)—for example, Hispanics and Whites have higher rates of sibling assault (Finkelhor et al., 2005)

# APPENDIX B

## TCSA CONTRACT

**A. Target Problems**
List in order of priority the most pressing problems (up to three) for immediate work. Identify each problem in a single phrase. For each, provide a problem rating: 0 = mild or not severe; 5 = moderately severe; 10 = extremely severe. Place initials of each member's ratings in spaces next to problem ratings.

**Problem #1:** ______________________________

Problem ratings ________ ________ ________ ________ ________

**Problem #2:** ______________________________

Problem ratings ________ ________ ________ ________ ________

**Problem #3:** ______________________________

Problem ratings ________ ________ ________ ________ ________

**B. Task Formulations**
Identify up to three tasks for each corresponding target problem. State using verbs as actions or steps to be taken (e.g., Jane will ask permission to use Mary's hairdryer before using it).

**Problem #1**

Task #1: ______________________________

Task #2: ______________________________

Task #3: ______________________________

**Problem #2**

Task #1: ______________________________

Task #2: ______________________________

Task #3: ______________________________

**Problem #3**

Task #1: ______________________________

Task #2: ______________________________

Task #3: ______________________________

**C. Rehearsed? Were tasks rehearsed during session (e.g., role played, problem-solved)?**
*Circle one:* Yes No

**D. Obstacles: Were potential obstacles to task implementation considered?**
*Circle one:* Yes No

# APPENDIX C

# Sample of Completed Contract*

## TCSA CONTRACT

**A. Target Problems**

List in order of priority the most pressing problems (up to three) for immediate work. Identify each problem in a single phrase. For each, provide a problem rating using this scale: 1 = mild or not severe; 5 = moderately severe; 10 = extremely severe. Place initials of each member's ratings in spaces next to problem ratings.

**Problem #1:** *Sibling fighting*

Problem ratings 7 (BM) 4 (PM) 8 (Mrs. M) ______ ______

**Problem #2:** *Parental favoritism*

Problem ratings 9 (BM) 3 (PM) 4 (Mrs. M) 7 (Mr. M) ____

**Problem #3:** *Distinguish parental treatment from favoritism*

Problem ratings 6 (BM) 9 (Mrs. M) ______ ______ ______

**B. Task Formulations**

Identify up to three tasks for each corresponding target problem. State if using as actions or steps to be taken using verbs (e.g., Jane will ask permission to use Mary's hairdryer before using it).

***Tasks for Problem #1***

Task #1: *Pete will ask Brian for permission to play with Brian's toys before he plays with them.*

Task #2: *Brian will calmly tell his mother when Pete does not ask permission.*

Task #3: *Brian will not hit Pete and Pete will not call Brian names.*

***Tasks for Problem #2***

Task #1: *When Brian claims Mrs. M was unfair, Mrs. M will ask Brian to explain and how could have done things more fairly.*

Task #2: *Brian will express perceptions of unfair treatment in a calm voice and saying, "Mom, I think you are being unfair."*

Task #3: *Pete will tell his mother when he felt that Brian was being treated unfairly.*

***Tasks for Problem #3***

Task #1: *Mrs. M will make a chart to record sibling disagreements, including descriptions of how she handled the boys' conflicts.*

Task #2: *Mr. M will call family meetings after sibling conflicts to let Mrs. M and Brian calmly talk about what occurred.*

Task #3: *Mrs. M will self-reflect after sibling fights, making honest appraisals of fairness.*

**C. Rehearsed? Were tasks rehearsed during session (e.g., role played, problem-solved)?**

*Circle one:* [Yes] No

**D. Obstacles: Were potential obstacles to task implementation considered?**

*Circle one:* [Yes] No

* From Martin Family Case Study in Chapter 8.

# APPENDIX D

## TCSA TASK REVIEW FORM

*Name:* ____________________________________________

Immediately following implementation of one of the contracted tasks, evaluate your success in carrying out each task using the following scale. Each family member should have their own form.

4 = Fully completed
3 = Mostly completed
2 = Partly completed
1 = Not completed
N = No opportunity to complete

Contracted tasks are usually meant to be carried out multiple times. Tasks may require a few attempts to complete. Space is provided for rating task performance for each time you try to carry it out. Some straightforward tasks may only have the option of rating as "fully completed" or "not completed."

| | Rating of Attempts | | | | |
|---|---|---|---|---|---|
| | 1st | 2nd | 3rd | 4th | 5th |
| ***Problem #1*** | | | | | |
| Task #1 | ____ | ____ | ____ | ____ | ____ |
| Task #2 | ____ | ____ | ____ | ____ | ____ |
| Task #3 | ____ | ____ | ____ | ____ | ____ |
| ***Problem #2*** | | | | | |
| Task #1 | ____ | ____ | ____ | ____ | ____ |
| Task #2 | ____ | ____ | ____ | ____ | ____ |
| Task #3 | ____ | ____ | ____ | ____ | ____ |
| ***Problem #3*** | | | | | |
| Task #1 | ____ | ____ | ____ | ____ | ____ |
| Task #2 | ____ | ____ | ____ | ____ | ____ |
| Task #3 | ____ | ____ | ____ | ____ | ____ |

**Identified Obstacles**

Identify obstacles encountered that led to scores of "1 = Not completed."

# APPENDIX E

## THE TCSA SEQUENCE

***Initial phase*** (from the first meeting until completion of the first contract)

1. Social stage
2. Provide TCSA overview and sibling education
3. Target problem formulation
   a. Problem identification and specification
   b. Identification of transactional sequences
4. Task selection
5. Identifying and resolving obstacles
6. Rehearsal
7. Contracting

***Middle phase*** (from completion of the first contract through the final meeting)

1. Social stage
2. Task review
3. Target problem review
4. Target problem formulation or reformulation
5. Task selection
6. Identifying and resolving obstacles
7. Rehearsal
8. Contracting

***Ending phase*** (the final meeting)

1. Target problem review
2. Identification of successful problem-solving strategies
3. Review of client problem situation in general
4. Discussion of future work and possible recontracting

# References


Adams, C. D., & Kelley, M. L. (1992). Managing sibling aggression: Overcorrection as an alternative to time-out. *Behavior Therapy*, *23*(4), 707–717.

Aguilar, B., O'Brien, K. M., August, G. J., Aoun, S. L., & Hektner, J. M. (2001). Relationship quality of aggressive children and their siblings: A multi-informant, multi-measure investigation. *Journal of Abnormal Child Psychology*, *29*, 479–489.

Anderson, K. L. (2010). Conflict, power, and violence in families. *Journal of Marriage and Family*, *72*(3), 726–742.

Appel, A. E., & Holden, G. W. (1998). The co-occurrence of spouse and physical child abuse: A review and appraisal. *Journal of Family Psychology*, *12*, 578–599.

Atwood, N. C. (2001). Gender bias in families and its clinical implication for women. *Social Work*, *46*(1), 23–36.

Bailey, D., & Reid, W. (1996). Intervention design and development: A case study. *Research on Social Work Practice*, *6*(2), 208–228.

Bandura, A. (1977). *Social learning theory*. Englewood Cliffs, NJ: Prentice-Hall.

Bank, L., & Burraston, B. (2001). Abusive home environments as predictors of poor adjustment during adolescence and early adulthood. *American Journal of Community Psychology*, *29*(3), 195–217.

Bank, L., Burraston, B., & Snyder, J. (2004). Sibling conflict and ineffective parenting as predictors of adolescent boys' antisocial behavior and peer difficulties: Additive and interactional effects. *Journal of Research on Adolescence*, *14*(1), 99–125.

Bank, L., Patterson, G. R., & Reid, J. B. (1996). Negative sibling interaction patterns as predictors of later adjustment problems in adolescent and young adult males. In G. Brody (Ed.), *Sibling relationships: Their causes and consequences* (pp. 197–229). Norwood, NJ: Ablex Publishing Corporation.

Bank, S., & Kahn, M. (1997). *The sibling bond*. New York: Basic Books.

Bateson, G., Jackson, D. D., Haley, J., & Weakland, J. H. (1956). Toward a theory of schizophrenia. *Behavioral Science*, *1*, 251–264.

Baum, L. R. (1998). Correlates of sibling violence. *Dissertation Abstracts International: Section B: The Sciences and Engineering*, *58*(11-A), 4442.

Beck, A. T., Steer, R. A., & Garbin, M. G. (1988). Psychometric properties of the Beck Depression Inventory: Twenty-five years of evaluation. *Clinical Psychology Review*, *8*(1), 77–100.

Bedford, V. H., Volling, B. L., & Avioli, P. S. (2000). Positive consequences of sibling conflict in childhood and adulthood. *International Journal of Aging and Human Development*, *51*(1), 53–69.

Begun, A. L. (1995). Sibling relationships and foster care placements for young children. *Early Child Development and Care*, *106*, 237–250.

Begun, A. L., & Berger, L. K. (2011). Sibling involvement in substances misuse and abuse. In J. Caspi (Ed.), *Sibling development: Implications for mental health practitioners*. New York: Springer Publishing.

Begun, A. L., & Mersky, J. (2011). Sibling relationships and out-of-home care. In J. Caspi (Ed.), *Sibling development: Implications for mental health practitioners*. New York: Springer Publishing.

Bem, S. L. (1974). The measurement of psychological androgyny. *The Journal of Consulting and Clinical Psychology, 42*, 155–162.

Bennett, J. C. (1990). Nonintervention into siblings' fighting as a catalyst for learned helplessness. *Psychological Reports, 66*(1), 139–145.

Berndt, T. J., & Bulleit, T. N. (1985). Effects of sibling relationships on preschooler's behavior at home and at school. *Developmental Psychology, 21*, 761–767.

Birtchnell, J., & Mayhew, J. (1977). Toman's theory: Tested for mate selection and friendship formation. *Journal of Individual Psychology, 33*(1), 18–36.

Boll, T., Ferring, D., & Filipp, S. (2005). Effects of parental differential treatment on relationship quality with siblings and parents: Justice evaluations as mediators. *Social Justice Research, 18*(2), 155–182.

Bornstein, M. H., Cote, L. R., Haynes, O. M., Hahn, C., & Park, Y. (2010). Parenting knowledge: Experiential and sociodemographic factors in European American mothers of young children. *Developmental Psychology, 46*(6), 1677–1693.

Bowen, M. (1978). *Family therapy in clinical practice*. New York: Brunner/Mazel.

Brennan, S. (2006). Sibling incest within violent families: Children under 12 seeking nurture. *Health Sociology Review, 15*(3), 287–292.

Brewer, A. A. (1999). Sexual disorders and sexual trauma. In R. E. Feinstein & A. A. Brewer (Eds.), *Primary care psychiatry and behavioral medicine: Brief office treatment and management pathways* (pp. 256–272). New York: Springer Publishing.

Briggs, H. E., & Rzepnicki, T. L. (Eds.). (2004). *Using evidence in social work practice: Behavioral perspectives*. Chicago, IL: Lyceum Books, Inc.

Brody, G., & Stoneman, Z. (1994). Sibling relationships and their association with parental differential treatment. In E. M. Hetherington, D. Reiss, & R. Plomin (Eds.), *Separate social worlds of siblings* (pp. 129–142). Hillsdale, NJ: Lawrence Erlbaum.

Brody, G. H., Stoneman, Z., & McCoy, J. K. (1992). Parental differential treatment of siblings and sibling differences in negative emotionality. *Journal of Marriage and the Family, 54*, 643–651.

Brody, G. H., Stoneman, Z., & McCoy, J. K. (1994). Forecasting sibling relationships in early adolescence from child temperaments and family processes in middle childhood. *Child Development, 65*, 771–784.

Brody, L. R., Copeland, A. P., Sutton, L. S., Richardson, D. R., & Guyer, M. (1998). Mommy and daddy like you best: Perceived family favouritism in relation to affect, adjustment and family process. *Journal of Family Therapy, 20*(3), 269–291.

Brotman, L. M., Dawson-McClure, S., Gouley, K. K., McGuire, K., Burraston, B., & Bank, L. (2005). Older siblings benefit from a family-based preventive intervention for preschoolers at risk for conduct problems. *Journal of Family Psychology, 19*, 581–591.

Bryant, B. K., & Crockenberg, S. B. (1980). Correlates and dimensions of prosocial behavior: A study of female siblings with their mothers. *Child Development, 51*(2), 529–544.

Bugental, D. B., & Happaney, K. (2002). Parental attributions. In M. H. Bornstein (Ed.), *Handbook of parenting: Status and social conditions of parenting* (Vol. 3, 2nd ed., pp. 509–535). Mahwah, NJ: Erlbaum.

Buhrmester, D. (1992). The development courses of sibling and peer relationships. In F. Boer, & J. Dunn (Eds.), *Children's sibling relationships: Development and clinical issues*. Hillsdale, NJ: Erlbaum.

Buhrmester, D., & Furman, W. (1990). Perceptions of sibling relationships during middle childhood and adolescence. *Child Development, 61*, 1387–1398.

Burns, D. D., & Nolen-Hoeksma, S. (1992). Therapeutic empathy and recovery from depression in cognitive-behavioral therapy: A structural equation model. *Journal of Consulting and Clinical Psychology, 60*, 441–449.

Burton, L. (2007). Childhood adultification in economically disadvantaged families: A conceptual model. *Family Relations, 56*(4), 329–345.

Button, D., & Gealt, R. (2010). High risk behaviors among victims of sibling violence. *Journal of Family Violence, 25*(2), 131–140.

Caffaro, J. (2011). Sibling violence and systems-oriented therapy. In J. Caspi (Ed.), *Sibling development: Implications for mental health practitioners*. New York: Springer Publishing.

Caffaro, J. V., & Conn-Caffaro, A. (1998). *Sibling abuse trauma: Assessment and intervention strategies for children, families, and adults*. Binghamton, NY: Haworth Press.

Caffaro, J. V., & Conn-Caffaro, A. (2005). Treating sibling abuse families. *Aggression and Violent Behavior, 10*, 604–623.

Campione-Barr, N., & Smetana, J. (2010). "Who said you could wear my sweater?" Adolescent siblings conflicts and associations with relationship quality. *Child Development, 81*(2), 464–471.

Canavan, M. M., Meyer, W. J., & Higgs, D. C. (1992). The female experience of sibling incest. *Marital Family Therapy, 18*(2), 129–142.

Card, N., Stucky, B., Sawalani, G., & Little, T. (2008). Direct and indirect aggression during childhood and adolescence: A meta-analytic review of gender differences, intercorrelations, and relations to maladjustment. *Child Development, 79*(5), 1185–1229.

Carlson, B. E. (2011). Sibling incest: Adjustment in adult women survivors. *Families in Society, 92*(1), 77–83.

Carlson, B. E., Maciol, K., & Schneider, J. (2006). Sibling incest: Reports from forty-one survivors. *Journal of Child Sexual Abuse, 15*(4), 19–34.

Carpenter, J. (2001). Coevolving social institutions: An example of status and markets (Chapter 4). In F. Adaman & P. J. Devine (Eds.), *Economy and society: Money, capitalism and transition*. Montreal, Canada: Black Rose Books.

Caspi, J. (2008). Building a sibling aggression treatment model: Design & development research in action. *Research on Social Work Practice, 16*(6), 575–585.

Caspi, J. (Ed.) (2011a). *Sibling development: Implications for mental health practitioners*. New York: Springer Publishing.

Caspi, J. (2011b). Future directions for sibling research, practice, and theory. In J. Caspi (Ed.), *Sibling development: Implications for mental health practitioners*. New York: Springer Publishing.

Caspi, J. (2011c). Highway patrolman: An application of sibling theory & research. In D. G. Izzo (Ed.), *Bruce Springsteen and the American soul: Essays on the songs and influence of a cultural icon*. Jefferson, NC: McFarland Press.

Caspi, J., & Reid, W. J. (1998). The task-centered model for field instruction: An innovative approach. *Journal of Social Work Education, 34*(1), 55–70.

Caspi, J., & Reid, W. J. (2002). *Educational supervision in social work: A task-centered model for field instruction and staff development*. New York: Columbia University Press.

Caya, M., & Liem, J. H. (1998). The role of sibling support in high-conflict families. *Journal of Orthopsychiatry, 68*(2), 327–333.

Cicirelli, V. G. (1994). Sibling relationships in cross-cultural perspective. *Journal of Marriage & the Family, 56*, 7–20.

Cicirelli, V. G. (1995). *Sibling relationships across the life span*. New York: Plenum.
Coady, N., & Lehmann, P. (2008). *Theoretical perspectives for direct social work practice: A generalist-eclectic approach*. New York: Springer Publishing Co.
Connor, D. F. (2002). *Aggression and antisocial behavior in children and adolescents: Research and treatment*. New York: Guilford Press.
Corcoran, K., & Fischer, J. (2000). *Measures for clinical practice: A sourcebook* (3rd ed., Vol. 1–2). New York: FreePress.
Crick, N. R., Nelson, D. A., Morales, J. R., Cullerton-Sen, C., Casas, J. F., & Hickman, S. E. (2001). Relational victimization in childhood and adolescence. In J. Javonen & S. Graham (Eds.), *Peer harassment in school: The plight of the vulnerable and victimized* (pp. 196–214). New York: Guilford Press.
Crouter, A., McHale, S., & Tucker, C. (1999). Does stress exacerbate parental differential treatment of siblings? A pattern-analytic approach. *Journal of Family Psychology*, *13*(2), 286–299.
Cuevas, C., Finkelhor, D., Clifford, C., Ormrod, R., & Turner, H. (2010). Psychological distress as a risk factor for re-victimization in children. *Child Abuse & Neglect*, *34*(4), 235–243.
Cuevas, C. A., Finkelhor, D., Ormrod, R., & Turner, H. (2009). Psychiatric diagnosis as a risk marker for victimization in a national sample of children. *Journal of Interpersonal Violence*, *24*(4), 636–652.
Culotta, C. M., & Goldstein, S. E. (2008). Adolescent's aggressive and prosocial behavior: Associations with jealousy and social anxiety. *The Journal of Genetic Psychology: Research and Theory on Human Development*, *169*(1), 21–33.
Cyr, M., Wright, J., McDuff, P., & Perron, A. (2002). Intrafamilial sexual abuse: Brother–sister incest does not differ from father–daughter and stepfather–stepdaughter incest. *Child Abuse & Neglect*, *26*(9), 957–973.
Daniels, D., & Plomin, R. (1985). Differential experience of siblings in the same family. *Developmental Psychology*, *21*, 747–760.
David-Ferdon, C., & Kaslow, N. (2008). Evidence-based psychosocial treatments for child and adolescent depression. *Journal of Clinical Child and Adolescent Psychology*, *37*(1), 62–104.
Deater-Deckard, K., Dunn, J., & Lussier, G. (2002). Sibling relationships and social–emotional adjustment in different family contexts. *Social Development*, *11*(4), 571–590.
Deater-Deckard, K., Ivy, L., & Petrill, S. A. (2006). Maternal warmth moderates the link between physical punishment and child externalizing problems: A parent–offspring behavior genetic analysis. *Parenting: Science and Practice*, *6*(1), 59–78.
DiGiorgio-Miller, J. (1998). Sibling incest: Treatment of the family and the offender. *Child Welfare*, *77*(3), 335–346.
Duncan, R. D. (1999). Peer and sibling aggression: An investigation of intra- and extra-familial bullying. *Journal of Interpersonal Violence*, *8*(14), 871–886.
Dunn, J. (1991). The developmental importance of differences in siblings experiences within the family. In K. Pillimer & K. McCartney (Eds.), *Parent–child relations throughout life*. Hillsdale, NJ: Erlbaum.
Dunn, J., & Kendrik, C. (1981). Social behavior of young siblings in the family context: Differences between same-sex and different-sex dyads. *Child Development*, *52*, 1265–1273.
Dunn, J., & McGuire, S. (1992). Sibling and peer relationships in childhood. *Journal of Child Psychology and Psychiatry*, *33*, 67–105.

Dunn, J., & Munn, P. (1986). Sibling quarrels and maternal intervention: Individual differences in understanding and aggression. *Journal of Child Psychology and Psychiatry, 27*(5), 583–595.

Dunn, J., & Plomin, R. (1991). Why are siblings so different? The significance of differences in sibling experiences within the family. *Family Process, 30*(3), 271–283.

Dunn, J., Slomkowski, C., & Beardsall, L. (1994). Sibling relationships from the preschool period through middle childhood and early adolescence. *Developmental Psychology, 30*, 315–324.

East, P., Slonim, A., Horn, E., Trinh, C., & Reyes, B. (2009). How an adolescent's childbearing affects siblings' pregnancy risk: A qualitative study of Mexican American youths. *Perspectives on Sexual and Reproductive Health, 41*(4), 210–217.

East, P., & Weisner, T. (2009). Mexican American adolescents' family caregiving: Selection effects and longitudinal associations with adjustment. *Family Relations, 58*(5), 562–577.

East, P. L., & Khoo, S. T. (2005). Longitudinal pathways linking family factors and sibling relationship qualities to adolescent substance use and sexual risk behaviors. *Journal of Family Psychology, 19*(4), 571–580.

East, P. L., & Rook, K. S. (1992). Compensatory support among children's peer relationships: A test using school friends, nonschool friends, and siblings. *Developmental Psychology, 28*(1), 163–172.

Edwards, M., & Weller, S. (2011). A sideways look at gender and sibling relationships. In J. Caspi (Ed.), *Sibling development: Implications for mental health practitioners*. New York: Springer Publishing.

Ensor, R., Marks, A., Jacobs, L., & Hughes, C. (2010). Trajectories of antisocial behaviour towards siblings predict antisocial behaviour towards peers. *Journal of Child Psychology and Psychiatry, 51*(11), 1208–1216.

Eriksen, R. E. (2010). Task-centred practice in Norway. In A. E. Fortune, P. McCallion, & K. Briar-Lawson (Eds.), *Social work practice research for the 21st century*. New York: Columbia University Press.

Eriksen, S., & Jensen, V. (2006). All in the family? Family environment factors in sibling violence. *Journal of Family Violence, 21*(8), 497–507.

Feinberg, M., & Hetherington, E. M. (2001). Differential parenting as a within-family variable. *Journal of Family Psychology, 15*(1), 22–37.

Feinberg, M., Reiss, D., Neiderhiser, J., & Hetherington, E. (2005). Differential association of family subsystem negativity on siblings' maladjustment: Using behavior genetic methods to test process theory. *Journal of Family Psychology, 19*(4), 601–610.

Felson, R. B. (1983). Aggression and violence between siblings. *Social Psychology Quarterly, 46*(4), 271–285.

Felson, R. B., & Russo, N. (1988). Parental punishment and sibling aggression. *Social Psychology Quarterly, 51*(1), 11–18.

Finkelhor, D. (1980). Sex among siblings: A survey of the prevalence, variety, and effects. *Archives of Sexual Behaviour, 9*, 171–194.

Finkelhor, D., Ormrod, R., Turner, H., & Hamby, S. L. (2005). The victimization of children and youth: A comprehensive, national survey. *Child Maltreatment, 10*(1), 5–25.

Finlkelhor, D., & Jones, L. (2006). Why have child maltreatment and child victimization declined? *Journal of Social Issues, 62*(4), 685–716.

Finkelhor, D., Turner, H., & Ormrod, R. (2006). Kid's stuff: The nature and impact of peer and sibling violence on younger and older children. *Child Abuse and Neglect, 30*(12), 1401–1421.

Finkelhor, D., Ormrod, R. K., & Turner, H. A. (2007). Poly-victimization: A neglected component in child victimization. *Child Abuse & Neglect, 31*(1), 7–26.

Fishman, S., Wolf, L., Ellison, D., Gillis, B., Freeman, T., & Szatmari, P. (1996). Risk and protective factors affecting the adjustment of siblings of children with chronic disabilities. *Journal of the American Academy of Child and Adolescent Psychiatry, 35*, 1532–1541.

Flanagan, K. (2003). Intervention with sexually abusive young people in Australia and New Zealand. *Journal of Sexual Aggression, 9*(2), 135–149.

Fortune, A. E. (in press). Development of the task-centered model. In T. Rzepnicki, S. McCracken, & H. Briggs (Eds), *From the task-centered approach to evidence-based and integrative practice*. Chicago, IL: Lyceum Books Inc.

Fortune, A. E., & Reid, W. J. (2011). Task-centered social work. In F. J. Turner (Ed.), *Social work treatment: Interlocking theoretical approaches* (5th ed.). New York: Oxford University Press.

Fosco, G., & Grych, J. (2010). Adolescent triangulation into parental conflicts: Longitudinal implications for appraisals and adolescent–parent relations. *Journal of Marriage and Family, 72*(2), 254–266.

Garcia, M. M., Shaw, D. S., Winslow, E. B., & Yaggi, K. E. (2000). Destructive sibling conflict and the development of conduct problems in young boys. *Developmental Psychology, 36*(1), 44–53.

Garey, S. (1999). Long-term effects of sibling emotional and physical abuse on adult self-concept and the associated guilt and shame. *Dissertation Abstracts International: Section B: The Sciences and Engineering, 59*(9-B), 5135.

Gass, K., Jenkins, J., & Dunn, J. (2007). Are sibling relationships protective? A longitudinal study. *Journal of Child Psychology and Psychiatry, 48*(2), 167–175.

Gelles, R. J. (1997). *Intimate violence in families* (3rd ed.). Thousand Oaks, CA: Sage.

Gelles, R. J., & Straus, M. A. (1988). *Intimate violence*. New York: Simon & Schuster.

Gellis, Z., & Reid, W. J. (2004). Strengthening evidence-based practice. Brief treatment and crisis intervention. *Special issue: Evidence-Based Practice in Healthcare and Mental Health, 4*(2), 155–165.

Gentry, D. B., & Benenson, W. A. (1993). School-to-home transfer of conflict management skills among school-age children. *Families in Society, 74*(2), 67–73.

Gershoff, E. T. (2002). Corporal punishment by parents and associated child behaviors and experiences: A meta-analytic and theoretical review. *Psychological Bulletin, 128*(4), 539–579.

Gershoff, E. T., Grogan-Kaylor, A., Lansford, J. E., Chang, L., Zelli, A., Deater-Deckard, K. et al. (2010). Parent discipline practices in an international sample: Associations with child behaviors and moderation by perceived normativeness. *Child Development, 81*(2), 487–502.

Gnaulati, E. (2002). Extending the uses of sibling therapy with children and adolescents. *Psychotherapy: Theory, Research, Practice, Training, 39*(1), 76–87.

Goeke, J. L., & Ritchey, K. D. (2011). Siblings of individuals with disabilities. In J. Caspi (Ed.), *Sibling development: Implications for mental health practitioners*. New York: Springer Publishing.

Goetting, A. (1986). The developmental tasks of siblingship over the life cycle. *Journal of Marriage and the Family, 48*(4), 703–714.

Goldstein, H. (1983). Starting where the client is. *Social Casework: The Journal of Contemporary Social Work, 64*, 267–275.

Goldstein, S. E., & Tisak, M. S. (2004). Adolescents' outcome expectancies about relational aggression within acquaintanceships, friendships, and dating relationships. *Journal of Adolescence, 27*(3), 283–302.

Goodwin, M. P., & Roscoe, B. (1990). Sibling violence and agonistic interactions among middle adolescents. *Adolescence, 25*, 451–467.

Gorey, K., Thyer, B., & Pawluck, D. (1998). Differential effectiveness of prevalent social work practice models: A meta-analysis. *Social Work, 43*(3), 269–278.

Graham-Bermann, S., & Cutler, S. (1994). The Brother–Sister Questionnaire: Psychometric assessment and discrimination of well-functioning from dysfunctional relationships. *Journal of Family Psychology, 8*(2), 224–238.

Graham-Bermann, S. A., Cutler, S. E., Litzenberger, B. W., & Schwartz, W. E. (1994). Perceived conflict and violence in childhood sibling relationships and later emotional adjustment. *Journal of Family Psychology, 8*(1), 85–97.

Graham-Bermann, S. A., & Levendosky, A. A. (Eds.). (2011). *How intimate partner violence affects children: Developmental research, case studies, and evidence-based intervention.* Washington, DC, US: American Psychological Association.

Green, A. H. (1984). Child abuse by siblings. *Child Abuse & Neglect, 8*, 311–317.

Gully, K. J., Dengerine, H. A., Pepping, M., & Bergstrom, D. (1981). Research note: Sibling contribution to violent behavior. *Journal of Marriage & Family, 43*(2), 333–337.

Haj-Yahia, M. M., & Dawud-Noursi, S. (1998). Predicting the use of different conflict tactics among Arab siblings in Israel: A study based on social learning theory. *Journal of Family Violence, 13*, 81–103.

Haley, J. (1976). *Problem-solving therapy: New strategies for effective family therapy.* San Francisco: Jossey-Bass.

Hanson, C. L., Henggeler, S. W., Harris, M. A., Cigrang, J. A., Schinkel, A. M., Rodrigue, J. R. et al. (1992). Contributions of sibling relations to the adaptation of youths with insulin-dependent diabetes mellitus. *Journal of Consulting and Clinical Psychology, 60*(1), 104–112.

Hardy, M. (2001). Physical aggression and sexual behavior among siblings: A retrospective study. *Journal of Family Violence, 16*(3), 255–268.

Haskins, C. (2003). Treating sibling incest using a family systems approach. *Journal of Mental Health Counseling, 25*(4), 337–350.

Heatherington, L., & Friedlander, M. L. (1990). Complementarity and symmetry in family therapy communication. *Journal of Counseling Psychology, 37*(3), 261–268.

Hepworth, D.H., Rooney, R.H., & Larsen, J.A. (2002). *Direct social work practice: Theory and skills* (6th ed.). Pacific Grove, CA: Brooks/Cole.

Hetherington, E. M., & Stanley-Hagan, M. (1999). Stepfamilies. In M. Lamb (Ed.), *Parenting and child development in "non-traditional" families* (pp. 137–159). Mahwah, NJ: Erlbaum.

Hoffman, K., Kiecolt, K., & Edwards, J. (2005). Physical violence between siblings: A theoretical and empirical analysis. *Journal of Family Issues, 26*(8), 1103–1130.

Hoffman, K. L., & Edwards, J. N. (2004). An integrated theoretical model of sibling violence and abuse. *Journal of Family Violence, 19*(3), 185–200.

Hotaling, G. T., Straus, M. A., & Lincoln, A. J. (1990). Intrafamily violence and crime and violence outside the family. In M. A. Straus & R. J. Gelles (Eds.), *Physical violence in American families: Risk factors and adaptations to violence in 8,145 families* (pp. 431–470). New Brunswick, NJ: Transaction.

Howe, N., Rinaldi, C., Jennings, M., & Petrakos, H. (2002). No! The lambs can stay out because they got cosies: Constructive and destructive sibling conflict, pretend play, and social understanding. *Child Development, 73*, 1460–1473.
Huang, K., Caughy, M. O., Genevro, J. L., & Miller, T. L. (2005). Maternal knowledge of child development and quality of parenting among White, African-American, and Hispanic mothers. *Journal of Applied Developmental Psychology, 26*, 149–170.
Hudley, C., & Graham, S. (1993). An attributional intervention to reduce peer-directed aggression among African-American boys. *Child Development, 64*(1), 124–138.
Ibabe, I., & Jaureguizar, J. (2010). Child-to-parent violence: Profile of abusive adolescents and their families. *Journal of Criminal Justice, 38*(4), 616–624.
Jackson, D. D. (1968). Family therapy in the family of the schizophrenic. In D. D. Jackson (Ed.), *Therapy, communication, and change*. Palo Alto, CA: Science & Behavior Books.
Jenkins, J. (1992). Sibling relationships in disharmonious homes: Potential difficulties and protective effects. In F. Boer & J. Dunn (Eds.), *Children's sibling relationships: Developmental and clinical issues* (pp. 125–138). Hillsdale, NJ: Erlbaum.
Jensen, V., & Eriksen, S. (2002). Sibling violence. In D. Levinson (Ed.), *Encyclopedia of crime & punishment* (Vol. 4, pp. 1513–1517). Newbury Park, CA: Berkshire References/Sage Publications.
Johnson, D. (2009). *A compendium of psychosocial measures: Assessment of people with serious mental illness in the community*. New York: Springer Publishing.
Jones, R. N., Sloane, H. N., & Roberts, M. W. (1992). Limitations of "don't" instructional control. *Behavior Therapy, 23*(1), 131–140.
Kaduson, H. G. (1997). Release play therapy for the treatment of sibling rivalry. In H. G. Kaduson, D. M. Cangelosi, & C. E. Schaefer (Eds.), *The playing cure: Individualized play therapy for specific childhood problems* (pp. 255–273). Lanham, MD: Jason Aronson.
Kanter, J. (1983). Reevaluation of task-centered social work practice. *Clinical Social Work Journal, 11*, 228–244.
Keery, H., Boutelle, K., van den Berg, P., & Thompson, J. K. (2005). The impact of appearance-related teasing by family members. *Journal of Adolescent Health, 37*(2), 120–127.
Kellogg, N., & Menard, S. (2003). Violence among family members of children and adolescents evaluated for sexual abuse. *Child Abuse & Neglect: The International Journal, 27*(12), 1367.
Kelly, F. D., & Main, F. O. (1979). Sibling conflict in a single-parent family: An empirical case study. *American Journal of Family Therapy, 7*(1), 39–47.
Kendall, J. (1999). Sibling accounts of attention deficit hyperactivity disorder (ADHD). *Family Process, 38*, 117–136.
Kennair, N., & Mellor, D. (2007). Parent abuse: A review. *Child Psychiatry and Human Development, 38*(3), 203–219.
Kennedy, D. E., & Kramer, L. (2008). Improving emotion regulation and sibling relationship quality: The More Fun with Sisters and Brothers Program. *Family Relations, 57*, 568–579.
Kerig, P. K. (1995). Triangles in the family circle: Effects of family structure on marriage, parenting, and child adjustment. *Journal of Family Psychology, 9*(1), 28–43.
Kessler, R. C., & Magee, W. J. (1994). Childhood family violence and adult recurrent depression. *Journal of Health and Social Behavior, 35*, 13–27.
Kettrey, H. H., & Emery, B. C. (2006). The discourse of sibling violence. *Journal of Family Violence, 21*(6), 407–416.

Kim, J. Y., McHale, S. M., Crouter, A. C., & Osgood, D. W. (2007). Longitudinal linkages between sibling relationships and adjustment from middle childhood through adolescence. *Developmental Psychology, 43*, 960–973.

Kingston, L., & Prior, M. (1995). The development of patterns of stable, transient, and school-age onset aggressive behavior in young children. *Journal of American Academy of Child and Adolescent Psychiatry, 34*(3), 348–358.

Kiselica, M., & Morrill-Richards, M. (2007). Sibling maltreatment: The forgotten abuse. *Journal of Counseling & Development, 85*(2), 148–160.

Kolko, D., Kazdin, A., & Day, B. (1996). Children's perspectives in the assessment of family violence: Psychometric characteristics and comparison to parent reports. *Child Maltreatment, 1*(2), 156–167.

Kominkiewicz, F. B. (2004). The relationship of child protection service caseworker discipline-specific education and definition of sibling abuse: An institutional hiring impact study. *Journal of Human Behavior in the Social Environment, 9*(1–2), 69–82.

Kowal, A., & Kramer, L. (1997). Children's understanding of parental differential treatment. *Child Development, 68*(1), 113–126.

Kowal, A., Krull, J., & Kramer, L. (2006). Shared understanding of parental differential treatment in families. *Social Development, 15*(2), 276–295.

Krahé, B., & Möller, I. (2010). Longitudinal effects of media violence on aggression and empathy among German adolescents. *Journal of Applied Developmental Psychology, 31*(5), 401–409.

Kramer, L. (2004). Experimental interventions in sibling relations. In R. D. Conger, F. O. Lorenz, & K. A. S. Wickrama (Eds.), *Continuity and change in family relations: Theory, methods, and empirical findings*. Mahwah, NJ: Erlbaum.

Kramer, L. (2010). Essential ingredients of successful sibling relationships: An emerging framework for advancing theory and practice. *Child Development Perspectives, 4*(2), 80–86.

Kramer, L. (2011). Supportive sibling relationships. In J. Caspi (Ed.), *Sibling development: Implications for mental health practitioners*. New York: Springer Publishing.

Kramer, L., & Gottman, J. M. (1992). Becoming a sibling: "With a little help from my friends." *Developmental Psychology, 28*, 685–699.

Kramer, L., & Kowal, A. (2005). Sibling relationship quality from birth to adolescence: The enduring contributions of friends. *Journal of Family Psychology, 19*, 503–511.

Kramer, L., Perozynski, L., & Chung, T. (1999). Parental responses to sibling conflict: The effects of development and parent gender. *Child Development, 70*(6), 1401–1414.

Kramer, L., & Radey, C. (1997). Improving sibling relationships among young children: A social skills training model. *Family Relations, 46*, 237–246.

Krcmar, M., Farrar, K., & McGloin, R. (2011). The effects of video game realism on attention, retention and aggressive outcomes. *Computers in Human Behavior, 27*(1), 432–439.

Kretschmer, T., & Pike, A. (2009). Young children's sibling relationship quality: Distal and proximal correlates. *Journal of Child Psychology and Psychiatry, 50*(5), 581–589.

Lashewicz, B., & Keating, N. (2009). Tensions among siblings in parent care. *European Journal of Ageing, 6*(2), 127–135.

Lauricella, A. M. (2010). Why do mummy and daddy love you more? An investigation of parental favoritism from an evolutionary perspective. *Dissertation Abstracts International: Section B: The Sciences and Engineering, 70*(9-B), 5868.

Lauritsen, J. L. (1993). Sibling resemblance in juvenile delinquency: Findings from the National Youth Survey. *Criminology, 31*, 387–409.

Laviola, M. (1992). Effects of older brother–younger sister incest: A study of the dynamics of 17 cases. *Child Abuse & Neglect, 16*, 409–421.

Leitenberg, H., Burchard, J. D., Burchard, S. N., Fuller, E. J., & Lysaght, T. V. (1977). Using positive reinforcement to suppress behavior: Some experimental comparisons with sibling conflict. *Behavior Therapy, 8*, 168–182.

Levitt, J., & Reid, W. (1981). Rapid-assessment instruments for practice. *Social Work Research & Abstracts, 17*(1), 13–19.

Linares, L. O. (2006). An understudied form of intra-family violence: Sibling-to-sibling aggression among foster children. *Aggression and Violent Behavior, 11*, 95–109.

Lisak, D. (1994). The psychological impact of sexual abuse: Content analysis of interviews with male survivors. *Journal of Traumatic Stress, 7*, 525–548.

Lockwood, R. L. (2002). Examination of siblings' aggression styles: Do sisters show more relational aggression than brothers? *Dissertation Abstracts International: Section B: The Sciences and Engineering, 63*(5-B), 2621.

Lucas, M. B. (2002). Sibling support as a protective process for children exposed to domestic violence. *Dissertation Abstracts International: Section B: The Sciences and Engineering, 62*(12-B), 5970.

Mackey, A., Fromuth, M., & Kelly, D. (2010). The association of sibling relationship and abuse with later psychological adjustment. *Journal of Interpersonal Violence, 25*(6), 955–968.

MacKinnon-Lewis, C., Starnes, R., Volling, B., & Johnson, S. (1997). Perceptions of parenting as predictors of boys' sibling and peer relations. *Developmental Psychology, 33*, 1024–1031.

Malley-Morrison, K., & Hines, D. A. (2004). *Family violence in a cultural perspective: Defining, understanding, and combating abuse.* Thousand Oaks, CA: Sage.

Marsh, P. (2010). Task-centred practice in Great Britain. In A. E. Fortune, P. McCallion, & K. Briar-Lawson (Eds.), *Social work practice research for the 21st century*. New York: Columbia University Press.

Martin, J. L., & Ross, H. S. (1995). The development of aggression within sibling conflict. *Early Education and Development. Special Issue: Conflict Resolution in Early Social Development, 6*(4), 335–358.

Martin, J., & Ross, H. (2005). Sibling aggression: Sex differences and parents' reactions. *International Journal of Behavioral Development, 29*(2), 129–138.

Martin, M. M., Anderson, C. M., Burant, P. A., & Weber, K. (1997). Verbal aggression in sibling relationships. *Communication Quarterly, 45*, 304–317.

Mattaini, M. A., & McGuire, M. S. (2006). Behavioral strategies for constructing nonviolent cultures with youth: A review. *Behavior Modification, 30*(2), 184–224.

McGuire, S., Manke, B., Eftekhari, A., & Dunn, J. (2000). Children's perceptions of sibling conflict during middle childhood: Issues and sibling (dis)similarity. *Social Development, 9*, 173–190.

McHale, S. M., & Crouter, A. C. (1996). The family contexts of children's sibling relationships. In G. H. Brody (Ed.), *Sibling relationships: Their causes and consequences* (pp. 173–195). Norwood, NJ: Ablex Publishing Corporation.

McHale, S. M., Crouter, A. C., McGuire, S. A., & Updegraff, K. A. (1995). Congruence between mothers' and fathers' differential treatment of siblings: Links with family relations and children's well-being. *Child Development, 66*, 116–128.

McVeigh, M. J. (2003). 'But she didn't say no': an exploration of sibling sexual abuse. *Australian Social Work, 56*, 116–126.

Means-Burleson, A. M. (2002). Aggression: Family and sibling correlates. *Dissertation Abstracts International: Section B: The Sciences and Engineering, 63*(6-B), 3015.

Miller-Perrin, C. L., & Perrin, R. D. (2007). *Child maltreatment: An introduction* (2nd ed.). Thousand Oaks, CA: Sage Publications.

Minuchin, S. (1974). *Families and family therapy*. Cambridge, MA: Harvard University Press.

Minuchin, S., & Fishman, H. C. (1981). *Family therapy techniques*. Cambridge, MA: Harvard University Press.

Mitchell, J. (2004). *Siblings: Sex and violence*. Cambridge: Polity Press.

Morrill-Richards, M. M. (2010). The influence of sibling abuse on interpersonal relationships and self-esteem in college students. *Dissertation Abstracts International: Section B: The Sciences and Engineering, 70*(8-B), 5176.

Morrongiello, B., Schmidt, S., & Schell, S. L. (2010). Sibling supervision and young children's risk of injury: A comparison of mothers' and older siblings' reactions to risk taking by a younger child in the family. *Social Science & Medicine, 71*(5), 958–965.

Mullen, E. J., & Bacon, W. F. (2003). Practitioner adoption and implementation of evidence-based effective treatments and issues of quality control. In A. Rosen & E. K. Proctor (Eds.), *Developing practice guidelines for social work intervention: Issues, methods, and a research agenda*. New York: Columbia University Press.

Munn, P., & Dunn, J. (1988). Temperment and the developing relationship between siblings. *International Journal of Behavioral Development, 12*, 433–451.

Naleppa, M., & Reid, W. J. (2003). *Gerontological social work: A task-centered approach*. New York: Columbia University Press.

National Center on Elder Abuse. (1996). Trends in elder abuse in domestic settings. *Elder Abuse Information Series, No. 2*. Washington, DC: National Center on Elder Abuse. Retrieved from http://www.ncea.aoa.gov/ncearoot/main_site/pdf/basics/fact2.pdf

Newman, J. (1994). Conflict and friendship in sibling relationships: A review. *Child Study Journal, 24*(2), 119–152.

Noland, V. J., Liller, K. D., McDermott, R. J., Coulter, M. L., & Seraphine, A. E. (2004). Is adolescent sibling violence a precursor to college dating violence? *American Journal of Health Behavior, 28*(1), S13–S23.

Noller, P., Feeney, J., Peterson, C., & Sheehan, G. (1995). Learning conflict patterns in the family: Links between marital, parental, and sibling relationships. In T. J. Socha & G. H. Stamp (Eds.), *Parents, children, and communication: Frontiers of theory and research* (pp. 273–298). Hillsdale, NJ: Lawrence Erlbaum Associates.

Noller, P., Feeney, J., Sheehan, G., & Peterson, C. (2000). Marital conflict patterns: Links with family conflict and family members' perceptions of one another. *Personal Relationships, 7*(1), 79–94.

Norris, F. H., & Kaniasty, K. (1994). Psychological distress following criminal victimization in the general population: Cross-sectional, longitudinal, and prospective analyses. *Journal of Consulting and Clinical Psychology, 62*(1), 111–123.

Nugent, W. (2010). *Analyzing single system design data*. New York: Oxford University Press.

O'Brien, K. M., & Crick, N. R. (2003). *Relational and physical aggression in sibling relationships: From hitting and kicking to ignoring and excluding, siblings do it all*. Unpublished manuscript, University of Minnesota, Minneapolis, MN.

O'Brien, M. J. (1991). Taking sibling incest seriously. In M. Q. Patten (Ed.), *Family sexual abuse, frontline research and evaluation*. Beverly Hills, CA: Sage.

Odling-Smee, J. F., Laland, K. N., & Feldman, M. W. (2003). *Niche construction: The neglected process in evolution*. Princeton, NJ: Princeton University Press.

Olson, R. L., & Roberts, M. W. (1987). Alternative treatments for sibling aggression. *Behavior Therapy, 18*(3), 243–250.

Orobio de Castro, B., Slot, N. W., Bosch, J. D., Koops, W., & Veerman, J. W. (2003). Negative feelings exacerbate hostile attributions of intent in highly aggressive boys. *Journal of Clinical Child and Adolescent Psychology, 32*(1), 56–65.

Ortiz, B. (1981). Birth order and marital satisfaction: A review of the literature. *Family Therapy, 8*(1), 29–32.

Ostrov, J., Crick, N., & Stauffacher, K. (2006). Relational aggression in sibling and peer relationships during early childhood. *Journal of Applied Developmental Psychology, 27*(3), 241–253.

Pakula, L. C. (1992). Consultation with the specialist: Sibling rivalry. *Pediatrics in Review, 13*, 72–73.

Patterson, G. R. (1984). Siblings: Fellow travelers in coercive family processes. In R. J. Blanchard (Ed.), *Advances in the study of aggression* (pp. 174–214). New York: Academic Press.

Patterson, G. R. (1986). The contribution of siblings to training for fighting: A microsocial analysis. In D. Olweus, J. Block, & M. Radke-Yarrow (Eds.), *Development of antisocial and prosocial behavior: Research, theories, and issues* (pp. 235–261). New York: Academic Press.

Patterson, G. R., Dishion, T. J., & Bank, L. (1984). Family interaction: A process model of deviancy training, *Aggressive Behavior, 10*, 253–267.

Perlman, H. H. (1957). *Social casework: A problem-solving process*. Chicago, IL: University of Chicago.

Perlman, M., & Ross, H. S. (1997). The benefits of parent intervention in children's disputes: An examination of concurrent changes in children's fighting styles. *Child Development, 68*(4), 690–700.

Phillips, D., Phillips, K., Grupp, K., & Trigg, L. (2009). Sibling violence silenced: Rivalry, competition, wrestling, playing, roughhousing, benign. *Advances in Nursing Science, 32*(2), E1–E16.

Pillemer, K., & Finkelhor, D. (1988). The prevalence of elder abuse: A random sample survey. *The Gerontologist, 28*(1), 51–57.

Piotrowski, C. C. (1999). Keeping the peace or peace of mind? Maternal cognitions about sibling conflict and aggression. In P. D. Hastings & C. C. Piotrowski (Eds.), *Conflict as a context for understanding maternal beliefs about child-rearing and children's misbehavior* (pp. 5–23). San Francisco, CA: Jossey-Bass.

Piotrowski, C. C. (2011). Patterns of adjustment among siblings exposed to intimate partner violence. *Journal of Family Psychology, 25*(1), 19–28.

Plomin, R., & Daniels, D. (1987). Why are children in the same family so different from one another? *Behavioral and Brain Sciences, 10*(1), 1–16.

Plomin, R., Asbury, K., & Dunn, J. (2001). Why are children in the same family so different? Nonshared environment a decade later. *The Canadian Journal of Psychiatry/La Revue canadienne de psychiatrie, 46*(3), 225–233.

Prochaska, J. M., & Prochaska, J. O. (1985). Children's views of the causes and "cures" of sibling rivalry. *Child Welfare, 64*(4), 427–433.

Raffaeli, M. (1992). Sibling conflict in early adolescence. *Journal of Marriage and Family Therapy, 54*, 652–663.

Ralph, A., Toumbourou, J., Grigg, M., Mulcahy, R., Carr-Gregg, M., & Sanders, M. (2003). Early intervention to help parents manage behavioural and emotional problems in early adolescents: What parents want. *Australian e-Journal for the Advancement of Mental Health, 2*(3), 1–13.

Ramos, B., & Tolson, E. (2008). Task centered practice. In N. Coady & P. Lehmann (Eds.), *Theoretical perspectives for direct social work practice: A generalist–eclectic approach*. New York: Springer Publishing.

Randall, T. (1992). Adolescents may experience home, school abuse; their future draws researchers' concern. *Journal of the American Medical Association (JAMA), 267*(23), 3127–3128, 3131.

Rapoza, K. A., Cook, K., Zaveri, T., & Malley-Morrison, K. (2010). Ethnic perspectives on sibling abuse in the United States. *Journal of Family Issues, 31*(6), 808–829.

Recchia, H., & Howe, N. (2009a). Associations between social understanding, sibling relationship quality, and siblings' conflict strategies and outcomes. *Child Development, 80*(5), 1564–1578.

Recchia, H., & Howe, N. (2009b). Sibling relationship quality moderates the associations between parental interventions and siblings' independent conflict strategies and outcomes. *Journal of Family Psychology, 23*(4), 551–561.

Reese-Weber, M., & Kahn, J. H. (2005). Familial predictors of sibling and romantic-partner conflict resolution: Comparing late adolescents from intact and divorced families. *Journal of Adolescence, 28*(4), 479–493.

Reid, W. J. (1985). *Family problem-solving*. New York: Columbia University Press.

Reid, W. J. (1987). Evaluating an intervention in developmental research. *Journal of Social Service Research, 11*, 17–39.

Reid, W. J. (1992). *Task strategies: An empirical approach to clinical social work*. New York: Columbia University Press.

Reid, W. J. (1993). Fitting the single-system design to family treatment. *Journal of Social Service Research, 18*(1–2), 83–99.

Reid, W. J. (1997). Evaluating the dodo's verdict: Do all interventions have equivalent outcomes? *Social Work Research, 21*(1), 5–18.

Reid, W. J. (2000). *The task planner: An intervention resource for human service professionals*. New York: Columbia University Press.

Reid, W. J. (2004). The contribution of operant theory to social work practice and research. In H. E. Briggs & T. L. Rzepnicki (Eds.), *Using evidence in social work practice: Behavioral perspectives*. Chicago, IL: Lyceum Books.

Reid, W. J., & Epstein, L. (1972). *Task-centered casework*. New York: Columbia University Press.

Reid, W. J., & Fortune, A. E. (2003). Empirical foundations for practice guidelines in current social work knowledge. In E. K. Proctor & A. Rosen (Eds.), *Developing practice guidelines for social work intervention: Issues, methods, and research agenda* (pp. 59–79). New York: Columbia University Press.

Reid, W. J., & Shyne, A. W. (1969). *Brief and extended casework*. New York: Columbia University Press.

Reid, W. J., & Donovan, T. (1990). Treating sibling violence. *Family Therapy, 17*, 49–59.

Rende, R., Slomkowski, C., Lloyd-Richardson, E., & Niaura, R. (2005). Sibling effects on substance use in adolescence: Social contagion and genetic relatedness. *Journal of Family Psychology, 19*(4), 611–618.

Reynolds, J. F., Dorner, L., & Orellana, M. F. (2011). Siblings as cultural educators and socializing agents. In J. Caspi (Ed.), *Sibling development: Implications for mental health practitioners*. New York: Springer Publishing.

Richmond, M., & Stocker, C. (2003). Siblings' differential experiences of marital conflict and differences in psychological adjustment. *Journal of Family Psychology, 17*(3), 339–350.

Riggio, H. (2000). Measuring attitudes toward adult sibling relationships: The Lifespan Sibling Relationship Scale. *Journal of Social and Personal Relationships, 17*(6), 707–728.

Rinaldi, C., & Howe, N. (1998). Siblings' reports of conflict and the quality of their relationships. *Merrill-Palmer Quarterly, 44*(3), 404–422.

Ronan, K. R., & Kazantzis, N. (2006). The use of between-session (homework) activities in psychotherapy: Conclusions from the *Journal of Psychotherapy Integration* special series. *Journal of Psychotherapy Integration, 16*(2), 254–259.

Rooney, R. H. (2009). *Strategies for work with involuntary clients* (2nd ed.). New York: Columbia University Press.

Roscoe, B., Goodwin, M. P., & Kennedy, D. (1987). Sibling violence and agonistic interactions experienced by early adolescents. *Journal of Family Violence, 2*(2), 121–137.

Rosen, A. (2003). Evidence-based social work practice: Challenges and promise. *Social Work Research, 27*(4), 197–208.

Rosenthal, P. A., & Doherty, M. B. (1984). Serious sibling abuse by preschool children. *Journal of the American Academy of Child Psychiatry, 23*(2), 186–190.

Ross, H., Ross, M., Stein, N., & Trabasso, T. (2006). How siblings resolve their conflicts: The importance of first offers, planning, and limited opposition. *Child Development, 77*(6), 1730–1745.

Routt, G., & Anderson, L. (2011). Adolescent violence towards parents. *Journal of Aggression, Maltreatment & Trauma, 20*(1), 1–19.

Rudd, J. M., & Herzberger, S. D. (1999). Brother–sister incest—Father daughter incest: A comparison of characteristics and consequences. *Child Abuse and Neglect, 23*(9), 915–928.

Rzepnicki, T. L., McCracken, S. G., & Briggs, H. E. (Eds.). (2012). *From task-centered social work to evidence-based and integrative practice: Reflections on history and implementation*. Chicago: Lyceum Press.

Sanders, R. (2004). *Sibling relationships: Theory and issues for practice*. Basingstoke, Hampshire: Palgrave.

Sanders, R. (2011). Siblings in practice. In J. Caspi (Ed.), *Sibling development: Implications for mental health practitioners*. New York: Springer Publishing.

Saudino, K. J., Wertz, A. E., Gagne, J. R., & Chawla, S. (2004). Night and day: Are siblings as different in temperament as parents say they are? *Journal of Personality and Social Psychology, 87*(5), 698–706.

Satir, V. (1983). *Conjoint family therapy*. Palo Alto, CA: Science and Behavior Books.

Scarr, S., & McCartney, K. (1983). How people make their own environments: A theory of genotype–environment effects. *Child Development, 54*, 424–435.

Schachter, F. F. (1985). Sibling deidentification in the clinic: Devil vs. angel. *Family Process, 24*(3), 415–427.

Schachter, F. F., Gilutz, G., Shore, E., & Adler, M. (1978). Sibling deidentification judged by mothers: Cross-validation and developmental studies. *Child Development, 49*(2), 543–546.

Schachter, F. F., Shore, E., Feldman-Rotman, S., Marquis, R. E., & Campbell, S. (1976). Sibling deidentification. *Developmental Psychology, 12*(5), 418–427.

Schachter, F. F., & Stone, R. K. (1985). Difficult sibling, easy sibling: Temperament and the within-family environment. *Child Development, 56*, 1335–1344.

Shulman, L. (2008). *The skills of helping individuals, families, groups, and communities* (6th ed.). Pacific Grove, CA: Brooks/Cole.

Siddiqui, A., & Ross, H. (2004). Mediation as a method of parent intervention in children's disputes. *Journal of Family Psychology, 18*(1), 147–159.

Silverman, J. B. (1999). Sibling violence: Its relation to childhood observation of caretaker violence and factors derived from the brother–sister questionnaire. *Dissertation Abstracts International: Section B: The Sciences and Engineering, 60*(5-B), 2368.

Simonelli, C., Mullis, T., & Rohde, C. (2005). Scale of Negative Family Interactions: A measure of parental and sibling aggression. *Journal of Interpersonal Violence, 20*(7), 792–803.

Singer, A. T., & Weinstein, R. (2000). Differential parental treatment predicts achievements and self-perceptions in two cultural contexts. *Journal of Family Psychology, 14*, 491–509.

Slomkowski, C., Rende, R., Conger, K. J., Simons, R. L., & Conger, R. D. (2001). Sisters, brothers, and delinquency: Evaluating social influence during early and middle adolescence. *Child Development, 72*(1), 271–283.

Smallbone, S., Marshall, W. L., & Wortley, R. (2008). *Preventing child sexual abuse: Evidence, policy and practice*. Devon, UK: Willan Publishing.

Smith, J., & Ross, H. (2007). Training parents to mediate sibling disputes affects children's negotiation and conflict understanding. *Child Development, 78*(3), 790–805.

Soli, A. R., McHale, S. M., & Feinberg, M. E. (2009). Risk and protective effects of sibling relationships among African American adolescents. *Family Relations, 58*, 578–592.

Stauffacher, K., & DeHart, G. B. (2005). Preschoolers' relational aggression with siblings and with friends. *Early Education and Development, 16*, 185–206.

Stauffacher, K., & DeHart, G. B. (2006). Crossing social contexts: Relational aggression between siblings and friends during early and middle childhood. *Applied Developmental Psychology, 27*, 228–240.

Steinmetz, S. K. (1981). A cross-cultural comparison of sibling violence. *International Journal of Family Psychiatry, 2*(3–4), 337–351.

Stocker, C., Ahmed, K., & Stall, M. (1997). Marital satisfaction and maternal emotional expressiveness: Links with children's sibling relationships. *Social Development, 6*(3), 373–385.

Stocker, C., & McHale, S. (1992). The nature and family correlates of preadolescents' perceptions of their sibling relationships. *Journal of Social and Personal Relationships, 9*, 179–195.

Stocker, C. M. (1994). Children's perceptions of relationships with siblings, friends, and mothers: Compensatory processes and links with adjustment. *Journal of Child Psychology and Psychiatry, 35*, 1447–1459.

Stocker, C. M., & Youngblade, L. (1999). Marital conflict and parental hostility: Links with children's sibling and peer relationships. *Journal of Family Psychology, 13*(4), 598–609.

Stormshak, E. A., Bellanti, C. J., & Bierman, K. L. (1996). The quality of sibling relationships and the development of social competence and behavioral control in aggressive children. *Developmental Psychology, 32*, 79–89.

Straus, M. A., Gelles, R. J., & Steinmetz, S. K. (1980). *Behind closed doors: Violence in the American family*. New York: Anchor Press/Doubleday.

Strawbridge, W. J., & Wallhagen, M. I. (1991). Impact of family conflict on adult child caregivers. *The Gerontologist, 31*(6), 770–777.

Suitor, J. J., Sechrist, J., Plikuhn, M., Pardo, S. T., & Pillemer, K. (2008). Within-family differences in parent–child relations across the life course. *Current Directions in Psychological Science, 17*, 334–338.

Sulloway, F. (1996). *Born to rebel: Birth order, family dynamics, and creative lives*. New York: Pantheon Books.

Sung, M., Lee, J., & Park, S. (2008, July). *Dynamics and politics of adult sibling and sibling-in-law relationships in South Korea: Continuity and change*. In Abstract book: Research papers (p. 159): Proceedings of the 100th World Congress of the International Federation of Home Economics, Lucerne, Switzerland.

Tannock, M. (2008). Rough and Tumble Play: An investigation of the perceptions of educators and young children. *Early Childhood Education Journal, 35*(4), 357–361.

Thomas, E. J., & Rothman, J. (1994). An integrative perspective on intervention research. In J. Rothman & E. J. Thomas (Eds.), *Intervention research: Design & development for human service* (pp. 3–23). New York: Haworth Press.

Thomas, R. M. (2004). *Comparing theories of child development* (6th ed.). Stamford, CT: Wadsworth.

Thompson, K. M. (2009). Sibling incest: A model for group practice with adult female victims of brother–sister incest. *Journal of Family Violence, 24*(7), 531–537.

Thyer, B., & Myers, L. (2007). Research in evidence-based social work. *Cognitive behavior therapy in clinical social work practice* (pp. 45–66). New York: Springer Publishing.

Tiedemann, G. L., & Johnston, C. (1992). Evaluation of a parent training program to promote sharing between young siblings. *Behavior Therapy, 23*, 299–318.

Titelman, P. (Ed.) (2008). *Triangles: Bowen family systems theory perspectives*. New York: The Haworth Press/Taylor & Francis Group.

Toman, W. (1959). Family constellation as a character and marriage determinant. *International Journal of Psycho-Analysis, 40*, 316–319.

Tracey, T. J. G., & Rohlfing, J. E. (2010). Variations in the understanding of interpersonal behavior: Adherence to the interpersonal circle as a moderator of the rigidity–psychological well-being relation. *Journal of Personality, 78*(2), 711–745.

Trotter, C. (2010). Task-centred practice in Australia. In A. E. Fortune, P. McCallion, & K. Briar-Lawson (Eds.), *Social work practice research for the 21st century*. New York: Columbia University Press.

Tucker, C. J., Updegraff, K., & Baril, M. E. (2010). Who's the boss? Patterns of control in adolescents' sibling relationships. *Family Relations: An Interdisciplinary Journal of Applied Family Studies, 59*(5), 520–532.

Tucker, M., Sigafoos, J., & Bushell, H. (1998). Use of noncontingent reinforcement in the treatment of challenging behavior: A review and clinical guide. *Behavior Modification, 22*(4), 529–547.

Turner, F. J. (Ed.) (2011). *Social work treatment: Interlocking theoretical approaches* (5th ed.). New York: Oxford University Press.

Turner, H. A., Finkelhor, D., & Ormrod, R. (2010). Poly-victimization in a national sample of children and youth. *American Journal of Preventive Medicine, 38*(3), 323–330.

U.S. Department of Health and Human Services, Administration on Children, Youth, and Families. (2007). *Child Maltreatment 2005*. Washington, DC: U.S. Government Printing Office.

U.S. Surgeon General. (2001). *Youth violence: A report of the Surgeon General*. Washington, DC: Department of Health and Human Services.

Updegraff, K. A., McHale, S. M., & Crouter, A. C. (2002). Adolescents' sibling relationships and friendships: Developmental patterns and relationship associations. *Social Development, 11*, 182–211.

Updegraff, K. A., McHale, S. M., Killoren, S. E., & Rodríguez, S. A. (2011). Cultural variations in sibling relationships. In J. Caspi (Ed.), *Sibling development: Implications for mental health professionals*. New York: Springer Publishing.

Updegraff, K. A., McHale, S. M., Whiteman, S. D., Thayer, S. M., & Delgado, M. Y. (2005a). Adolescent sibling relationships in Mexican American families: Exploring the role of familism. *Journal of Family Psychology, 19*, 512–522.

Updegraff, K. A., Thayer, S. M., Whiteman, S. D., Denning, D. J., & McHale, S. M. (2005b). Relational aggression in adolescents' sibling relationships: Links to sibling and parent–adolescent relationship quality. *Family Relations, 54*(3), 373–385.

Volling, B. L., & Belsky, J. (1992). The contribution of mother–child and father–child relationships to the quality of sibling interaction: A longitudinal study. *Child Development, 63*(5), 1209–1222.

Volling, B. L., & Elins, J. L. (1998). Family relationships and children's emotional adjustment as correlates of maternal and paternal differential treatment: A replication with toddler and preschool siblings. *Child Development, 69*(6), 1640–1656.

Vuchinich, S., Wood, B., & Vuchinich, R. (1994). Coalitions and family problem-solving with preadolescents in referred, at-risk, and comparison families. *Family Process, 33*(4), 409–424.

Wagner, V. S., Hunter, R., & Boelter, D. (1988). Sibling rivalry and the systemic perspective: Implications for treatment. *Journal of Strategic & Systemic Therapies, 7*(3), 67–71.

Walker, J. S. (1999). The effects of children's caretaking behavior and distress: A conceptual and empirical investigation. (ProQuest Information & Learning). *Dissertation Abstracts International: Section B: The Sciences and Engineering, 59*(9-B), 5116.

Walsh, J. A., & Krienert, J. L. (2007). Child–parent violence: An empirical analysis of offender, victim, and event characteristics in a national sample of reported incidents. *Journal of Family Violence, 22*(7), 563–574.

Walters, M., Carter, B., Papp, P., & Silverstein, O. (1988). *The invisible web: Gender patterns in family relationships*. New York: Guilford Press.

Watson, M. F., & McGoldrick, M. (2011). Practice with siblings in a cultural context. In J. Caspi (Ed.), *Sibling development: Implications for mental health practitioners*. New York: Springer Publishing.

Watzlawick, P. (1977). *How real is real? Confusion, disinformation, communication*. New York: Random House.

Weisner, T. S. (1987). Socialization for parenthood in sibling caretaking societies. In J. B. Lancaster (Ed.), *Parenting across the life span: Biosocial dimensions* (pp. 237–270). Hawthorne, NY: Aldine de Gruyter.

Weisner, T. S., & Gallimore, R. (1977). My brother's keeper: Child and sibling caretaking. *Current Anthropology, 18*(2), 169–190.

Welfare, A. (2008). How qualitative research can inform clinical interventions in families recovering from sibling sexual abuse. *ANZJFT Australian and New Zealand Journal of Family Therapy, 29*(3), 139–147.

Whipple, E. E., & Finton, S. E. (1995). Psychological maltreatment by siblings: An unrecognized form of abuse. *Child & Adolescent Social Work Journal, 12*(2), 135–146.

Whitchurch, G., & Constantine, L. (1993). Systems theory. In P. G. Boss, W. J. Doherty, R. LaRossa, W. R. Schumm, & S. Steinmetz (Eds.), *Sourcebook of family theories and methods: A contextual approach* (pp. 325–355). New York: Plenum Press.

Whiteman, S. D., Bernard, J. M. B., & Jensen, A. C. (2011). Sibling influence in human development. In J. Caspi (Ed.), *Sibling development: Implications for mental health practitioners.* New York: Springer Publishing.

Wiehe, V. (1997). *Sibling abuse: Hidden physical, emotional, and sexual trauma* (2nd ed.). Thousand Oaks, CA: Sage Publications.

Williams, S. T., Conger, K. J., & Blozis, S. A. (2007). The development of interpersonal aggression during adolescence: The importance of parents, siblings, and family economics. *Child Development, 78*(5), 1526–1542.

Yu, J., & Gamble, W. (2008). Familial correlates of overt and relational aggression between young adolescent siblings. *Journal of Youth and Adolescence, 37*(6), 655–673.

Yu, J. J. (2008). Reexamining aggression and social affordance in sibling relationships: Taking a closer look at neglected characteristics. *Dissertation Abstracts International: Section B: The Sciences and Engineering, 68*(11-B), 7693.

Zukow, P. G. (Ed.). (1989). *Sibling interaction across cultures: Theoretical and methodological issues.* New York: Springer-Verlag.

Zukow-Goldring, P. (2002). Sibling caregiving. In M. H. Bornstein (Ed.), *Handbook of parenting: Being and becoming a parent* (2nd ed., Vol. 3, pp. 253–286). Mahwah, NJ: Lawrence Erlbaum.

# Index

Made in the USA
Middletown, DE
18 August 2021

46296141R00156